BAREFOOT ANGEL

Second Edition

PEGI HANDLEY

Barefoot Angel by Pegi Handley

This book is written to provide information and motivation to readers. Its purpose is not to render any type of psychological, legal, or professional advice of any kind. The content is the sole opinion and expression of the author, and not necessarily that of the publisher.

Copyright © 2020 by Pegi Handley

All rights reserved. No part of this book may be reproduced, transmitted, or distributed in any form by any means, including, but not limited to, recording, photocopying, or taking screenshots of parts of the book, without prior written permission from the author or the publisher. Brief quotations for noncommercial purposes, such as book reviews, permitted by Fair Use of the U.S. Copyright Law, are allowed without written permissions, as long as such quotations do not cause damage to the book's commercial value.

ISBN: 978-1-952822-99-5 (Paperback)
ISBN: 978-1-952822-98-8 (Digital)

Library of Congress Control Number: 2020939798

Printed in the United States of America.

THE TRUTH ABOUT OUR childhood is stored up in our body, and although we can repress it, we can never alter it. Our intellect can be deceived, our feelings manipulated, our perceptions confused, and our body tricked with medication. But someday the body will present its bill, for it is as incorruptible as a child who, still whole in spirit, will accept no compromises or excuses, and it will not stop tormenting us until we stop evading the truth.

—Dwight D. Eisenhower

CONTENTS

CHAPTER ONE 1

CHAPTER TWO 9

CHAPTER THREE 21

CHAPTER FOUR 29

CHAPTER FIVE 39

CHAPTER SIX 45

CHAPTER SEVEN 57

CHAPTER EIGHT 65

CHAPTER NINE 73

CHAPTER TEN 87

CHAPTER ELEVEN 117

CHAPTER TWELVE 129

CHAPTER THIRTEEN 139

CHAPTER FOURTEEN 155

CHAPTER FIFTEEN 165

CHAPTER SIXTEEN 183

CHAPTER SEVENTEEN 189

CHAPTER EIGHTEEN 195

CHAPTER NINETEEN 207

CHAPTER TWENTY 213

CHAPTER TWENTY-ONE 227

CHAPTER TWENTY-TWO 237

CHAPTER TWENTY-THREE 265

CHAPTER TWENTY-FOUR 271

CHAPTER TWENTY-FIVE 287

CHAPTER TWENTY-SIX 323

CHAPTER TWENTY-SEVEN 345

CHAPTER TWENTY-EIGHT 361

CHAPTER TWENTY-NINE 365

CHAPTER THIRTY 373

CHAPTER THIRTY-ONE 383

CHAPTER THIRTY-TWO 397

CHAPTER THIRTY-THREE 401

CHAPTER THIRTY-FOUR 411

CHAPTER THIRTY-FIVE 419

CHAPTER THIRTY-SIX 427

CHAPTER THIRTY-SEVEN 435

CHAPTER THIRTY-EIGHT 443

CHAPTER THIRTY-NINE 453

CHAPTER FORTY 461

EPILOGUE 471

CREDITS 481

CHAPTER ONE

I bent forward and gently kissed Jeff's forehead. He looked so peaceful in his coffin. He was so handsome, a good looking kid. His most outstanding feature was his gorgeous hazel eyes, with long curled lashes. If I weren't his mother I'd say he had sexy eyes. I touched his cold, hands, unappealing in their lifelessness.

Soft music tiptoed gently through the slumber room in an attempt to weave a false peace into the room. Spicy carnations punctuated the sweet fragrance of roses. The walnut coffin at the back of the room was simple but nice. It had been so hard for me to pick out that coffin to lay my son in...forever.

How could this be happening? It didn't seem possible that Jeff was dead. He was only sixteen...why had he been robbed of a chance to grow up...have children of his own? He had been born on my twenty-first birthday, a wonderful birthday present. He'd been my baby for nine years before his brother came along.

I patted his hair. Maxine Hadley, owner of the funeral parlor, had allowed me to fix it.

As I continued to stroke his hair, my vision suddenly blurred. Jeff's body in the casket faded slowly into the background and then a small bundle, wrapped in brown paper, floated into my field of vision. It looked like a tiny mummy…the image was frightening but vaguely reminiscent of something I couldn't identify.

Damn, what is this? I'm losing my mind, that's what's happening. God, please don't let that happen again! I dug my nails into the palms of my hands to fight a smothering darkness which threatened to choke off consciousness.

"Mrs. Newman…Mrs. Newman, are you all right?"

The voice sounded hollow—far off in the distance and I felt the floor drop from under me.

Mrs. Hadley grabbed the chair which I reeled into. I clawed my way back into reality, clutching the arms of the chair as though they could lift me to sanity.

With so little time left to see Jeff, I carefully got to my feet and moved slowly back to my place beside the casket. Once again, the vision of the tiny bundle appeared, replacing the actual body of my son in his coffin. I heard a soft, muffled baby's cry. In the shadows of the slumber room, I shuddered, and began sobbing. Tears choked me as I collapsed again into the chair. The vision brought as much distress as the loss of my son.

What does it mean? Is God trying to tell me something? I know I'm losing it. The words made circles in my mind like a mantra.

I purposefully made myself look again toward the coffin. I could see the side of Jeff's lifeless face. Again he evaporated before my eyes and in his place the tiny bundle wrapped in paper appeared, accompanied by the muffled cries of the baby.

I forced myself to concentrate—to rid myself of the image by recalling the still vivid scene at the hospital when Jeff died. I remembered every minute detail, from the time I got the call that Jeff was on his way by ambulance to the emergency room.

The dispassionate voice on the other end began, "I'm sorry to call with bad news, but your son Jeff has just been in an automobile accident. An ambulance is taking him to Keweah Delta Hospital. "He asked me to call you.

I remember thinking, if Jeff had asked the lady to call his mother and gave her the telephone number, then he couldn't be hurt too badly.

Yet fear mauled my mind. Oh, Pegi, calm down, I told myself. Why do you always get like this? It's your fear of blood. You're afraid you'll see Jeff covered with blood, and you'll panic.

Hurriedly, I made three telephone calls—one to my husband, another to a friend Merle, and the last to my daughter Shaunda. I hadn't known Merle long. We'd both come into AA the same week. He was a doctor and I knew he'd be a good person to have by my side.

We all arrived at the hospital at about the same time, just as Jeff was being lifted onto the gurney in the emergency room. I remembered the faint smell of antiseptics. The artificial lighting flooded the long corridor, giving it an eerie glow. Polished floors glistened, the sterile white walls seemed to vibrate with bright white light. A harsh, impersonal voice over the intercom echoed through the empty hallways: "Dr. MacMillan, call extension 233. Dr. MacMillan, please call extension 233."

A medical figure in white-starched uniform and white crepe-soled shoes spoke to Jeff in muted whispers. Jeff argued with the doctor and nurses, begging them not to put those straps on him. He kicked and swung his legs and arms in every direction. I didn't see any wounds, thank God, or a drop of blood. Surely he couldn't be hurt badly.

A nurse wheeled a square aluminum machine on a table over beside Jeff. It was a cylinder-shaped instrument on the end of a coil. It had several knobs, and I knew it had voltage. The nurse positioned it on Jeff's chest while another nurse stood at Jeff's head, stroking his hair and talking to him.

The doctor turned and saw me standing in the doorway. "Who are you? Are you related to this young man?" His voice cracked in a brusque uncaring tone.

"Yes, I'm his mother."

At that moment, one of the nurses cried out, "His heart has stopped."

Jeff sat straight up. His eyes flickered with a sudden change. "Daddy!" he called out in a voice tinged with alarm. The doctor looked up at the spot on the ceiling where Jeff's eyes had stared, then he turned suddenly and closed the door right in my face.

A fist of iron grabbed at my heart, and I found myself struggling to draw a breath. I was standing only inches from the closed door. I had a right to be with Jeff. I was his mother! How could the doctor be so cruel?

Had Jeff really called for his Daddy, or had I misunderstood? Jeff's father had been dead almost ten years. Surely, Jeff wouldn't be thinking about his Daddy at a time like this. It must have been something to do with shock. And what was wrong with his eyes? They had looked so strange.

A loud thumping sound came from the room behind the closed door. It sounded as if Jeff's body had fallen to the floor.

One, two, three times. Again and again...Thump! Thump! Thump! A sudden realization forced me away from the door; a rush of hot tears seared my cheeks. Suddenly a disheveled and obviously distraught young woman ran toward me.

"Are you Jeff's mother?" she asked breathlessly.

I nodded. "Yes..."

She seemed to choke on the words. "My little girl was killed in the same accident. We were in the pickup with my boyfriend. He was towing Jeff down the mountain road. You know the last hill, the one coming down from the dam on Highway 198? We were on that last big hill. My boyfriend had a blowout, and we went over that steep embankment. In less than a hundred feet, we would have been on flat land."

She stopped for a moment, in an obvious attempt to compose herself. Trembling violently, with tears streaming down her face, she fumbled in her purse for more tissues. Then, keeping her eyes lowered, she drew a breath and seemed to gain a measure of self-control.

"My little girl went through the windshield and was killed instantly. She was only four years old. If my boyfriend lives, he'll be a vegetable for life." Then she raised her anguished eyes to mine. "Jeff is fine. He climbed up the side of that rocky hill and flagged down a motorist."

I was stunned by what she'd told me. "I just saw Jeff. He was talking to the nurses and doctors. I saw him moving both legs and arms, so I know they weren't broken."

"I hope he's okay," the young woman said.

We went to the parking lot with Merle and my family. Merle was a general practitioner. "Please, Merle, go into that room and find out what they're doing with Jeff."

"Pegi, I can't do that. I have no authority in this hospital," Merle answered. In minutes, I saw the doctor walking across the parking lot toward me. It was the same doctor who had closed the door in my face.

"I'm Dr. Burgess," his fingers fiddled with the stethoscope hanging around his neck. "I'm sorry, Mrs. Newman, your son just died."

He said it with all the compassion of a mechanic telling me that my car needed new brakes. The shock was overwhelming. I grabbed him, beat against his chest with both fists, screaming, "No! No! No!" My husband and Merle pulled me off the doctor…Oh God how can you do this to me? Now, as I remembered that painful event, I kept my eyes on the coffin, making sure Jeff was still in it. I had no faith in God. I had hated Him before, and hated Him even more now for taking my son. But my mind continued to present the scene of Jeff calling out to his Daddy in the emergency room. Had he really seen his father when he died? How could that be possible?

"Are you all right, Mrs. Newman?"

I looked up and realized that Mrs. Hadley had come back into the room. She seemed genuinely concerned. I just nodded not wanting to interrupt a memory of Jeff's last Christmas.

Jeff and I had argued back and forth about the Christmas tree. I had been drinking far too much. After Jeff finally decorated the tree for his younger brother Danny, I climbed on a chair to put the star on top, lost my balance, and fell into the tree, shoving it through the window.

I was enraged and ashamed with myself and angry with Jeff for wanting that stupid tree. I wouldn't let Jeff pick up the pieces. I made him go to bed, and kept drinking until I finally passed out.

To my surprise the next morning, the tree was standing upright. Plastic had been placed over the broken window, and Danny's presents were under the tree. When Danny asked about the broken window, Jeff just laughed.

"Santa must've fallen through the window. He must've been in an awful hurry to get out before you woke up. I bet he even heard you waking up." Jeff laughed and laughed while his delighted little brother stared at the tree. Jeff's mischievous eyes flashed. How I loved those eyes when they shined like that. And that little crooked grin he had, just like his Daddy's.

My thoughts continued to bounce back and forth, carrying me back to the time when Jeff was young.

Stop this thinking! I told myself. Pegi your son is lying in a coffin—he's dead. I willed my mind to stop serving up memories of bad times. Stop! Stop! Stop! The pungent, sweet fragrance of the carnations in the slumber room brought me back to the realization that it was really Jeff in that simple coffin. My mind made an abrupt U-Turn, remembering all those nights that I drank myself into a stupor at the golf course bar. Jeff had called me every ten minutes, asking me to come home. Why didn't I go home? Why? I couldn't pull myself away from that bar stool. I had to stay until I drank myself into a fog.

I had always yearned to make up all those years to him.

Now I'd never be able to...

I couldn't stop the bittersweet memories. As he grew older, he'd walk to the golf course and sneak into the bar. In a desperate attempt to get me to stop drinking, he would grab my purse with the car keys and all my money. But it didn't stop me. I'd just charge my drinks and have somebody drive me home. I'd go back the next day, pay the tab, and get my car. God, I would give anything to rewind the tape recorder of my life—do it differently.

Now, I remembered Jeff driving me home, when he didn't even know how to drive a car. Drunkenly, I had offered instructions.

I kept trying to push the painful memories away, but they lingered like uninvited guests, moving farther and farther into the past...

Jeff was six years old, and admitted to Exeter Memorial Hospital for a tonsillectomy. A nurse with a urinal stood beside his bed, trying to coax him into giving her a urine specimen.

"No!" Jeff cried. "I won't give you my pee. What do you want that nasty stuff for? I don't have to do that. No!" He spotted me standing at his door. "Mommy, do I have to do that?"

I loved his spunk. Now, I kept my eyes averted from the coffin. I was terrified that Jeff's sweet spirit might not be there again—that it would be replaced by the evil vision of the baby mummy—the bundle whose muffled cries assaulted my ears.

What did the intrusion of this dark vision on my grief mean? In the days following Jeff's funeral, the mystery of the bundled baby slowly began to unfold.

CHAPTER TWO

Months wrapped in grief crept by following Jeff's funeral, and I felt like part of my identity had vanished with him when his young life was ripped away from me. He had been my guardian angel when I was drinking—had cared and watched over me, as I had done for Mama and my own siblings. History had indeed repeated itself, I began to realize. I tried to fill the emptiness of the dark void with busy projects, anything to keep my sanity.

When I was exhausted and tired the thoughts bombarded me. Thoughts of my childhood marched across my mind in platoons, leaving me staring into space like my Mama had done. Maybe if I gave in to the remembrances they would tell me what the vision of the terrifying baby mummy—the crying bundled baby—had meant...

A picture began to form:

The lady chased Mickey and me out to the front yard. "Peggy, mind your brother now. We got work to do helpin' your mammie."

Taking Mickey by the hand, I pulled him into the yard. He was my brother, and I was taking really good care of him. Looking into the house I wanted all those ladies to see what good care I was taking of him. It was really hard for me to control him. He kept trotting off. One minute he cried for Mama, the next he wanted to run off chasing the other kids, or climbing onto the cars that lined the dirt road that were up on big blocks. And there were hundreds of them in all shapes and color. Many had been there since the day were arrived, and that included ours.

One of the ladies hollered from the house, "Now Peggy, you mind your little brother. Don't hurt him while we're busy. Ya' hear me, Peggy?"

Shaking my head up and down, up and down, with Mickey in hand I ambled on.

Other ladies ran back and forth in and out of our house, carrying in pails of water. Each time, one of them would pour it into a tub on the stove before going back to the pump for more.

"You know how that youn'gun is" she chanted. "Always picking on her little brother," one woman said. "Peggy is just plain contrary. She has a temper, just like that Daddy of hers." "I ain't contrary, am I Mickey?" I wandered past a window of my house. Why wouldn't they let me in? What were the ladies doing to my Mama?

Barely taller than Mickey, my dirty cotton panties hung to the ground, sopping wet. I stepped out of them.

We could see Mama and Daddy's bed through the door—a big, shiny, iron bed. The walls echoed with her cries. In a corner were piles of towels. The small room was strewn with towels, clothing, and trash. All the windows and doors were open to let the breeze blow through.

Mama was sick. She'd been in bed a long time. Neighbor ladies kept going in the house, checking on her. Every time one came to check on Mama, we poked our heads through the front door, only to be chased away.

Most of the ladies were in the house, now. A barking dog and the crow of a rooster covered the sounds of Mama's sobbing cries, but I could hear her when she screamed. I could hear her voice resoundingly outside, between the sounds of the animals. I worried that Mama was hurt bad. If these ladies would let me in, I was sure I could make my Mama all better. I'd crawl up on the bed with her.

Rubbing her hands on an apron, made from feed sacks, one woman ran to the front door and hollered, "Miss Matty, it's time. Hurry! I need y'all now. Winnie's pains are only minutes apart."

Miss Matty, getting up from the step, puffing hard, wiped the sweat from her forehead with a rag, then stuffed it into her pocket. "I'll be right there. Oh, mercy." She hurried into our house, pausing to glance back at me. "Peggy, you watch that brother of yours. Don't let him get into the street."

Poking my face into the screen, I yelled, "I want my Mommie!" All the ladies stood at the end of Mama's bed. I couldn't see my Mama at all, but I could sure hear her. She was crying louder and louder. She was crying worse than I'd ever heard anybody cry, and it frightened me. It must have scared Mickey, too, because he started to cry.

That ole woman pushed out the door. Yanking me around to face her, "young lady I told you you're Mommie is sick. Now you listen to me or I'm going to swat you a good one."

I turned my back to her, with my arms folded across my chest, "she's my Mommie, not yours."

It wasn't long before I heard a baby cry, but I didn't know where the cry was coming from. I listened intently for another cry, and when it came again, it sounded like it was coming from my house.

"Baby, baby Mickey." Mickey just sat not caring about all the commotion.

My heart pounded. I was scared. Suddenly I knew why Mama was crying so. Somebody had cut her. Then I heard the cry again. That took my attention away from the blood. This time, it was a big, loud, strong cry. I was really surprised. Did a baby make Mama cry?

"Listen, Mickey," I said, raising my head. "Can you hear? Baby…a baby crying."

The ladies sounded happy as they ran back and forth… attending Mama, then to the kitchen, and back again to Mama. One was busy picking up all those bloody rags. The blood made my stomach turn 'til I thought I'd puke, but the ladies were happy, so I guessed it was all right.

Finally, a lady came to the door, "Peggy, Mickey, you have a new little baby brother!"

"See, Mickey! Me told you baby…"

Mickey just shook his head and ambled on.

I ran up to the door and tried to peek in. The big ladies still hid my view of the bed, but I could hear the baby.

A few women were in the kitchen washing rags. One kept all the rest of them laughing. Another went back and forth, hanging the rags across the rickety fence out in back of our house. She dumped the pail of water out in the back yard, and it went clear across the yard, leaving a big swirling mud hole.

After most of the ladies had gone, one of them finally let Mickey and I into the house. Mickey just took one look and meandered off, but I went right up to the bed to see my new brother. I could almost reach the top of Mama's bed.

Mama held the tiny baby tight in her arms. He was wrapped tightly in a light, faded pink blanket. I felt the fluffy blanket while I peered at the bundle.

Beside the bed was a big box with a pillow on top. Another soft, pretty blanket was draped over it. On the side of the box were two bright, shiny handles.

Mama leaned over and showed me my new brother, but I wasn't tall enough to see him very well. I reached for the tiny hand that shot out of the blanket and jerked in mid-air. He was still screaming. That was the squalliest kid that I'd ever heard! Way after dark, Daddy came in. He took one look at Mama and said, "Another kid. Good thing it's another boy.

That's what we need...lots of big, strong boys. Maybe some day he'll be big enough to pick cotton."

The straight chair squeaked loudly when Daddy plunked himself down and let his elbows drop to the table. With the toe of one shoe, he slipped the other shoe off, then used the toes of that foot to slip off the other shoe. He scratched one foot with the other while he pulled his sweat-stained shirt off and put on another smelly one.

"Torn shirts, shoes that don't fit...I'm tired as hell. And I have to come home from a hard day's work with no hot meal and three squalling kids."

"Oh, Melvin, there's plenty of food in there," Mama said softly. "The neighbors brought food all day."

"Yeah, but it's not hot or good. Just their leftovers, I bet." Daddy got up and went into the kitchen to check out the offerings. I listened as he puttered about. Then he came back with a plate full of food, slouched down, and started eating. That didn't stop his complaining, though.

"When you gonna' get up, Win? I'll be glad when these kids are grown up and can help in the fields. He wiped his mouth with the back of his hand. I'll never know why I came out here to California. Promise of a better job. Promises, promises!" Daddy tore his shirt off and threw it in the corner on top of other stuff. "And how long's it been, now, since you picked cotton? Three days? When can you go back into the fields, Win? We need that extra money."

"Stop your worrying, Melvin, here, put this baby in the drawer." She held my new brother out to him.

Daddy glanced at the little bundle in Mama's arms and shook his head. "I'm not touching that kid, not me. You want him in that drawer, you get up and do it yourself." He opened up drawers, slamming them shut, then stormed out of the house with his shirt in one hand, "I'm gonna go play cards."

I watched Mama slowly get out of bed, put the tiny baby in the drawer, tucking the edges of the blanket tight around him. The drawer was brown, polished bright. I thought it made a nice bed.

I sat on my knees in front of the new baby and took his little hand in mine, "I'm your big sis," I told him. "And this is your big brother Mickey."

The baby screamed back at me.

I wrapped my hand in the soft folds of the blanket and held tight. The baby's pink mouth was wide open, and I saw that he didn't have any teeth. Mickey tried to stuff his bottle into the baby's mouth.

"We gonna' have scads of these," I told Mickey. "Daddy just said so."

Pretty soon, Mama was up and back in the field picking cotton. She named the baby Brian, and she took all three of us, my two brothers and me, to the fields with her. Leaving us under the big old shade tree, Mama lugged that heavy sack, dragging it on the ground as she worked away from us. She was just like all the rest of the dirty workers, moving slowly up one row, then down the other, reeking of old, smelly socks, wet, stinky clothes, and tobacco smoke.

Mama swayed against the weight of the lumpy cotton sack, shifting it from one side to the other as she eased herself down the long rows of cotton. Before long, she was just a dot on the other side of the field. But I could always spot her by that red and white bandanna she wore. I could spot her anywhere, by her walk and her jesters.

Looking back toward our tiny houses, they sat on big cement blocks with holes in them. I could see all the way under them to the next house and the next. Each with a decapitated sagging porches and hordes of kids in the front yard. Hundreds of clothes lines everywhere. Mostly hung gleaming white diapers, and tiny cotton panties. Hundreds of them. A few overalls in the mix, but not near as many diapers. Orange trees dotted the area here and there. Dozens of the tiny houses had gardens and in the evenings the men worked their garden until dark.

I watched the big men as they worked, their dusty overshoes wrinkled down at the back, their glazed eyes fixed on the rows of cotton. Most never changed their clothes, and those who did wore them six days straight. One old man wore a work shirt with bright, striped suspenders that held up his pants.

When Brian woke, he shrieked loudly. Mama always heard him, and she'd come running. She'd sit under the shade of the big cottonwood tree, then unbutton the top buttons of her dress and take out her heavy breast. Milk oozed from her nipple as she tried to poke it into Brian's screaming, jerking mouth. Mama rocked and softly patted Brian while she sang "Hush Little Baby, Don't Say a Word." Sometimes, Mama even yodeled softly to our new baby. I loved it when she yodeled. That was my favorite, and she did it well. And could she ever whistle.

In no time Brian was back asleep. Mama placed him on his pallet and turned to me before going back out to the field. "Now, Peggy, you watch your little brother for Mama."

"I will, Mama," I promised. "I love my new baby."

Sometimes Mama didn't come when Brian first woke up, and I'd talk to him to keep him quiet so Mama could pick more cotton. I could tell that my new brother really liked me. Sometimes when he fussed, I'd give him a taste of my bottle.

On cold morning my brothers and me sat by a big crackling bond fire on scratchy wool army blankets. Mickey and me spent a lot of time swatting at the fire, and dipping our long sticks into the hot, red coals.

The boss paid the workers with thin metal coins that could only be spent at one community store. No other store would take it.

Like my Mama and Daddy, most of the workers at Tagus Ranch had come from Texas and Oklahoma to seek their fortunes in California. They had hordes of kids, lots more than my family. They all worked in the fields. The more kids they had to work the fields, the more money the family had. Some worked ten to twelve hours a day, dragging heavy cotton sacks behind them, up one row and down the other.

Big tractors pulled trailers full of cotton to the gin. They came back and forth from early morning 'til dark, up and down the dusty country road. Sometimes the kids played in the trailers of cotton. Then one day, one of the kids drowned in the cotton; the grownups said he "smothered", and after that, nobody could get into the trailers.

After all the pickers were done, the threshing machine would come in and clean up the mess. I watched the big machines vanish around the bend in the road and wished the pickers would come back with their swearing, laughter, quarreling, screams, and cries.

When a new worker was hired by a field boss, one of the first things he was asked was, "Do you have a pocket watch?" If he did, the boss would take his watch from him and hang it on a nearby tree. In a rough, loud voice that carried over all the noisy trucks and tractors, he would shout, "The only times here are noon-time and quitting-time. We have two loud horns. When you hear them, you'll know what time it is." The tiny town of Tagus Ranch was located right off the main highway. The road spun off to the right, a single lane of gravel cutting between row-after-row of small, single-story shacks, all in straight lines. There was a haphazardness to the road, with hundreds, or maybe thousands, of people milling about. In the middle of the houses was one store where everyone bought their dry goods.

A tall tree shaded our house from the heat, throwing a large shadow across the whole front yard. An ancient, rusted truck sat on blocks in one front yard, under the sprawling trees. Two babies in diapers played in a swing made from a rubber tire that hung from a rope in one of the trees. The children next door, both naked, played in a makeshift sandbox.

My Daddy got really sick. He couldn't work, and sometimes he couldn't even walk. He coughed and wheezed all the time and was always out of breath. It was hard for him to smoke, but he always tried.

After a while, some men came and took Daddy to a hospital. Later, the men came back to our house and set up a big, green tent under the trees in our back yard, where it was cool. They spoke quietly to Mama, like they didn't want us kids to hear.

When they came back later with Daddy, I could see right away that he was even sicker than before. The hospital must have made my Daddy sicker, cause he sure wasn't like that before.

The big, strong men put Daddy on a cot in the tent. "Now you kids be careful, ya' hear," one of them told us. "Your Daddy is real sick, and what he has is catching. It's something real bad, and you don't want it."

Mama said, "Daddy has to sleep outside in the fresh air. That will make him better."

Mama spoon-fed Daddy liquid medicine hundreds of times a day, for coughing.

I stood at the canvas flap opening and watched my Daddy sleep on the cot. He coughed a terrible, hacking cough. He coughed non-stop, and couldn't even walk because he coughed so badly. From inside the house, I could hear him struggling for breath even when he was outside in the tent... My Daddy was really sick. More than a hundred times a day Mama slid her finger into Daddy's mouth and reaching deep, drew out a long gray string of phlegm, pulled it out and slung it outside. Daddy snatched an enormous breath then. People said tuberculosis was "con-ta-gious," and nobody could be in the same room with Daddy except Mama.

"Mama is Daddy nurse," I told Michey.

Mickey didn't care. He didn't know what a nurse was. I didn't either.

Mama positioned her old, squeaky rocking chair where she could rock and nurse Brian while taking care of Daddy at all times. Every time she went into the tent she had to change clothes. And she changed again when she came out. She said her dress was filled with the germs of what Daddy had. Mama really didn't have that many dresses. She was real busy washing her dresses. Mama couldn't work in the fields anymore because she had to take care of Daddy. She looked thin and tired. Mostly, she just stared into space, never saying much. She never sang anymore like she used too, not even to Brian.

Sometimes when she sat in the rocking chair with Brian, she spoke of the cars that drove to our house. "Can't you see them, Peggy? Look, see all the dust they leave behind?" Other times, she'd say, "What did they want, Peggy? Who were those people?"

"What people, Mama?" I asked.

"The people in the car!" Mama shouted.

"There were no people," I said, looking around the dusty road. "Nobody drove up."

Getting up, she'd walk out into the dirt filled road. "Come here, Peggy!" She'd pointed at the ground. "See these tire tracks? Now, don't tell me a car didn't drive in."

"But Mama, I don't see no car."

I never saw the cars or the dust, nor did I hear the car doors slam that Mama claimed to hear. She'd just rock baby Brian with that strange look on her face.

Piles of stuff grew in the corners of the house between the dust balls and other clutter of rags and clothing strewn about. Mama just rocked, looking into space.

Daddy was taken away. Mama said he was too sick to live at home, and the children couldn't be around him.

He had to go live in something called a sanitarium. A sanitarium was something like a hospital for people who were sick. He'd have to stay for a very long time. Mama said we would be moving far away from Tagus Ranch so we would be close to Daddy.

In my mind I wondered, Is Mama sick too? My Mommie is different, and I don't know why.

CHAPTER THREE

Daddy was taken to the tuberculosis sanitarium in Springville, California, located in the foothills of the Southern Sierra. In the '30's, treatment for TB consisted of isolation, and living in the mountains with clean, fresh air. It was thought that TB could be prevented by isolation and quarantine of those who had it, and it was important to move the diseased from contaminated surroundings.

Death from TB was five times higher among the poor. It was largely a disease of poverty and malnutrition. The best treatment was a proper diet, rest, and fresh air. One of the most useful remedies developed at the time was artificial pneumothorax. This involved the injection of air into the chest cavity, which gave the lungs a rest.

We hadn't been to our new house long when Daddy's mother and his niece came out to see him. Grandma Bearden was a sweet little lady. My cousin Johnny Mae was 11 years old and so happy to see me. She said to me, "i cried for days when you left Texas."

"You did?...Why."

"I stood outside the door when you were born. I was so excited to have a cousin. They wouldn't let me see you for three days."

"Three days,...why?" I asked.

"That was just the rules. Germs everyone was scared of germs. That's what killed my mama when I was born. So when you came along nobody could go near you. I remember too...not when my mama died, but when you were born."

"And I suppose, they still are....look at Daddy and his germs...I guess that's what he has". At least Mama doesn't have to always be changing her dress now that Daddy is in the hospital." But I soon found out that when she went to the hospital to see Daddy, she had to put a robe on over her dress.

The fence behind our house was high and brown, with the boards nailed so closely together I couldn't see through. Big knotholes filled many of the boards. I went along, wiggling my toes in the straggly patches of grass until I came to a hole that I could almost peek through by standing on my toes. I got a box and crawled up on it. I looked through the hole and saw an eye peeking back at me. I moved back a few steps just as a tiny hand appeared. It belonged to a boy about my age. The little boy whispered to me, "I can't play with you. My Mommy says you have a germs."

There's that word again...GERMS. "I don't have the germ, my Daddy does," I whispered to the boy.

"Well, I still can't play with you. I'll get a whopping I'd never forget."

When I came close again, the hand was gone, and all I saw was an area that looked as wild and needed much attention...junk was everywhere..

Every day, I climbed on the box in search of the boy. I never saw him again, and I never told Mickey. I knew Mickey would scare the boy away for good.

We lived on Main Street in a tiny white house with a white picket fence. Next door was a church but I didn't know what a church was.

The house had many big trees in the yard, and under them were piles of orange, gold, and brown leaves. They seemed to multiply on their way down. The piles were knee high, and Mickey and I ran through the leaves to hear them crackle underfoot.

It was a wonderful house, like none I'd ever lived in before. We had an inside toilet. This was the first time I'd ever seen a toilet inside the house, but we still peed outside when we had to go. We also had lots of furniture. Mickey and I slept in one bed, and Mama slept in the other. Brian slept with Mama.

From our front yard, Mama pointed out the big, long, yellow building high up on the hill. I could just barely see the rooftop. "That's the hospital where your Daddy is."

"Can Mickey and I go see Daddy?" I asked.

"Not now. The doctors don't want any of us to catch TB." "Mama, what is TB? Is it a real bad disease?"

"Yes, the doctor said it was bad," she answered. "We have to be careful that we don't catch it."

I wondered how long it would be before we would see Daddy again.

The big door of our house looked out onto the side yard, at the church next door. The doors of the other houses looked out onto the street. The other houses were old, narrow, and tall. Those across the street sat high on a hill. Raising my head high and getting up onto my toes, I stretched to look at them. The gardens were all well-cared for, the lawns fresh, green, and trimmed neatly, were watered almost every day. Tall flowers sprinkled everywhere. Orange and lemon trees dotted the area on both sides of the street. Between every house on the hillside, a fence went way down the hill to the road.

"Those are called 'picket fences'," Mama said. "See how every board is straight and perfect, like a line of wooden soldiers?"

Huge pots at the front doors were filled with bright red and pink flowers. Mama called them geraniums.

Ger-an-iums, I silently savored the word on my tongue. That's a funny word, and hard to say, too. I liked our new town and our new house.

Adding to the excitement in town were street races. Loud noises of squealing tires and roaring engines echoed through the narrow streets. Young men would spend hours with their head under the hood of a hot rod, engulfed with puffs of smoke.

Logging trucks zoomed up and down the winding, narrow, mountain road. And they didn't slow down. Our little house shook when the trucks barreled past. They made awful screaming noises down the curvy road. People could hear the trucks coming for miles, and stayed out of the street when they roared past. The big trucks never so much as even slowed down.

Across the street from our house was a big hotel made of brick and brown-painted wood. It had lots of windows and a big porch facing our house and the mountains. Just under the hotel was a bar. Around the corner was the post office.

On our side of the street, across from the hotel, was a liquor store.

An elderly man owned the liquor store. Outside the store were stacks of newspapers. Inside, metal shelves held row after row of magazines, and there were racks of candy, gum, and cigarettes.

The old man had boxes filled with geraniums—only his were dead. It was fun to spy on him. He always watched Mickey and me over the top of his glasses. He wore a puke-colored plaid flannel shirt and baggy pants, and his pockets always bulged and sagged.

Mickey asked, "What's in that man's pocket, Peggy?" "Those, young man, are my tools," the man answered.

"Tools just like your Daddy has. Haven't you ever seen your Daddy's tools?" He pulled pliers, a screwdriver, and hammer from his pocket and showed them to Mickey.

"My Daddy don't have none of them. My Daddy's in that hospital." Mickey pointed to the big hospital on the hill.

"Yeah, I heard. That's real bad to be in there, sure is." He stood on his toes and stretched out his arms to latch a board on a signboard to a hook over the door to his store. On the board were big, bright red letters: "CLOSED". I was only four, and I couldn't read yet. But I planned to "learn myself how, and real soon."

The man rubbed at the white stubble on his chin, pushed the big sign into place, and locked the board with a big padlock placed at each corner.

"You sure do talk funny, mister," I told him.

Laughing, he said, "Yeah, suppose I do. That's German. Don't suppose you know what German is, do ya?" "No, mister. What is it?"

"When you grow up and go to school, ya'll learn." He turned sharply and went up the street.

"Come on, Mickey, let's cross the street," I said. "Give me your hand. We don't want one of those big trucks to smash us. I wonder where Mama is?" She always seemed to be gone lately.

Sunday nights, people walked back and forth past the shops and the cafe. Young couples, old women, old men, groups of teenagers. Mostly they strolled near the homes or walked leisurely through town. Some had long, dreadful faces. Some were silent. Many chatted, and the young ones giggled. Others sat on porches of their houses. Everyone hollered to each other.

"Good evening, Mr. Wells!"

"Nice day, huh, Tom? Gonna be hot before we know it." Cars coughed down into town, later returning up the hill toward home. Mama rocked and stared into space.

Mickey and I watched everyone.

Out near the Tule River was a soda spring. All day Saturday and after church on Sunday, cars lined up while people waited to fill their jugs with the soda water. People came from miles around for soda water.

After we'd lived in our new house for a while, when Daddy came home, he was always mad the minute he stepped into our house. I guess he was mad because he had to stay in that old hospital for so long. I never knew why Daddy came home. I know he wasn't cured, because he always became sicker and went back to the hospital. He'd drink and smoke so much he made himself sicker. Then he started hitting my Mama. I tried to protect her. I didn't want Daddy to hit my Mama. Mama never fought back, but boy, I sure did!

Then he started beating me, too. He chased us out of the house, then locking the doors so we couldn't get if. Then we heard the crashing of glass. Daddy broke all the dishes and what ever else was with in his reach.

Late at night I climbed those high step to the door of the house next door that they called a "church". I'd heard it told that Jesus lived there. I knocked and knocked but nobody ever came to help my Mama.

The next day Daddy went back to the hospital, and I was sure glad he did. What a mess he'd left for us to clean up. Not only was our house a mess, so was Mama. Both eyes blue and puffy. Her lip swollen and bleeding. Handfuls of hair everywhere. And to begin with, she didn't have much hair.

Late one afternoon, just about dusk, I crawled under Mama's bed to hide from Mickey and Brian. It was dark and spooky under there, with lots of dust. The bed springs were rusty and full of dust. One of Daddy's shirts was wadded up in a corner.

Gobbed-up newspaper scattered about, I touched the heap and it was soft. Unwrapping the paper, it stuck but came right off when I pulled, paper clung in places. It looked like a big piece of bloody meat, it had that same awful, sweet icky smell.

It jiggled when I touched it. I wiped my bloody finger on the floor, leaving a long, thin brownish-red line. I touched the meat again, this time harder. It wobbled and jiggled. What is it? I thought. It was sticky too.

Rolling out from under the bed I sneezed, then ran to get Mickey. The bloody meat was gone when we returned. A big bloody splotch remained on the floor.

I looked all over the room, and found that in the closet there was a tall brown paper bag, filled with bloody rags. They had that same sickly, sweet smell. I couldn't stop wondering about the awful, jiggly piece of meat under Mama's bed. Who had put it there?

CHAPTER FOUR

Across the river, down by the soda spring stood a huge old barn. Every Saturday night, people came from all over the valley, with their children, for a big dance.

Leaving Brian home—he was asleep, anyway—I led Mickey to the barn dance. We always went real early so we could find a good place to sit and watch the dancers. From a bale of hay outside, we gazed at the dancers through huge open barn doors, listening to the hootchy-cootchy music. We tried to get inside the big barn several times. The man at the door would always say, "Give me fifty-cents."

"What's that?" I asked.

"Money. Go get me fifty-cents from your parents and I'll let you in."

The next week, I handed him a hand full of change. "That not enough, young lady. I need fifty-cents for the two of ya'. And your Mommy will have to be with ya' too." A western string band entertained the cowboys and their ladies from nine till fight time. The children danced jigs with their grandfathers and daddy's. Some of the children danced together, in one long line, to the tune of "Cotton

Eye'd Joe." Sometimes the boys faced one way, and the girls faced the opposite.

They had guitars and banjos, piano and drums. If the fiddle player wasn't playing, she danced and tapped her foot in time to the music. I liked her the best. I loved to watch her twirl, with her skirt going high over her head. Her top was pulled off her shoulders. She twirled and stepped high to the rhythm of the music, while she played her fiddle and sang. "Get along little dogie, yippi ki yeah, yeppi ki yo."

People danced a two-step around the dance floor. The band played roadhouse music, country style—Lone Star rag and honky-tonk blues. My favorite song was "The Wabash Cannonball." I'd get so excited every time I heard it. I learned all the words. Wasn't no time at all that I'd sit with Mickey and sing to him, right along with the band.

I always liked seeing Dodge at the dances. His name was Mr. Dodge, but everybody called him "Dodge". He was my most favorite person. He danced with all the little girls. They all ran and swarmed around him the minute he walked into the dance hall. Almost every time he'd come outside, pick me up into his big arms and dance with me. I was face to face with his pokie whiskers and kept my face turned away from him. But I wanted to dance. I didn't like his stinky, smelly breath, right in my face. He smelled like Daddy.

Sometimes he danced with all the children, and everyone loved Dodge. My heart throbbed with excitement when I saw him, because I knew he'd come outside and dance with me.

The dance contest was the biggest thrill of the evening. People gathered in front of me, blocking my view. I was in heaven, standing on my tiptoes to catch a glimpse of the dancers in the middle of the crowd. Then I spotted Mama.

"I never knew she could dance like that," I whispered to Mickey. My heart was filled with excitement just watching her. She rocked with beautiful rhythm. She rocked from heal to toe. I just couldn't believe my eyes, and I couldn't pull them from her. I'd never seen my Mama like this. She was all smiles,.as I watched. The minute the dance was over, taking Mickey by the hand we shoved our way threw the people across the dance floor. But Mama could not be found. I looked everywhere for her. Had I dreamt that I'd seen her. I kept bumping into everybody looking for Mama. Looking up at the sky flooded with brilliant stars which seemed to twinkle in time to the music. The hillsides boomed with the sounds of yipping dancers who stomped and stretched their studded boots to the floor, trying to imitate the country crooner's hip and shake. The cowboys grinned at their ladies. But angry by now, I couldn't see Mama. Where had she gone? I whispered to myself A lady in a full skirt plucked away on the fiddle as she stepped high to the music. Another sucked on a silver harmonica. It looked like that harmonica was glued right to her mouth. Those two were my favorites.

Way in the back, a man sat on the heels of his boots playing the spoons. Beside him, another man did something with his finger in his mouth, while he hit his hand back and forth against his pant leg.

Outside, men gathered around cars passing a big brown bottle between them, each taking a big swig. Several fights broke out. Later, the men seemed to change. They didn't talk well, and their words were slurred. They acted silly, staggering and wobbling around with blank, hollow looks in their eyes. Most of the men and women outside pulled off their pants and wrestled. I never understood that.

Some of the things they said, Mickey and I didn't understand. One of the men was always stumbling around saying something about "give a dog shit." His words were fast and angry. Another's mouth opened and closed like a fish when he talked.

Dodge would dance the Hoky Poky with me in the dark of the night, behind the big old trees and shrubs. He always told me, "this is our little secret, just yours and mine, okay?" "I won't tell nobody, Dodge." And I never did. I liked for him to dance the Hoky Poky with me. His big arms picked me up and he swung me high around his neck. He'd hold onto my legs that hung around his big neck, with my little bare bottom at the back of his neck.

He ran and jumped with me. Stopping, he put his right foot out and sang.

> "Put your right foot in,
> put your right foot out,
> put your right foot in,
> and shake it all about.
> You do the Hoky Poky
> and you turn yourself
> about. That's what it's
> all about!"

Dodge screamed and shouted, and I laughed with bubbling joy while he danced with me straddling his neck. Much, much later after I'd gotten to know Dodge real well, every time he saw me, he'd joke and tease me. Sometimes, he'd toss me a coin. Late at night when I saw him, he'd give me a piggy back ride on his back. Sometimes he'd take his shirt off, and later, he always took his shirt off when I rode on his back. I really did like Dodge, and I felt safe with him. "I love you, Peggy," he told me. "I love you just like you were my very own little girl."

"I wish you were my Daddy," I said. "Can you be my Daddy?"

"Let's just pretend that I'm your Daddy, okay? It'll be our secret, only ours. Nobody else will know."

"Okay. Just you and me will know."

Later, while dancing the Hoky Poky, Dodge raised his big arms and lifted me off his neck. Ducking his head, he lifted me over and sat me on the back of a big, rusty truck. He sang to me, moving his feet in and out in a dance pattern. With his big hand, he touched my nose.

Dodge was always putting his hands in my pantie. He said he liked me best when I didn't wear any panties. His fingers hurt me really bad.

I smelled a whiff of Dodge's nasty breath. His 'thing' poked out the bottom of his shirt. It was big, purple, and hard.

> "Put your right finger in,
> put your right finger out,
> put your right finger in,
> and toss it all about!"

He rubbed my nose and laughed. "Now the mouth... open up wide."

"Put your right finger in,
put your right finger out,
put your right finger in,
and turn it all about!"

"Open mouth...open mouth wide for Dodge. That's a girl, that's my girl."

His dry, cracked finger poked in my mouth. It didn't taste very good. Dodge laughed, and I did too, 'cause I thought it was supposed to be great fun.

The one they called Perce slumped over and dozed early in the evening. He always wore a crumpled calf-roper's hat and shredded coveralls. Scrubbed up, Perce was a pleasant fellow, shaggy-haired and innocent-eyed. But he wasn't scrubbed up often. 'Bout as often as me. He dozed while his friend, Shorty, limped around or sat alone at a table, his boot tapping with the music.

Directly, Shorty got up and danced around the floor all by himself. Sometimes a little girl would run over to him and he'd grab her, and the two of them would dance off together. He'd drop her off where he had picked her up and, two-stepping in a trot, go back to where he had been sitting with Perce.

Many men chased their ladies through the tall grass. Mickey and I saw one cowboy pull something off his lady's legs while she sat on the seat of his pickup. I wondered what those things were that the man pulled off the lady's legs. My Mama didn't wear nothing like that. I pulled up my dress and looked at my bare bottom. I didn't have anything like that, either.

Creeping closer to the edge of the truck, I peered into the big, creaky, rusty bed. A moment later, I saw something else: pink flesh...pink toes. Curly brown hair between white legs. Her eyes were closed, and she had such soft, white flesh. She was so pretty that I couldn't move. She looked dreamy-eyed. She was full of laughter, locked together with this man. Their cries of abandon mingled with the laughter of children from the barn and the country music.

I felt vaguely uneasy and didn't know why. Why am I frightened of these men? I wondered. All the ladies are locked naked with men. Everybody is doing "it". Everywhere I go, everyone is doing "it". Even my Mama and Daddy—Mama with other men.

Hidden under a tree, a man stood outside and took his big purple thing out of his britches. I couldn't take my eyes off it, and I couldn't see what he did with that thing. It was different from my little brothers', so big and ugly looking as he held it in his hand. In a way, it seemed frightening. After he put it back in his britches and zipped up his pants, he walked toward me. When he got even with me he paused, glanced down at me. He reached out a hand, touched the top of my head, and I twisted away from under his palm.

"Peggy?" he said, smiling.

Along the mountainside, naked bodies locked together on the green grass, their labored cries of ecstasy mingled with the western band and sound of laughter.

Weeks later, Dodge's game turned into a different kind of game.

Lifting me high onto a tall haystack, Dodge sang the Hoky Poky and danced. His pants were unbuttoned, and his shirt tail hung out over the front of his pants.

"Open your mouth wide for old Dodge," he instructed me. "Put your pee-pee in..." Taking his thing, he tried to put it in my mouth.

"Huh? Ugh...no," I protested. "I don't like that." "Come on, sweetheart," he said in a low voice. "Dodge won't hurt you. You know that, don't you?" Again, he took his thing ugly, hard and throbbing, he rubbed that ugly smelly thing on my face.

Panic! My lips squeezed tight, I shook my head. My legs turned to jelly.

"Put your pee-pee in...Come on, open wide, sweetheart. Open wide for Dodge. Pull your pee-pee out..." Dodge continued to sing as he slid his hand in between my legs.

> "Put your right finger in,
> put your right finger out,
> put your right finger in,
> and turn it all about,
> You do the Hoky Poky, and you turn yourself about"

Dodge's singing faded.

"Doesn't that feel good, honey?"

"Yuck!" I pushed Dodge away. "No!" I shouted. "I don't like this game."

"Come on, sweetheart," he begged. "Come on, do it for Dodge. I thought you liked the Hoky Poky. I thought you liked old Dodge."

"I do like to dance the Hoky Poky, but I don't like this one!" I cried. "It's not the same as the dance." As I walked home I kept trying to brush off the thick, sticky, dry and cracked substance that clung all over me.

The music and stars that filled my heart with joy earlier, now seemed to stare down at a chilly nightmare. Why had Dodge changed the game to a nasty thing? Was it my fault? What had I done? Why did Dodge want to pee pee in my mouth.

Early the next morning as I lay in bed with my brothers I couldn't get Mama out of my head. And Mama never came home.

It was the beginning of a pyramid of guilt which would build through the years. The stars watched my innocence beginning to fade that night like Mama and the excitement of the music.

CHAPTER FIVE

In 1942, I attended my first day at school. The school yard was covered with lush green grass. My heart pounded with electric excitement. With jumbo grins the children sidestepped about, buzzing with laughter. They all carried paper sacks or lunch boxes.

"What are those?" I asked a little girl.

With her finger in her mouth, she said shyly, "My lunch." The girl giggled to another as if it was a great secret. Lunch? What's that?

I stood aside shyly, twisting my dress and watching all the children being hugged by their mothers. A long, slobbery Sugar Daddy sucker hung from my mouth. I stole a sucker every day from the old German man at the grocery store. If I couldn't get it in the mornings, I always managed to in the evenings. I'd pull it way out until it was just a thin line. Slobber dripped onto my chin, and the skin under my chin was always chapped from the moisture.

I watched the children being embraced by their mothers. Many wiggled their way into their Mommies' rounded arms, up against the softness of their breasts. I closed my eyes and pretended that my Mama was hugging me that way. I didn't know why my Mama wasn't with me, since all the other kids had their mothers with them.

Artwork decorated the classroom walls, bright splashes of color and shapes on display. I stared at the pictures.

My teacher was a tiny old lady, bent at the waist, with fuzzy red hair. She looked like a brillo pad my Mama used to scrub pots with. She went to the black wall and picked up a long white stick she called "chalk." She wrote her name in big letters on the black wall. "My name is Miss Tarr." With the long piece of chalk, she touched each letter, spelling it out: "M I S S T A R R". The ABC were written out at the top of the black board in large block letters. I copied them to carry home and read to my brothers.

I went to school without shoes or a coat. My clothes and body were all the same dirty color. I wore no under panties. My dark brown hair was long, thick, and straight, hanging in oily strings around my face. Each strand was so dirty it made my hair look very, thick. My feet were dirty, thick, and calloused. I wore the same painfully small dress during the day and to bed that night. The sash on my dress dangled at my sides; the other girls' sashes were tied in big, pretty bows. The minute I noticed one little girl, I loved her. Her hair was in long ringlets, and bounced as she jumped around. She had those holes in her cheeks like my brother Brian. Her eyes were pale blue. She wore the prettiest dress I'd ever seen. I wanted to touch her smooth, white face and her dress.

I wanted to hold her hand, but she pulled away from me.

I tried to focus on the other children. They didn't look like me. They were all squeaky clean. They seemed to practically shine. A chill cut through me, just looking at those other children. I knew that I wasn't like them.

They whispered to each other and pointed at me, snickering. They wouldn't play or talk to me. Instead, they just stared, a smile on their mouths that told me they were laughing at me. I tried to pretend I didn't care, but of course I did. Their giggles and snickers sank deep into my mind. A knot of fear grew in my stomach like a live thing.

One of the first days in school, Miss Tarr went down the rows of students asking each of them if they knew what nationality they were. I held my hand high in the air and waved. I couldn't wait my turn, 'cause I knew the answer to her question.

Finally, before Miss Tarr got to me, she said, "All right, Peggy. You seem to know what your nationality is. Will you tell the class?"

Excitedly I said, "Half of me is Okie, but I don't know what the other half is."

Miss Tarr laughed, and the rest of the class roared with laughter. Right off I knew that I'd said the wrong thing. But I didn't know what was wrong. It must be because I'm an Okie, I thought. Now I don't want to be one.

The teacher stopped to tie the other little girls' sashes, but not mine. I wondered why, wishing she would tie my sash, too.

"Miss Tarr, will you tie my sash in a bow like you did for Margie?" I smiled big, hoping she would.

"Run along, Peggy," the teacher said. "Yours won't stay. Your sash is in strings. Run along now."

There was just a note of meanness in her voice. She didn't smile at me as she did with the other children.

My lip quivered a bit, and hot tears stung my eyes. I didn't let anybody see them. They don't like me. The words made big circles in my mind as I tried to do my work. Nobody likes me...I don't know why, I haven't done anything wrong. Why doesn't Miss Tarr like me?

The little girl was dressed in a pretty starched and ironed dress, with her hair tied on each side of her head in puppy tails, with bright, neat bows. She was so pretty and spotlessly clean. She looked like something that should be put on a shelf somewhere, just to look at.

I wanted to play with her, to touch her. But when I tried, she jumped out of the sandbox and ran away screaming in the nastiest way possible. "Miss Tarr! Miss Tarr!"

I'd never seen anything as wonderful and prissy as that girl. I chased after her, reaching out to touch her stiff pinafore.

I thought the ruffles on her dress were about the prettiest I'd ever seen. The ruffles on my dress hung limp and shredded, the lace torn off in spots. Why don't I look like her? I thought, wishing I had a dress like hers.

She slapped my hand away and screamed at me, spraying spit. "Don't touch me! Look at how dirty your hands are!"

I kept on feeling her ruffles. I didn't think my hands were very dirty. Then I ran back to the sandbox, and she started screaming again. "Miss Tarr! Peggy just went to the bathroom in the sandbox."

With short, little steps, Miss Tarr came running to the edge of the sandbox. With her hands on her hips, she asked, "Did you go potty in the sandbox, Peggy?"

Quietly, I said, "Yes, Miss Tarr. What's wrong with that?" Miss Tarr yanked me from the sandbox by my ear and dragged me to the classroom. When she finally let go of my ear, it was numb.

Miss Tarr shook her finger in my face and talked about all sorts of things I'd never heard of. "Rules." With spit flying from her lips, she called me a "stupid Okie" and "the scum kid."

"I'm not a Okie, and I'm not stupid." My tightly closed knuckles were white. I wanted to hit her right in the nose.

"Well, what are you?"

"I don't know, but I'm not a Okie."

"Well, your Mama sure is, so that makes you an Okie."

"Well, she ain't no more, 'cause I'm gonna tell her not to be!"

The class giggled noisily. "You're the one that said you were an Okie," one boy yelled at me.

"Well, I may have told you that, but I'm not no more!"

The class roared with laughter. Miss Tarr waved a ruler in one hand and pulled me by the sleeve of my dress until we were nose-to-nose. "Don't you back-talk me, you hear?" She shoved me into the dark cloakroom. "You're as common as dirt. Now stay in there!"

I lost my balance, tripped, and sprawled onto the wooden floor, face down. But I didn't cry. I wouldn't give her the pleasure of seeing me cry.

I crouched in the narrow cloakroom and listened to the lesson through the door, even holding up my hand when I knew the answers. One part of me knew it was unfair, but another told me that I was always the bad one. After all, nobody else ever got into trouble.

Miss Tarr was always angry when I asked "stupid questions," as she called them. Instead of smiles and words of encouragement, I got smacks from her ruler.

But life was about to give me another harsh smack.

CHAPTER SIX

We hadn't been in Springville long when it was discovered that Mickey and I had tuberculosis.

I watched while Mama stood in our front yard and talked with a man in a long, white coat. I could tell by his clothes that he was from the hospital. They spoke in muted whispers. I couldn't hear their words, but I knew they were talking about me, and I knew it was bad. I could tell by the way they acted that it was a secret.

Finally, Mama called me. "Peggy, get your brother and go with Dr. Winn to the hospital. I'll be right over."

"Why? Can I see Daddy?"

She didn't answer, so I went to get Mickey.

The man took us by the hand and led us into the doorway of the huge building. The glare of the polished floor and the echoes of muffled voices bounced off the cold, enamel painted walls. The place was full of loud, threatening voices. Two nurses came into the room. One took Mickey while the other took me, and they practically dragged us into a small room with a big stall and hose. Turning the water on they hosed up down. After turning off the water the two nurses each took one of us and both scrubbed and scrubbed us until we were both red and raw. The one nurse filled my hair with something green out of a bottle. Pulling and rubbing my hair she scrubbed me again. I was screaming and crying, my eyes burned and people in white gowns were running from every direction, watching.

After we were bathed we were dressed in dresses and carted off back to another room with just two metal beds and a toilet. The whole room looked like metal painted the same green color as the rest of the hospital. I choked on a breath, and the smell of antiseptics made my eyes water. I hated the smell. A nurse told me to get into bed—Mickey too.

I pushed back the covers of my bed with my feet and slid to the back, with my head against the wall. I was filled with deep-seated churning I did not understand. I began to shake, but I wasn't cold.

I loved the bed, though. The sheets felt crisp, cool and smooth. "We don't have these things at home," I told Mickey. They warmed up when I crawled in. I'd never seen such clean, warm, and cozy blankets. I didn't mind staying in the bed all the time, because it felt so good.

At night, when everyone was gone, I'd sneak into bed with Mickey. I had never slept without him and Brian.

I missed Brian and wondered if Mama was taking good care of him. I sure hoped so. I wished I could see him, but the doctor said I couldn't, that I might give him my old TB. I wished that I could give it to somebody, 'cause I sure didn't want it.

The door was metal, with a tiny window in it. All day long, people peeked in the window at us. The sound of other steel doors opened and banged shut all the time.

Footsteps echoed down the big, wide hall. Sometimes we heard someone speak softly—a voice easily heard in the empty hallway.

Daddy sometimes came to the door and talked to Mickey. I huddled in the corner away from Daddy, watching from a curled-up position in my hospital bed. I was scared out of my hide. I was terrified of the awful hospital.

Then a doctor and nurse I'd never seen before came into our room. They wore white coats, and stethoscopes hung from one's neck. The other stethoscope was stuffed into the nurses pocket. I immediately jumped under my bed.

The doctor pulled a chair close to my bed. "Come on out, Peggy," he said quietly. "I'm Dr. Rush, and I won't hurt you. You need to be examined."

Mickey lay on his stomach and tried to coax me out. "They won't hurt you, Peggy. Come on out." Taking my hand, Mickey helped me out from under the bed. "My sister is scared of you," he explained to the others.

"Can your sister talk?" the nurse asked, pretending to study a stack of papers in her hand.

"Sure, she can talk." He turned to me. "Talk, Peggy, talk. They want to know if you can talk. Come on, Peggy, talk!"

I just shook my head "No."

"Well, I guess she can hear," said the nurse. She left the room.

Before long, two others came back and rolled us down the long hallway. I was still afraid, but I was also fascinated by all the people I saw. Some were in those big chairs with wheels, like the ones Mickey and I were in. Many strolled along wearing long robes and slippers.

We were wheeled into another echoing room with a lot of big, shiny machinery and a long examining table. I jumped from the chair with wheels and hid under the metal table, making a terrible clang as I scurried for its protection. I was terrified. I'd never been in a hospital before. Everyone was a stranger, and I was away from my Mama. I didn't understand what was happening and was afraid of what could happen next. I wanted to go home.

I wouldn't even look at any of those people. I kept my eyes closed as I crouched there, drawing my legs up to ease the knot that had grown in my stomach.

Finally, after listening to the doctor's calm, persuasive voice, I crawled out. The nurses lifted me onto the table, and I listened to all the clanging sounds as they gave me instructions about how to breathe. How stupid, I thought. I know how to do this. Has Miss Tarr told them I'm an Okie and Okies don't know how to breathe? I listened while Mickey was put on the table.

The nurses were all dressed in crisp, white, starched jackets. They wore high hats and a big white bandage over their mouths.

"Why is that thing over your mouth?" Mickey asked. "It's called a mask. We don't want to pass your germs around," one of the nurses said.

"I have a germ? What's a germ?"

"It's a disease that you can pass on to someone else. Then they'll have TB, too."

Oh, that's why the kids don't like me—I have a germ. The thought somehow seemed to strangely lay a comforting hand on all the hurt they had caused. Now there was a reason.

"It's going to be all right," the nurse reassured us. Every racing heartbeat seemed to tell me, *It's not either! Something bad is happening!* I watched, terrified, as a nurse slipped a big black band around Mickey's arm and pumped it up. She tucked a tiny silver disk under the band, then put the other end in her ears. When she finished, she took a big piece of gauze with a clear, colorless liquid, and smeared it all over the side of his ribs. After that, she took another piece of gauze with a bright, orange liquid, and painted Mickey's entire side with it.

"What are you doing to my brother?" I asked.

She turned to smile at me. "Well, Peggy, at least we know that you can talk!"

"It's okay, Peggy," Mickey said. "It don't hurt."

When she finished, she wrote something on a paper clipped to a piece of metal. Then she came over to me and started doing the same thing she'd done to Mickey. The big, black band on my arm was too tight, and it hurt when she pumped it up. Then she yanked the band from my arm with a ripping sound.

The doctor took a tiny bottle and put a very long needle into the top. I had that feeling in my stomach again, and knew that something nasty was about to happen. I had never seen anything like that shiny tray filled with all kinds of stuff.

I listened carefully as the doctor told Mickey, "This will burn a little, but it won't hurt. All you'll feel is a lot of pushing, pressure."

I watched intently as they felt around with their thumbs on Mickey's chest. Mickey flinched.

Then they brought the same tiny bottle with that long needle over to me. I pushed myself with the back of my heels as far as I could go.

"It's okay, Peggy," Mickey said. "It won't hurt. See, it didn't hurt me." He turned so that I could see his side.

I wrapped my arms around my chest and wouldn't let loose. "I won't let you near me. I won't!" I screamed, cried, and kicked, backing further into the corner. I wished I could slip right through the wall and come out on the other side, then I could run away from these people. "Stay away from me!" I threatened.

The nurse hurried out, and came back a few minutes later with Daddy.

"Peggy, it won't hurt," he promised. "It's just a little bee sting." He lifted his robe aside to show me where he had gotten "shots." "They do it to me every day."

When Daddy came toward me and started to grab me, I kicked him away. I stood up on the bed, ran to the end, and jumped off. "Don't come near me!" I screamed.

The doctor led Daddy out the door. "Let's leave her alone for now."

In a few minutes, they returned with another doctor. He was tall, lean, and well scrubbed, dressed in white matching slacks and shirt. He was clean-shaven with dark hair cut short and slicked to the side. With him were about five or six nurses.

Pure panic shot through me. All I could hear was the sound of my own heart pounding. Had I not opened my eyes at that precise moment, I knew they would kill me. "Don't hurt me!" I begged, drawing up my legs. "Stop! Stop!" Three of the nurses grabbed me and pinned me to the bed.

One uncurled my arms that were tight around my chest, while another held them tight. Another held me down onto the bed with her knee in my side, and one held my legs straight. My stomach churned, and I shivered violently. I felt the coldness as they rubbed that liquid on me. I felt thumbs feeling for the bones in my side. I was scared out of my mind with fear of that big needle. They pushed hard, then harder. Within just seconds, I'd had the shot. It was all over, and all of the nurses left.

"See, it's done," the doctor said. "It didn't hurt nearly as bad as you thought, did it?"

Rubbing my chest, I shouted defiantly, "Yes, it did too hurt. I bet you never had one of those shots with that long needle." I drew my knees up to my chest, and wrapping my arms around myself, buried my head. From that moment on, the people in white took up residence inside my head. Along with the words "something bad is happening" and "the kids don't like me". They all rode a merry-go-round when the lights were off at night.

Every other day, I had this treatment...one side one time, and the other side the next. Every time, I'd fight them. Many times, I'd run out of the room and hide. One time I escaped and ran home. Mama took me back to the hospital. Other times I hid in the basement, but that was a spooky place. I really didn't know which was worse, the shot or the basement. They also fed us spoonfuls of a liquid they called cod- liver oil. It had a nasty taste, and after many days of taking it, Mickey and I both stunk of it.

Every night, we were given a spoonful of pure sugar with turpentine on top of it. It was awful tasting, too.

Other times, we were taken in a big chair with big wheels on both sides. They rolled us down the big, wide hall to a room where the nurse said they took a picture of our chest. I wished I could be alone with this chair. I wanted to wheel up and down, up and down the big hallway. Mickey and I could really have had fun racing.

They slid trays of food under the door for us and we gobbled down our food, using our fingers. We picked up the dish and licked it clean, then licking our fingers like lollipops. We'd never had food like this. The nurses stood outside our door and laughed as they watched us.

One cold day, all the nurses coming on duty carried brightly wrapped packages. Some hung big red, blue, and green glass balls in the hallways with huge silver things they said were snowflakes. Two nurses draped long garlands of greenery and tiny lights among the treasures on the bookshelves.

One hung a line of cards with scenes of horses in the snow, and a little round man all dressed in red, with a long white beard.

Our room was right across the hall from the nurses' station, and we watched the goings on with wide eyes.

A few days later, a man dressed in high boots and a long, heavy coat carried in a small green tree. The nurses set it in the window of the office. Now it was hard to look into their station, but we watched everyone decorating the tree with big glass balls and long silver strings. Mickey and I watched in fascination.

"Sure is pretty, huh, Mickey?"

"Uh huh," he agreed, his mouth hanging open.

One nurse brought us a piece of hard, striped candy. "What's this?" I asked.

"Why, it's Christmas candy," she said cheerfully. "Haven't you ever heard of Christmas candy before?"

"No," we answered at the same time.

After that, one of the nurses brought us a piece of candy every day.

"This is homemade fudge," a nurse said. "I made it myself. I went home last night and made it just for the two of you."

We gobbled the fudge and asked for more. "What's going on?" I asked.

"Why, it's Christmas. You know…when Santa comes."

"Who's Santa?" Mickey asked.

She stared at us. "You mean, you've never heard of Santa?" Then she smiled. "Well, you're in for one big surprise." She hurried out of our room. When she returned, she carried a small book. "I'm going to read you a story." As she turned the pages, we saw pictures of dancing reindeer and a red and white Santa.

"T'was the night before Christmas, and all through the house " Her words were slightly muffled through the mask.

She read the whole story to us while we touched the pages in wonder. For the next few days, nurses spent their afternoons showing us how to cut out strips of colored paper and loop them together to make chains. We hung them around our door. One nurse even put our chains on her tree.

We were thrilled to help decorate their Christmas tree. Mickey and I thought that was the greatest thing anybody could do, letting us help.

It was my very first Christmas, I was so excited, and couldn't wait to see Santa. Mickey and I were watching from our window when a big Jeep drove into the parking lot. Santa Claus was dressed all in red, just like in the picture book. His cheeks were bright pink beneath his big white beard. He slung a big, heavy bag over his shoulder and walked slowly up the high steps.

I wanted to talk to him, to feel him, and touch him. I was excited and couldn't wait to sit in his lap. Suddenly a terrible thought came to me: What if he got nasty like Dodge when I sat on his lap?

We waited a long time before he came in to see us. When he finally arrived at our room, I was too scared to talk to him. He spoke for a short while to Mickey, and gave Mickey and me a big stocking full of candy, apples, an orange, nuts, and his very own toy.

As Santa turned to leave he left a stocking on a chair, "This is for you young lady," he told me. A tag hanging on the side read "Girl." I came alive every morning playing with my wonderful toy.

I had just started school when I had gotten sick and had to go to the sanitorium. I was disappointed because I couldn't go to school. A lady came to the hospital one day a week to teach us, but it wasn't like my real school. She was dressed in white, like the nurses, and wore that big bandage over her mouth.

Dressed in gowns, under panties, and socks, the children gathered in a big room while the teacher read the lessons to us.

Mickey went home first. He didn't have TB anymore. I had to stay all by myself and Mickey couldn't even come to visit. I kept running away and finally they had to keep my door locked. I was terrified out of my mind being there alone. Finally, when it came time for me to leave the hospital I ran to pack my toy, and could scarcely wait to see Mickey and Brian.

Mama came to walk me across the street; she was wearing that big, ugly dress—the one she always wore day and night. I knew I'd soon be having another brother, but I really hoped for a sister.

Red, white and blue flags flew all over town.

Scotty was born on July 4, 1943, while we lived in the house in Springville. I remember Mama bringing him home from the county hospital.

Mrs. McDonald stayed with us while Mama was in the hospital. She had a houseful of girls. I liked all the girls. Mrs. McDonald curled my hair like hers. It was very painful, but I didn't cry.

Mama was gone an awful long time. I felt grown-ups were witless. Mama didn't have to go to any stupid hospital when Brian was born. Why did she have to go now? I couldn't seem to keep up with the big people. One said one thing, then another would come along and say something else. And besides, why didn't she just go to the same hospital where Mickey and I had been? She didn't have to go so far away.

Scotty was my third brother. I was six years old, and every night the first star appeared in the sky, I'd wish for a sister. I was terribly disappointed, but in no time at all, I fell in love with my new baby brother. Scotty was adorable, with his golden ringlets. He had golden curls just like my friends from school. How I loved golden curls.

As Scotty grew older, the more he became the sister I had wanted so badly. I'd sit for hours, curling his hair around my finger. In no time, his long curls hung past his waist. I put him in dresses.

As soon as Scotty could talk, he named me "Sissy". From then on, everyone called me Sissy.

"Dress me too, Sissy!" Brian would say, as I dressed Scotty.

As they both got older, they wore dirty bib overalls held by one strap. Scotty still looked like a girl, and most people thought he was. When he got older, a grown-up would say, "What an adorable little girl."

"You-son-ya-beach!" Scotty would yell. "Me no girl, huh Sissy?"

CHAPTER SEVEN

As long as I could remember, Daddy was in the tuberculosis institution. He came home only occasionally. I don't know if he was released, or if he simply walked away. Daddy was always sick, even when he was home. He drank and smoked until he had to go back to the hospital.

I always knew when Daddy was coming home from the sanitorium because I could hear him as he walked down the street, and smell his cigarette. He had a slight gimp. He always told stories about how a milk cow had stepped on his ankle when he was young. He also said, "That was the end of my boxing career."

He'd come walking home late at night.

The minute he would appear at the door, he'd stand erect, eyes sweeping the room like a bobcat surveying the hillside hunting for prey. He'd come in screaming and yelling. It was like watching a volcano erupt. He would move slowly turning into a burning thing which seemed to feed on itself, flaring into a firestorm—an angry goblin or demon who threatened to destroy everything in his path.

"Where's that whore?" he'd scream. "Everybody in town knows you're a whore, Winnie."

I could smell beer, whiskey and sweat, but I smelled my own fear stronger than all three. I lived with that voice and fear everyday. I knew what it could do, how it could sound. It stabbed right down into the heart and soul of my little cringing self.

Mama was always scared, would run from her room. The minute Daddy saw her, he backed her into our bed right across us. She would crawl against the wall and curl herself into a knot. Sometimes she crumbled to the floor. Pulling her up, Daddy would slap her and her head would snap back like a loose rag doll. Looking me straight in the eyes, he'd scream, "Your Mama's a whore—your Mama's a whore! I want you to know that."

I always thought that Mama must have deserved the beatings because Daddy said she was a whore. When I could escape the beatings, I'd run under the cover of darkness to the house next door. I'd knock and knock, pound on the big door, looking for that wonderful man they called "Jesus". But Jesus never answered. At times I knocked on that big door until my knuckles bled.

One night, frightened by the noise, Scotty began to squall. Mickey ran outside too, and Brian always wrapped his arms around his legs to hold them steady while he balanced on the edge of the tattered sofa bed and peed. Then he ran on out into the yard and hid from Daddy. Shy and quiet, nobody ever heard one word from Brian.

Daddy beat Mama and threw her out of the house. "Take this bawling kid with you!" he hollered.

Mama ran back for Scotty, then came out to sit under the big trees and nurse him. Scotty was quiet while Mama sobbed.

Daddy made us stay outside all night, even when it rained. Our hiding place offered little relief from the rain and cold, and none from the fear of our Daddy. Sometimes we had to stay there for days.

I played pretend games with my three little brothers and listened to Mama cry.

When Daddy was drunk and provoked, I obeyed him as though he held a whip. I took my three brothers and went to the bridge that crossed the Tule River. There, we hid in the crawl space between some rocks.

As I grew older, I'd fight back. I tried to help Mama, but Daddy beat me, too.

Daddy began taking Scotty with him to the bars, where Scotty learned to curse like a trooper. The men in the bars thought it was funny, which only made things worse. Scotty still sucked on his bottle. It was either hanging from his mouth or in his hip pocket. He carried it with him everywhere.

He'd go up to one of the men in the bar, hit him on his leg, and say, "Hi Hank. You ol' son ya' bitch!"

When Daddy started taking Scotty to the bars, I coaxed Scotty into bringing his hamburger out to share with us. While Scotty was in the bar, I made many trips to check on him. He was often asleep on the floor at Daddy's feet under the poker table.

The men gave Scotty a sip of their drink. One filled his bottle. The drunken men howled.

One man roughed up Scotty's hair and said, "Damn, Melvin, this is a cute kid. Hey, give Melvin another drink, will ya'?"

"Me know, me cute kid," Scotty said.

"How do you know you're a cute kid, Scotty?"

"Me Sissy told me so."

Laughing, Hank would buy Scotty a hamburger, and my brother would run home with his hamburger in a paper sack.

"Come on, Sissy, me give you supper," he'd announce his arrival. "Me got supper for us. Hurry, Sissy." He'd run into the house and plop down on the couch. He'd give me a bite, then he'd take a bite.

Mama and Daddy went to the bar every night. When they came home, their fights began. One night when they got back, Daddy reminded me of a dog, ready to latch his teeth onto anything.

Walking backward, Mama pawed at the air, screaming. Turning, she threw herself out the door, landing on the steps on her belly. Her face filled with terror, blood spurted from her nose. Her face twisted in pain.

Blood frightened me more than anything. I'd run and hide, yet I peeked out to watch. I always expected Daddy to kill my Mama.

As Daddy beat Mama, I saw a cruel grin spread across his face. Before he spoke, goose bumps rose on me when I heard that syrupy voice. I always knew when his viciousness was about to erupt.

Mama closed her eyes and cried, "Oh Melvin don't!"

Seconds later Daddy backhanded her. Her face twisted and Mama fell to her knees. She rubbed her arm and stared up at Daddy.

He fumbled with his trousers, pulling at his big leather belt before unzipping his pants. Reaching for Mama, he yanked her by the hair into a kneeling position and shoved his pee-pee into her mouth.

Tears ran down my Mama's face, and she looked at me the whole time she performed what looked to be a horrible punishment.

Daddy finally pushed her away. He stood over her, his legs spread apart to keep his pants from falling to the floor as he smoothed out his shirt tail. Still standing over Mama, pulling up his pants with a smirk, he walked out of the house.

Like Mama, I felt broken and helpless. Grabbing our blanket we ran out into the night. I sobbed and began crying uncontrollably, closing my eyes and hiding my face. The horror I'd witnessed made it feel like the life was being sucked right out of me.

The Springville Inn was across the street from our house. It was full of steady drinkers, reeking of stale liquor and cloudy smoke. Drunken laughter echoed from the tall ceilings.

Daddy was at a poker table, his hat pushed to the back of his head. Scotty was asleep on the floor at his feet.

A man spotted me peeking in the back door. "Hey, you, I hear you have a hair-trigger temper just like that Daddy of yours." He gave me a slobbering grin.

One lady with dirty blond hair, was twisting on the high bar stools. It looked like a playground ride. A cowboy stood beside her with his foot on the rung of the stool and his arms wrapped tight around her waist.

I wanted to go inside too, like Scotty. I wanted to crawl up on one of those high stools and turn round and round. There was a cigarette machine and a nickelodeon—a bulging, bright thing with a glow of purple, red, and yellow. Air bubbles danced through the hollow letters that spelled "WIRLITZER". The big bright, fancy letters marched across the top of the nickelodeon. I longed to run my fingers across the colorful sides and try to catch the bubbles.

While living in the Springville house, I remember people jumping for joy and dancing in the streets hollering, "The war is over! The war is over!"

Standing in front of my house, it was a joyous day, filled with cheers and shouting. Horns, whistles, sirens, and the old school bell rang out continuously as everyone expressed their feelings of thrill, joy, and relief. People danced in the streets, shaking hands, hugging and kissing. Others threw papers, confetti, and streamers into the streets. A band played, and banners waved high in the sky. Moms and Grandmas hugged each other and screamed, "My husband is coming home soon."

Others shouted, "My son's coming home!"

I saw one woman drop her head into her hands and sob. "My son will never be coming home."

There were many solemn moments also, and many looked sad. I was puzzled and had no idea what it was all about, but my thoughts wanted to relate it somehow to my personal situation. Oh! That's what's the matter! There's a war! What's a war? Is my war over? Oh boy! My Daddy won't hurt me no more. War…my war is over, too. Suddenly, it all made sense. That's what happened! That's why my Daddy beat me. That's why others called me names. We were having a war. That makes sense. Now things are going to be more better. Now my Daddy will be nicer to me. Oh boy, the war is over.

It was wall-to-wall people. Everyone was shouting. People I didn't even know kissed me. The small street through Springville was jammed. People wandered around as if they had no control over where they were going.

The next morning, all the businesses in town were closed. The Springville children used red, white, and blue chalk to draw big pictures of the United States flag all over the sidewalks.

But I was to find my own war continued. There had been no armistice in the battleground of our home.

CHAPTER EIGHT

Nobody was looking as I sneaked into the bar. I jumped on the stool and spun around and around, watching myself in the mirror. I had never before seen what I looked like, and it was amazing to be able to gaze at myself. I grinned big; I squinted my eyes. My face was tiny in the looking glass. I'd never seen anything like it. Maybe down at the river, I'd seen my reflection, but this was different. It was like a dream. Then I started looking at myself in different positions; I posed upside down, then right side up on the stool. I posed myself over, under, around sideways.

I sat back on the stool, swirling my finger around the lip of an empty glass, listening to the squeaking sound it made. I stared at my eyes in the mirror. I didn't know exactly why I did this, but I kept staring into those two hazel eyes looking back at me. I was surprised at how I looked—a tiny, round face with a lot of dark curly hair. I thought, I like how I look. I don't look ugly like everybody says. I wonder why everybody says I'm ugly? I didn't want to look away from those eyes. I seemed more real to myself now that I saw my face and I no longer felt like I was walking behind something that I'd never before seen.

I'm not ugly, and I'm going to tell those kids at school that I'm not! I vowed to my reflection.

"Give me another one," the man said, his words slurred. "Make it whiskey, this time."

While their backs were turned, I scooted out the back door.

The very first time I went to the bar alone at night, it was both exciting and scary at the same time. Usually, Mickey was with me.

Watching the people dancing from high on the hill behind the Springville Inn, I was fascinated by all the laughter, and wished more than anything else that I was big enough to go in. The toilets were outside, so it would be easy for someone to spot me.

After a while, a man came out the back door. When I thought it was safe, I moved my head from behind the tree. For an instant, my eyes locked with his. They seemed evil. I was scared half out of my wits. He was a tall, balding man, not much older than my Daddy. He went into the dirty bathroom. When he came out, he motioned at me with his head as he walked to the edge of the building. When he reached the side of the building, he turned and watched me again. Again, he motioned with his head for me to come. I still didn't move. Finally he said, "Come'ere, girl."

I just stared.

"Did you hear me? Come here."

I was shy and afraid. The man's gray eyes glared straight at me, while his hand jerked at his crotch. His knuckles were bulging and pale in contrast to his ruddy, red face.

"If you'll come here, I'll give you a quarter."

"No, you'll hurt me like my Daddy does." My mouth seemed filled with cotton.

He grinned, but it was a cruel, nasty smile. "Why, I'd never hurt a pretty little thing like you. What would make you think that? Now come here, Peggy. Isn't that what they call you 'Peggy'?"

Pretty. He called me pretty. No one had ever called me pretty. Maybe he's not mean like Daddy, I argued with my inner sense.

Reaching into his tight pockets he said, "Here, let me give you a quarter."

"A quarter? You're gonna' give me a quarter?"

"Yes, Peggy. Peggy is your name, isn't it? I'll give you a quarter, if I can touch you."

"Just touch me, that's all?"

"Yes, that's all. I like to touch pretty little girls like you."

"No!" I screamed, and ran home. I never looked back to see if the man was watching me.

The next morning, when Mickey, Brian, and I were playing in our front yard, the man drove by our house. He waved and hollered, "Hi, Peggy."

"Who's that?" Mickey asked.

"I don't remember his name, but I seen him at the bar. Last night he said he'd give me a quarter if I'd let him touch me."

"Sissy, why didn't you let him touch you?" Mickey asked. "I could sure use that quarter. Let's go back there. Maybe he'll still give you a quarter."

It was a long time before we saw the man again at the bar. Mickey and I went back to the bar almost every night, looking and waiting for him. Yet every time he went by my house, or I saw him around town, he'd always wave or speak to me. By now, I felt like I knew him; however, he didn't show up at the bar again for nearly a month. The night he did come Mickey and I were both behind the tree and he walked right up and started talking to us. He took two quarters out of his pocket handing one to Mickey and one to me. "You kids buy yourselves a soda pop, you hear?" He turned and went back into the bar. We didn't see him anymore that night. The next time we saw him, he said, "Hi, Peggy. Do you want another quarter?"

"Yeah, if you'll give Mickey one, too." "Will you let me feel your body?"

I didn't like the sound of that. "Why?"

"Your body is young and sweet. I just want to feel it." "Go ahead, Peggy," Mickey urged. "Let him feel your skin. That's all he wants to do."

The man reached out his huge, gnarled hand toward me. I could feel his heat; his closeness suffocated me. He smelled of strong whiskey, like Daddy. My heart beat in time to the words. No! He'll beat me, just like Daddy. He'll hurt me! He zigzagged toward me and I felt a sudden grip on my arm. There was a commanding strength in his fingertips.

"No!" I squirmed out of his grasp, out of his reach. "Ya' ain't got nothing to worry about," he said.

I ran for home, with Mickey right on my heels.

I jumped in bed with Brian and Scotty. I hadn't been in bed long when I felt Mickey crawl in bed with us. I pretended like I was sleeping.

The next morning, I hopped out of bed long before anyone else was up.

Later, Mickey said, "Sissy, you know Mama gets money from the men, and she gives it to Daddy. It wouldn't hurt if you'd get money from the men and give it to me."

"No!" I yelled. "I won't let him touch me. He'll hurt me just like Daddy! I won't do it."

Over the next few days, I saw Mickey talking to the man. Staring at them, I could sense a dark evil emanating from the man's darting, penetrating eyes. Then Mickey stuffed something into his pocket, and rapidly patted it.

Days later Mickey said, "Peggy, you know we need that money. I promise I'll stay right with you if you'll let that man touch your body. He isn't going to hurt you. I promise you, Sissy. He won't hurt you."

"I don't need no money, and you know it!" I screamed. "I can get anything I want without dumb ol' money!"

"Do it for me. Just one time. That's all, just one time. Please, Peggy, please."

"Well…" His pleading eyes got to me. "We'll see…well, maybe."

On Sunday mornings, I liked to stand at the edge of our yard and listen to the music coming from the big house next door they called the "church". Twisting my dress, my bare bottom shining, I'd gaze at all the people entering. Most of the people gave me a snarling sneer as they hurried past me. I always looked for the wonderful man they called Jesus.

One man hand-in-hand dragged his little girl past me on their way into the big house. "Don't look at her, Beth." My heart pounded from his harsh words.

Scotty peered from behind me with his thumb in his mouth. He fidgeted silently, with my dress twisted in the fist of one hand.

"Oh, Mister, he's not home," I shyly said.

"Who's not home?" The man asking looked at me with a strange expression.

"The man who lives there, that man they call Jesus. He's not home."

"How do you know He's not home?" He seemed to be holding back laughter.

"Because I knocked and knocked on his door last night and he didn't answer."

Shaking his head all the way up the walkway the man laughed like it was the best joke he'd heard in a long time. Finally, he took a handkerchief out of a jacket pocket and wiped at his eyes.

I closed my eyes and listened to the music coming from the big house. They were singing "Amazing Grace." Wishes presented themselves to my mind, I wish I could go inside with all the people. Just one time. Why can't I be like'em? When I grow up, I'm gonna have a family just like they do. I liked the loudness of the music, just like in the bar and the songs of Jesus. I especially liked "Yes, Jesus Loves Me." The shouts of "Amen!" and "Hallelujah!" made me feel warm and tingly. I listened and longed to be born again. "Washed whiter than…" but I didn't understand whiter than what?

Mama complained about my hearing, but I really didn't notice that I couldn't hear well. I seemed to hear what I wanted to hear. I noticed I'd miss a word now and then, but I really wasn't concerned like everyone else was.

I wondered why they sang that song, when I knew Jesus didn't love me and beside I knew he really didn't live in that big house. I didn't know why he didn't love me, when he loved everyone else. I heard the man say that Jesus loved all his children. Wasn't I one of his children?

I'm different. I know I am. I'm not like the rest of the people, and I don't know why, I told myself. Sometimes I seethed with belligerence.

I stood outside listening and ached to go in. I still hadn't seen the man they called Jesus.

I rationalized, I can sneak in without anyone seeing me. Why not? They'll be busy singing. I sneak in other places, even the bar when nobody even knows it. Shrugging away my thoughts, I took a deep breath and propelled by resolve, made my way eagerly to the door. I started to push through, and was overcome by the music.

"What a friend I have in Jesus, all our sins and grief to bear!

What a privilege to carry, Everything to God in prayer." Holding the heavy door, I realized that Scotty was beside me. The big door creaked open slowly, and a moment later I was standing in the center aisle of a breathtakingly beautiful place.

Suddenly, I felt big, powerful hands grabbing me from behind, and a gruff voice rasped in my ear, "No, you don't!"

"Huh?" I uttered a startled cry.

Tugging on the hem of my dress, Scotty asked, "What's wrong, Sissy?"

The hands pulled me back, then he let go of my shoulders. The door swung back into place.

I spun around and looked up into an old man's big face. The wiry, gray-haired man stared at me. His dark, wrinkly face and jawline jutted out from the taut skin of his neck. His big hand with sharp fingernails dug into my shoulder, pushing and pinching me; the cords in his neck tightened like Daddy's did before he would hit Mama.

"Not that way!" he said as he turned me around, pushing me ahead of him out the big, wooden door. He told me I couldn't come in. "This is for adults. Kids go to Sunday school downstairs."

"Hi, Mary Jane," I greeted a girl one morning as she was going to church with her Daddy.

Her Daddy dragged her by the hand. "Come on, Mary Jane. She's just trash." Mary Jane kept looking back at me as her Daddy led her into the church.

Her Daddy was the man who had wanted to touch my body.

CHAPTER NINE

I don't know why we moved so far from town to the old, smelly hog farm. It took us all day to walk to town and back home. The hogs were owned by an insurance man from Porterville. The house was a tired, dark, wood-framed building—a run-down shanty. The yard was nothing but puffs of dry dirt. Bullets had peppered the barn and hog shed leaving pockmarks in the siding.

The hogs were huge, over eight hundred pounds. Sometimes a mother sow had babies, usually at least a dozen. The owner of the hog farm always came right after the piglets were born to castrate the piglets. The ones who weren't castrated were "killer hogs." We thought they were all killers and never got near them.

My brothers said the hogs snorted continuously. I don't know why, but I couldn't hear them snort. Sometimes I watched them sniff at the messy ground around the feeding trough. They rooted all day for bits of food that had spilled from the previous night's feeding.

We only had cold water. There was a bathroom, but for some reason, we couldn't use it. There was a big bathtub that was almost as orange as Daddy's chest.

We used the outhouse, which was a long way from the house. The wooden walls had faded to a dull gray, and cobwebs covered the door. Mama had to get a crowbar to get the door open the first time. It made a screeching sound. Mama swept more cobwebs aside with the crowbar. Inside the house, one bare light bulb hung from the ceiling. Sometimes we had electricity. When we didn't, we used coal-oil lamps. In the winter, the wind whipped through the cracks in the walls.

Wild animals were all around, even wild boar. We saw raccoons, skunks, deer, coyote, fox, mountain lions, and bobcats. In the spring, I looked beside the road for opossums that had been killed by passing automobiles. Searching the opossums pouch for the babies, and if I found them I would always have to pry them off of their dead mother's nipple. The babies hung on for dear life. I was never able to keep even one alive.

Our front yard was big and sprawling. A clump of scraggly wild fig trees concealed most of the dilapidated old cabin. A rickety picket fence which was bleached gray from the sun surrounded it. The gate hung limply from its hinges.

The back of the house sat in the hollow, barely held up by rotten posts. The old wood porch looked like it was about to sag to the ground with a sigh of relief. We didn't have a door, neither on the porch nor into the front of the old house, and we had only a tattered screen door on the back. Out back, under a cement stand-pipe covered by dark, rotten boards, an old, deep well was hidden. The sides of the well were green with moss. We spent hours dropping rocks into the well. My brothers put their ears down to listen to the rocks hitting the water below. Or we'd holler into the well to hear our voices echo.

"I don't hear it," I always crowded closer in order to hear. "Oh, Sissy, you never hear," Scotty said, mocking Mama. He didn't know that I couldn't hear. He'd just heard Mama say that I couldn't hear. I thought my hearing was just fine, as far as I was concerned.

The house was sparsely furnished and had one bedroom. The porch went across the front of the house. In the summer, we slept on the porch, but when it turned cold, we dragged our mattress into the living room.

An old icebox sat in the kitchen. When Daddy came home, he always brought a block of ice for his beer and whiskey. He never brought home food.

Mama had a treadle sewing machine, but I don't remember her sewing very much. She never made dresses for me. When we had needles, I tried to sew.

A splintered pine table with a dented tin top sat in the middle of the kitchen floor. There were a couple of old "heir's" trunks, as Mama called them, one with broken hinges.

A hot water pipe ran through the wood cookstove, and we had hot water only in the winter. The water went down the drain and into a big mud puddle just on the outside of the wall.

A door in the kitchen led into Mama's and Daddy's bedroom, which had an iron bed frame with a sagging mattress and springs. Every time Mama or Daddy turned over, it squeaked and groaned loudly. The mattress was thin and dirty. It rippled and sagged.

Just past our back yard was the dump. The edge of a rocky cliff protruded over a tangle of scrub brush, rock, and moss. It was surrounded by litter: beer bottles; soda bottles; paper wrappings; an old, dirty, high-top work shoe. A trickle of dirty water dripped from the end of a pipe. A monument of trash leaned against the trunk of one of the trees. There were piles of broken wringer washing machines, wagons with the wheels missing, wash buckets, rubber hoses, some short, some longer, hundreds of tires still on broken wooden rims, and plain old garbage-collecting flies.

An old tattered sofa sat on its side at the back of the house, under a big tree. When I sat with my knees deep into the sofa, I could feel the springs stabbing at me. No matter where I sat, no matter how I shifted or which way I turned, the springs poked my knees.

In the floor of the old house were cracks big enough to stick my whole arm down into the dirt below. Once I found some pocket change in the dirt, so I always searched for more.

We found old, dirty mattresses from the neighbors' dumps that we dragged inside and threw on the floor. Most were full of holes, and some had springs poking through. The cotton was in lumps. Brian peed on them, and over time they got lumpier and lumpier.

Every day during the hot summer, we dragged our dirty mattresses outside to dry. By nightfall, they'd be dry, and we'd haul them back onto the front porch. They never dried in the winter.

We had a table with a couple of chairs, and we used apple crates turned up on end for more kitchen chairs. Daddy always leaned back against the wall in his chair, twisting his feet around the back legs. Eventually, he broke the legs off. In the cold winter months, we all slept together to keep warm—except for Brian. If we were lucky enough to find an extra mattress, we dragged it home for him. No one ever wanted to sleep with Brian, and he didn't want to sleep alone.

At times, he'd go to sleep in bed with the rest of us, but after he fell asleep, Mickey and I would move him to the other bed. When we got older, my three brothers slept together.

I made a room divider out of orange crates on the front porch, where my mattress was. I hung blankets from the ceiling, and the area served proudly as my very own bedroom. I crawled into my small, safe place, retreating into the cubbyholes. It was a good way to keep away from Daddy. It was my private play space.

I liked to sit in the boxes alone. I'd draw or make paper dolls, making up stories, speaking quietly to myself. I'd cut a row of paper dolls out from the Sears catalog and line them against my wall. An old, tattered quilt was even spread on the floor like an oriental rug, and in one corner a rag-doll slept in a cigar-box crib.

Sometimes I'd dream of how it would be "if I was you, and you was me." If I could look exactly like you do, and you could look like me. I'd rather be you any old day, was the theme of my make believe.

Lined around the wall like an audience, sat all the stuffed animals and dolls I'd gathered from the neighbors' dumps: teddy bears with stuffing long gone, clowns, soggy and black with mold, smelly and dirty. There was one broken doll with brown hair painted on its head, and wearing off making her appear as though she had a bad case of the mange. Her blue eyes couldn't blink, but she had bright red painted lips, curved up into a smile. My ragtag audience were my "friends".

I sewed buttons on for eyes. "Green Frog" had yellow eyes. I made pupils by sewing a black button on top of a yellow button. This was my very first experience at sewing. Then I made their shoes, and then made some for myself and my brothers. I collected pictures of shoes from the catalog and tried to copy the pictures when I made our shoes. More than anything in the world, I wanted my very own shoes. But the only ones I had ever had were the ones we found from the neighbors' dumps.

I collected white and pink buttons from other clothing. Stuffing up the holes with cotton I pulled from the mattress, I'd paint a tiny girl's face, using the holes for eyes. I would glue the tiny face onto a piece of paper, then color a girl's body. As I got older, I learned to patch, then appliqué and embroider. I patched my own clothes.

The school kids laughed and poked fun at me because of my patched dresses. They laughed when my clothes had rips and tears, and laughed at my dresses that looked like patchwork quilts on two legs.

Scotty named the stuffed animals. We'd sit hidden and play with them for hours. There was "Butter Butt", who had been Scotty's favorite when he was three. "Miss Piggy" was right up near the front. For years, she shared the bed with Scotty and me. Gradually, Scotty was weaned from his animals. Only at night, he tucked one deep in the crook of his arm.

Sometimes the flies stuck to me. I'd lie on my bed early in the evening and watch the flies bang against a hot, naked light bulb. I would even watch the flies "do it." That surprised me. Even the flies were "doing it." Everybody and everything was "doing it."

I got a funny feeling when I saw two people doing it. I even felt funny when I watched the flies do it. The way I felt was frightening in a way, but with a warm edge. I couldn't figure out the tingling feeling I felt when I saw animals or people "doing it"—it was sickening, yet exciting.

Daddy always got to bathe first when he was home. After he was through he stood at the door clean-shaven and erect, his pants and shirt were finely pressed with sharp creases running down his trousers.

Mama added more hot water, then she bathed.

I was next in line after Mama. Sometimes I put little Scotty into the tub with me. Mama added more hot water before the next one bathed. Whoever took a bath last used dirty, black water. It took Mickey and me both together to pull the tin tub outside to dump the water. By the time we managed to get the tub outside, most of the water had sloshed out. Sometimes we just dumped the bath water out inside the house. It seeped down through the big cracks in the floor and puddled under the house.

Sometimes a man in a big black Hudson brought food to Mama. She called them "commodities". He had flour and lard, oatmeal, and canned milk. Sometimes he brought sugar or, if none was available, plain corn syrup. I made glue from white flour and water. I thought, huh, flour and water mixed together made glue. Add an egg and sugar, you got cake. I could never figure that out. I wondered about it a lot.

Another thing we received were bed sheets. Hundreds of them. They were all for small beds, but sometimes Mama sewed them together for her bed. We made diapers and towels out of them, too. We even papered our walls with them to keep the cold air from coming through the cracks. Mama sewed them together with padding inside and made quilts. Daddy braided them to make a rope.

While standing in line waiting with the neighbors for our commodities, I listened to all the other women talking. They said the bed sheets were left over from the war.

The outhouse was fly-infested in the summer months. The farm workers used it during grape season. When I was older, I used the nearby fields. I refused to stand in line with those workers. Someone always tried to touch me. White streaks of lime covered the stinky gray-brown mass down below.

When Daddy wasn't around, there was a line to our house. Mama entertained the men. The men would unzip their pants and sit on a straight chair. I always watched them suspiciously as they drifted by. Mama's face always seemed to be pinched and thin. She was usually clad only in a simple faded cotton house dress. One of the babies always clung to her legs. She wore no under panties. Mama would pull up her dress and straddle the man like she was sitting in his lap, yet she still stood on both feet. It looked like she jumped up and down with both her feet on the floor, doing their sex things. I didn't really know what the sex thing was. A part of me told me it wasn't right and made me feel bad, but another part made me feel kind of good.

It never took long. The man would get up, zip up his pants, and the next man would sit down in the chair. I learned to recognize the familiar sounds they made, and I knew when it was about to be finished.

We dressed in rags. Our bodies were tanned and crusty with dirt. The waist of my dress was up under my arms, and the buttons down the back were all gone. I didn't wear anything underneath.

Rain water always caused white streaks to run down Scotty's arms and legs. It left polka dots on his feet. Scotty's stomach was swollen from lack of food. The hunger pangs never seemed to go away. When I did eat after a long time without food, it would make me sick, and I'd puke.

Daddy always had a car, which he probably won in poker games, but before he went back to the hospital, he managed to get rid of the car. I don't know if he sold it, or lost it the same way he'd gotten it. He never left Mama with a car. Maybe she couldn't drive.

Daddy gambled all the time. Most of the time he went to Porterville. "It's a bigger town, and easier to win," Daddy said. Porterville was a long way from our house. Mama and Daddy sometimes took us with them and left us in the car. I remember sometimes waking up in places that weren't familiar to me.

Sometimes we children hitchhiked to town. The townspeople picked us up at first, but stopped after they realized how crude, rude, stinking, and uncivilized we were. We perfected a technique that worked almost all the time. My brothers would hide behind a bush and leave me beside the road with my thumb out. Because I was alone, farmers stopped. Then we'd all jump into the car, crawling over or under whoever else was in the car.

People always asked my brothers if I could talk.

"Oh, not that again," Mickey said. "Talk, Sissy! Talk, so they won't ask me again."

I'd just shake my head.

"Why does everybody ask me that?" Mickey shouted at the driver.

"Well, I never heard her speak," the man said. "I thought she couldn't talk."

"Well, she can. She just doesn't like to talk in front of strangers."

It wasn't long before everyone caught on that my brothers hid in the bushes. Then nobody picked us up. We didn't walk on the road. We'd go by way of the river, or over the hill. We didn't mind. Sometimes it took us all night.

We slept in barns, stole apples, rabbits, sugar, and flour if we could. We took vegetables and fruit from our neighbors' gardens, and stole eggs from the henhouse—sometimes even the hen. However, food was the only thing we stole.

I didn't like taking chickens. They were too noisy. Besides, my brothers loved to chop off the chickens' heads and watch them run around our yard headless. It scared the dickens out of me to see all that blood splattering all over the ground.

We also took things that the neighbors threw into their dumps. We scavenged broken toys, shoes, blankets, and always the clothes, no matter what kind of shape they were in. Even if I couldn't wear them, I used the buttons.

Daddy shot deer in the nearby mountains. He gutted and skinned them, cutting them in half and hanging them high in a tree so the wild animals couldn't get them. Later, he'd send Mickey and I to get it.

Mickey and I shot buzzards and cooked them for us when Mama and Daddy didn't come home. We seemed to manage somehow to get food. Maybe not enough to keep our stomachs full, but enough to keep us from starving.

A dirt road led to our house. In the hot summer, it was inches deep with powdery dust. In the distance, the old outhouse sagged to one side. The trail back and forth from the house to the outhouse and around the yard was barren and dusty from all the traffic.

In the summer months, Mama pulled her rocking chair onto the front porch. She'd rock back and forth, always in a daze, looking straight ahead, never blinking. After a while, she'd say, "Who was that, Sissy?"

"Who's who, Mama? I didn't see anybody."

"That car that drove up. Who were they? What did they want?"

"Nobody drove up, Mama."

Slowly, Mama would get out of her rocking chair, dragging her feet as she walked out to the drive. "Come here, Sissy. See these car tracks? Now who was here?"

"Mama, I didn't see nobody."

"I'll swear, Sissy. You don't hear nobody, and you don't see nobody. I don't know what I'm gonna do with you. Wish I knew who drove in."

Words jumped into my mind, now I can't see! First I couldn't hear, and now I can't see! I don't know about the hearing, but I know I can see. But the words chipped away silently at my already badly damaged self-esteem.

A grape vineyard and berry patches bordered the property to the north. In season, they furnished us with plenty of "pickin's." Behind the vineyard and the berry patches, the mountains climbed high, nothing but tall, dark trees, brush, and rocks. We kids knew every tree and rock on that mountainside.

Mama always saw an old cabin, up on the mountain; sometimes a two-story cabin with a window in the attic. "See that old cabin?"

"I don't see no cabin, Mama. Mickey, Brian, and me have been all over that mountain, and there is no cabin up there. There's cabins and barns on this side of the mountain, but none on that one."

"Yes, there is," she would always insist. "I'm looking at it. And there's a young girl with long yellow hair in the attic window. She's waving a white scarf at me. I don't know why you don't see her, Sissy."

Here we go again, I thought, I can't see. Must be something bad wrong with Mama, 'cause I know that I can see and hear.

We had a neighbor to the north at the dead-end of the road. Mrs. Henry was blind, and her husband was deaf. They both talked funny, and I couldn't understand them. I called him Henry, and I called her Mrs. Henry. The old people brought us food, and sometimes Henry fetched me to help Mrs. Henry.

Inside their house were threadbare furnishings, holy artifacts of big crosses over the doorways, and big, colorful pictures of the man called "Jesus". The heat would swell around me, joining with the smells. The old man always wore his pajama top under a dirty pair of overalls.

The kitchen was all white and yellow, and showed signs of neglect and confusion. A bowl on the table had a rim around the edge, and there was a cup half-filled with cold, stale coffee. Mrs. Henry showed me how to clean vegetables from her garden and taught me how to cook.

One day, she gave me lunch. It was something she'd prepared for dinner the night before, and it was all gritty with sand from her garden. I thought that was how it was supposed to taste. I watched as she stuffed a chicken and told me how to do it. I liked the old couple, because they were good to me and gave me food.

One evening on my way home, I took a chicken along with me. I didn't ask, but I knew they wouldn't care. They had hundreds of them. That night I cooked chicken for my brothers. I didn't have all the ingredients to stuff it like Mrs. Henry showed me, but I didn't care, and neither did my brothers.

On many nights, guided by the moon, Mickey and I would set out to steal chickens. Occasionally, little twinges of guilt picked at my insides, but it was matched by the excitement of the moment—the wonderful prospect of food for myself and the other kids.

As we stumbled across the moon-washed scrub brush and rocks, watching out for wild boar or mountain lions, out searching for their own chickens, my mouth would always water, just anticipating the food.

The sudden splashes of guilt never stopped me from stealing. While it had started with sneaking Sugar Daddy-Suckers out of the old German man's store, it was to become the ugly seeds that grew into a fomenting pattern in the future—seeds which worked like the yeast Mrs. Henry put into her bread.

CHAPTER TEN

My knees pressed into the seat of the car, I looked out the back window and gazed at the moon—a large yellow disk shining brightly in the sky. It lit up Porterville enough to see well in the darkness.

I spotted a bloody dog digging through mounds of garbage, and decided to get a closer look while my brothers slept. I'd watched the dirty, wounded dog for several months. Quietly, I opened the car door, trying not to wake up my brothers because I knew they would be hungry. I gently closed the car door and crept around the other parked cars in the lot. I laid down on my stomach and slid under one of the cars. With my chin propped on my fists. I looked under the cars and across the big lot at the wretched dog.

I wondered where he lived and what had happened to him. I knew the townspeople didn't like him—just like they didn't like me. Men cursed and yelled at him every time they saw him. They threw rock at him, like the kids did to me.

I wouldn't treat him like that if he'd let me near him, I vowed. I'd take care of him just like I did my brothers.

I would even let him come into our car to stay warm, and maybe he could also keep us warm. I'd never had a dog before. Daddy said we couldn't feed a dog. If the dog would just give me one little bitty chance, I'd show him.

Foam flecked his nose. His coat was long, thick, matted, and lifeless. He was streaked with blood, mud, and burrs and looked wickedly mean. I froze when he looked at me. His back leg was caked with dried blood. It looked broken. He couldn't stand up on three legs very long. One side of his head was a big lump. Puss oozed from his chest, and I saw bone through a large hole between his two front legs. He limped backward on one of his front legs, cocked his head and looked at me with his lip snarled back.

He pulled some food from the trash dump, a little at a time, seeming mad with starvation, and holding the putrefied meat with one of his front paws tore at it ravenously. I could tell his mouth was sore. He tried to eat fast, gobbling down the food.

I gazed around, feeling scared. My hands quivered, and my heart beat fast. He did not take his eyes off me, even while he ate. I didn't know what he might do, since he seemed so desperate.

It was cold. My fingers were frozen. Rubbing my hands together briskly, I opened and closed my fingers. I wished I'd kept those old gloves, but Scotty wanted them to keep his little hands warm. Without the warmth of my brothers, I was cold.

I'd heard men in the bar call him a wolf. Sometimes they looked at him and argued among themselves about whether he was a dog or wolf.

"Look at those eyes," one said. "If those aren't wolf eyes, I never saw a wolf."

Another man had said, "His Daddy may have been a wolf, but I know damn well his Mama was no wolf."

"Damn, I know I killed that wolf the other night. I could swear I did," another man said.

"Nah, he ain't no wolf. If he was a wolf, he'd be up on that hill with his mate. You know they mate for life and never stray from their dens."

"If he was a female, you might be right."

"Look at those pads. Did you ever see a dog with pads like those? I know he's part wolf."

Another time, a man said, "I shot that bastard the other night. I caught him killing my chickens."

I crawled on my hands and feet, creeping closer, trying not to let my teeth chatter. My breath made white smoke. Staring hard at the dog, I hoped to see a slight sign of friendship in his eyes. Somehow, I had to let him know I wanted to be his friend. I needed him for warmth, and I just knew I could get him into our car. I'd lured many a squirrel to my hand. Why not this dog?

Propped on my elbow, I stared at the dog. Minutes passed, and he didn't take his eyes off me. I continued to move slowly, talking to him quietly. The dog glanced at his paw. His matted hairs sprang apart and stood on end when he looked at me. He put his ears back and lifted his upper lip, displaying jagged teeth. A ferocious sound came from deep in his throat. He snarled and growled.

I didn't budge. After a while, he quieted.

Getting up, I crept closer. He snapped at my feet, and I danced back a step or two. "Hey, what's gotten into you, boy?"

He gave me a wary look, but after a while, the hairs along his back flattened again. He stopped growling and stood motionless, staring at me. He just panted, never moving his eyes from mine.

I stepped toward him again, but the dog lunged at me more ferociously than before, growling deeper and snapping repeatedly at my legs, driving me backward. I stumbled over my own feet and fell on my butt.

The minute I was down, the dog slithered away. He moved fast, but I knew he was badly injured.

My teeth chattered with the sudden release of tension, and my heart pounded. I didn't move. I stayed motionless until I was certain the dog wasn't going to harm me.

The next night, Daddy parked in the same spot. The store across the street had closed. All the fruit and vegetables had been moved inside. The sidewalk was empty and spooky on that side of the street. Shadows grew taller. Earlier, the bright floodlights hanging from the awning outside the store had brightened the colors in the display of fruits and vegetables. Now it was dark.

Although the store was closed, I could hear the owner Mr. Hull screaming at me, "You wild thing, get out of here!" I never knew why nobody wanted me to eat. Everywhere I went, someone was hollering at me for eating. It was okay for others to eat, but not me. Why? Why did people hate me so?

Then I saw him! Inch-by-inch, the dog dragged himself on his stomach to the trash bins at the back of the store. Around him was all the garbage he'd pulled from the trash. I spoke to him softly. He had eaten through most of the papers and cardboard to get food. He had to eat fast before somebody caught him, and was not above taking what did not belong to him. How well I understood, I'd done the same thing.

"Come here, boy," I called. "Come here. Come here, fellow, come here. What would be a good name for you... maybe Patches"?

He continued to watch me.

I heard loud noises behind me, and then Mama screamed. Swiftly, with his tail between his legs, he fled, dragging his leg behind him.

Before I could get back to the old car, Mama and Daddy staggered down the street from the bar. Both were drunk and fighting in their usual manner.

When Daddy saw I was out of the car, he ran after me, got me by my hair, and dragged me down the sidewalk while taking his belt out of his pants. I begged him not to beat me.

"I'm not doing nothing, Daddy! I'm not doing nothing. I just wanted to go to the toilet. Really, Daddy, really."

Not being able to get his belt out of his pants soon enough to suit him, he spotted a big stick poking out from the mounds of trash. He stopped, still holding me by my hair, shook the stick loose from the rubbish.

He hit me on the backside and across my legs with the stick, time and time again, and gave me a final blow along the side of my head.

"I wasn't doing nothing, Daddy! Really I wasn't, really, Daddy."

Awake now, my brothers pressed their faces against the car window.

"Don't give me none of your lip, girl," Daddy said. Then he kicked me hard in the back as he shoved me into the car, right on top of my brothers. He stood outside and pulled long strands of my hair from between his fingers. His eyes looked like they belonged to a wild animal. He opened the car door and got in. "You're just like your mother. Nothing but bitches, both of ya."

The top of my head was numb, and I felt a smooth, empty patch where my hair had been. There was a ringing in my ears that lasted for many days.

I didn't understand why I was always in so much trouble with Daddy. I had to search for food. Why did he get so mad at me? I wished somebody would kill him. I hate you! I thought to myself.

At least he didn't hit my brothers. I would really have killed him if he had. I figured that if I wore him out, he wouldn't have the energy left to beat them.

Daddy got out again, and my heart dropped. I shuddered every time he opened the car door. I fought off a surge of fear, huddling in the corner. I thought he was going to pull me out again.

"Toss it over! Toss it over!" Daddy's eyes were wild. He grabbed the crank, then went to the front of the car and cranked the Dodge until it started. He threw the crank back onto the floorboard. The old car sputtered around the buildings and out onto the narrow streets, grinding gears finally caught up with the racing engine as Daddy drove toward home up the twisted, mountain road.

Halfway into a sharp, blind curve he sped up, hitting the brakes at the same time. We skidded crossway, with the back end of the car going around the corner first. At the same time, he frantically spun the wheel with one hand one way, then back the other, barely keeping the out-of-control car from skidding off the highway into the steep canyon below.

My brothers were awake and searching around for food that I usually had for them. I'd messed around with that wild dog and helped him with his food, but I'd forgotten about my three hungry brothers.

"Where's our food, Sissy?" they whispered. "Didn't you get us any food tonight?"

Scotty's lip puckered. I could see that he wanted to cry, but didn't dare. Scotty, was the baby, only two. At eight years old, I was the oldest. Being the oldest, Mickey and I had gone many days without food, and were used to it, but not Brian and Scotty.

As we rounded the corner, the headlights of the car caught a glimpse of Patches standing in the shadows. He had a different look in his eyes...one of understanding, I thought. It wasn't that wild, hard stare I'd seen in the past. As the lights hit him, he ducked under what was left of an old car skeleton overgrown with weeds. It sat forlornly along the railroad tracks.

Was this Patches home? I would try to find out tonight after Daddy and Mama had passed out.

I awakened in a stupor. I hadn't remembered falling asleep, after hours of trying to find the dog. In a fog, I'd forgotten that I'd climbed in the broken down car along the side of the railroad tracks.

Breathing the stale air salted with the layers of rust on the old car, I realized abruptly that I had followed the dog to the car. Then, I must have fallen asleep.

I felt a thump under the car. I remembered I'd been trying to coax the dog out from beneath it, but I must have fallen asleep. Panicking, I wondered what time it was.

I scrambled to my feet and ran from the wreck. I could tell by the movement of the dog that I had scared the daylights out of him. I'd never been this noisy around him before. I could still see people near the bars so it couldn't be too late. I ran and got back into the broken down wreck. It was just a shell made of cold metal. How could I have fallen asleep in this cold and drafty thing?

I felt the dog moving under me. Suddenly, his head appeared through the tall weeds and he looked at me. He licked his lips. I got a good, close look. His jaw looked bad. Was it broken? His mouth was grotesquely swollen. No wonder he was so skinny and had such a difficult time eating. The chill wind whistled, nipping me painfully with cold pinches.

I watched the dog, never taking my eyes off him. He lay in the tall weeds appearing to be trying to sleep. He opened one eye at a time guarding himself.

I didn't want to leave Patches, but I had to find food for my brothers. I couldn't let them go another night without anything to eat. I looked out the front of the windowless car and could see the street sign. A red neon beer sign blinked off and on at the front door of the bar.

I watched a tall, black, Indian man standing across the tracks right in front of the packing house, watching people going into the bar. A lady entered the back door. She wore gigantic spike heels that made her look ten feet tall. Her dress was full-skirted with gobs of petticoats underneath. She swayed and twisted as she walked, as though she expected everyone to watch her. Her blouse was off the shoulders. Her silky white skin glowed under the street lamp.

Out of the corner of my eye, I caught a movement. I wheeled around and saw a dark, shapeless form. My hands shook, and I suddenly felt the need to get out of the car. I didn't want to be trapped in there. No matter how much I frightened the dog, I had to get away.

Every night while Mama and Daddy drank in the bar and my brothers slept, I waited for the dog. He would always show up eventually. I watched him from a distance as he dug through the mounds of garbage.

He ignored everyone else, but it seemed like he waited for me. Some nights I met him at the trash barrels. In the early days before his injuries healed, I left food out for him so he wouldn't have to dig for himself.

As Daddy drove the mountain road toward home, I could see the dog watching us through the opening in the trees. Sometimes he followed, running along the mountain road. Every night, he came a little bit closer than the night before.

A few nights later, we were parked in the same spot, a place which seemed like our second home. In so many ways, it was better than our home, because we could get food behind the markets and the packing houses.

In the early evening, we watched the townspeople coming and going with their arms full, carrying sacks of food. A bright red-and-white wrapper of Wonder Bread poked from the top of a paper sack. Some carried a bottle of milk tucked in their arms, or it swung in a hand at their side. Milk was one thing we rarely had.

Daddy threatened me with my life to not ever let the townspeople know we were hungry. It was almost impossible to not show that I was hungry. I know people watched us scamper after a half-eaten sandwich, an orange, or an apple they'd thrown away.

"Watch this," a young girl said. "Hey Peggy, here." She pitched an apple at me. I jumped for the apple and caught it. When I turned back toward the girl and her friends, they were halfway down the block, looking back, giggling.

My brothers were my best friends—my brothers were my only friends. When you're sleeping in cars and living in the streets the way we lived, we didn't have time for friends. We searched for food long after all traffic had stopped and the stores were closed. We slept in the car in the early hours of the evening, prowling the town for food in the time before dawn. We generally found plenty of food to take home and were constantly amazed at all of the good food that the stores threw away.

In Porterville, there was a school downtown. In the summer, when it was warm, we would go to the school grounds and play. I'd put Scotty in the big swing and I'd swing him high, higher, soaring into the sky. Other times, I'd hold him on my lap and swing because I liked to swing, too. His tiny hands gripped the big chain links while my feet scuffed the earth below and we would swing upward into the dark sky.

On our way back to the car, we'd stop off at the ice house and pick up ice to suck on. Sometimes, late at night, we found big blocks of ice that we'd take home and put in our icebox.

Everything was quiet and still. I crept out of the car, being careful with the car door. I did not want to wake up the boys. If they were awake, they could get out of the car and run all over the town. We caused a lot of excitement.

I kept moving to stay warm. Being careful not to be noticed, I walked close to the bar. I wanted to see all I could. Sometimes, someone would give me a nickel or two... sometimes even a dollar, if I'd show them my bare bottom. The back door of the bar was closed, but when someone went in or came out, I could hear laughter and people talking. At times I could see the people standing up at the bar. A record player whined shrill western music. I could even hear Mama laughing—she had such a strange laugh.

What was it like in there? How did it feel to be warm? Mama and Daddy ate in the bar. Why didn't they bring food out for us? I couldn't ask my Daddy—he might beat me again.

A bald man with squinty eyes opened the back door. The twist of his mouth suggested cruelty. He pushed his glasses up on his nose and leered at me. My skin crawled, and I froze. Behind him I could hear ice rattle in a bucket and see things inside.

While the man held the door open, I stood quietly, taking in all the excitement going on inside the bar. A woman winked, and left with a man out the front door. A man eating near the front window watched them. I was tantalized by the smell of frying food.

High above the bar hung a painting of horses with riders roping cattle in clouds of dust. Just under the painting was a long mirror filled with faces. I wished I could get a closer look. Against one wall were booths full of people. Along another wall was a long, skinny table, with a man at each end throwing a small, heavy, flat disk back and forth. At the back was a poker table, and a game was in progress. Voices rose and fell in a mix of words and laughter.

The man pitched a cigar toward me, turned on his heel, and went inside. The door closed on that colorful world.

I headed back toward the car and then I saw the dog watching me from behind a building. With my knees bent and my hand out, I walked toward him, speaking softly. When I was within a few feet of him, he turned and ran a few feet away, then stopped and turned to look at me again. I spoke quietly, and he sped away. From the side of the building, he watched me for a moment before disappearing into the night.

I hurried to the trash cans and found scraps of meat. I had left plenty for him, and then took the rest for my brothers and me. I knew he was watching me from somewhere nearby. I ran behind the market where I could always find all sorts of meats to leave out for him.

The sky darkened, as if a storm were moving in. Darkness hung heavier under the trees. Gathering the sacks of food, I took them back to the car before the storm hit. I toted the food, making several trips not knowing how long the storm would last, and I had to make sure we had enough to eat.

Suddenly the storm was on us, bringing heavy thunder and wind that lashed through the narrow streets. It rattled the windows of the downtown hotel. Lightning streaked across the dark sky, and rain pounded down on me.

I watched the dog, cringing in the shadows of the trees as the sky lit up. The rain came down hard, forming colorful puddles on the hoods of parked cars. Images shimmered in every pool of water. I didn't see any lights in the houses and stores.

Running for cover in the wee hours of the morning to our shack, we returned home and shivered under the covers. Late that same evening we headed out again to town so that Daddy could gamble. It rained for days, and we hadn't eaten. I knew Scotty was hungry, and I told him maybe we'd be able to find food tonight.

"I'll read you the story of Fuzzy Duck," I offered.

He liked that idea, so we settled down into the damp seat. I hadn't been reading for long when Scotty fell asleep. I wondered where the dog was, or if he'd run away. I hoped he'd found a dry place to stay.

The wind screamed. Every second or two, lightning lit up the sky. The thunder rumbled and raged. The sky darkened and became scarier. Lightning blinked again and the wind raked the trees with a threatening hand. Finally, the storm passed in a dark velvet stillness. The sky seemed to open up, and the stars winked at the mischief of the storm.

I crept from the car to search for food. All the trash bins were empty except for rain water. I ran to the market. The trash bins there were sopping wet. I went through all the mushy, gooey stuff, but nothing was worth taking. I scurried to all our secret places: packing houses; restaurants—everything was full of water.

As I came back down a side street toward the car, I approached the bar where Mama and Daddy were. The red neon beer sign blinked off and on. The door of the bar was propped open by a tall stool. A cowboy stared out at me as I ran by.

"What's yore hurry, baby?" he called out to me. His hair was stubby short and the cheeks were sunken to the bone in small, molded caves. His nose was crooked, with large clumps of hair in the nostrils.

I momentarily stood still, paralyzed with fear, and then sprinted across the tracks to begin probing in one garbage can after another. Suddenly I froze when I heard that familiar K-Plunk of Daddy's belt buckle. Turning around, I came face to face with him. The end of his belt was wrapped around the palm of one hand, the buckle hanging loose. I scooted back as he swung, the buckle and belt wrapped around both of my legs, locking them together.

"I saw you run past the bar. Don't say one word, you hear me? Not one word." He laughed a mean, frightening laugh. Pulling the belt loose he kept swinging his belt at me, roaring and cussing. Daddy clenched his fist tightly around the end of the belt, releasing his fingers before tightening them again into a ball. In, out! In, out! His muscles shifted beneath his shirt. Trying to duck under his arm, he stepped in front of me, blocking my way. His black-brown eyes usually had an icy appearance, but now his gaze was like a hot poker.

He grabbed me, catching me by my jacket between the shoulders. I struggled against him, screaming, "Lemme go! Lemme go!" I tried to wrench free of that iron grip, ducking and twisting, first one way, then the another. I slid free from my jacket.

"I'll get you yet." The muscles in Daddy's arms tightened into knots, and the veins in his neck stood out like big throbbing ropes. He seemed to tire and staggered against a building. But his eyes were still hot as a coal stove.

I hightailed it down the street, my bare feet flapping against the pavement. I crossed the parking lot and ran on down the railroad tracks, never looking back. I knew that when he did get me, I'd have it double hard. At least, I'd saved myself this time.

It had rained and stormed for many nights. We had been alone in the car for what seemed like days without food, except for some vegetables. Scotty was so fussy that it was hard to keep him entertained.

Slowly, from behind one of the buildings, the dog appeared. He had something in his mouth. He moved cautiously, tail between his legs, watching in every direction. He was dripping wet, and I could see his ribs.

Moving slowly, he sat under the trees that lined the street, never taking his eyes off me. Then he put down what he'd been carrying in his mouth, and ran off. Stopping, he looked back. When he reached the side of the building, he sat there watching me. Once again, he came out and dropped something else in the same spot where he'd left the first. He trotted back and forth each time, carrying something and leaving it under the tree. He watched me closely after every drop, as if he were trying to tell me something.

I sat motionless and watched. My heart pounded in my chest. Something in his eyes was different, but I didn't know what. "Patches, you'll be my special friend. Patches! Come here, Patches!"

His ears perked up when I called him. I told him, "You know your name already, don't you?" I crept from the car. Patches pressed his ears back, arched his neck, and narrowed his eyes. He drew back his lips, and growled in warning.

I wasn't frightened, though. He was my friend. I got within an arm's length of him, before he made a leap for me with his ears back and those big teeth showing. He growled a low frightening rumble in his throat, then leaped past me. The dog ran and stopped at the side of the building to watch me as before. His tail wagged back and forth, and his tongue hung out as though he was laughing.

I was so happy that I had forgotten to find out what he'd left under the tree. Running to it, my eyes widened when I saw what he had left there. Food—lots of food.

I never dreamed in a million years this dog would realize we were half-starved kids. Had he brought this food for us? I moved toward him. "Is this for us, boy? Patches. I wish you could speak to me, Patches."

He ran around in circles, then jumped up on his two hind legs, coming down on all four in an obvious display of delight. He'd run off a few feet, then come back as if he wanted to play. I could tell he was happy. He circled around me.

I stood motionless, watching. Fear suddenly replaced my surprise. He'd never been this close to me before. Never. As suddenly as he'd come, he disappeared.

I gathered up all the food and climbed back into the car. I wakened my brothers. They didn't believe me when I told them how I'd gotten it.

"Huh uh, Sissy," echoed Scotty as I handed him a weenie. My brothers teased me endlessly as we ate. They giggled about the big whopper of a lie they claimed I'd told, about the dog bringing the food to me.

Suddenly the car door opened and Daddy said, "Come on, we're getting out of here. I'm sick of your shit." He shoved Mama into the Dodge and slammed the door behind her. I pretended to be sleeping.

On our way home I saw Patches standing at the side of the road. I watched him out the back window. He followed us for miles, running, his ears bouncing in the wind. His coat was still a mess from the storm. I sent him wordless "thank you's".

Though it was dark, I could see. Stars lit up and filled the sky with speckles of light. Now and then one fell, and I'd watch it streak down. I wondered where it landed, and if I would be able to find it. The stars were thick all over the sky. I didn't remember ever seeing so many. Some were as big as hen's eggs, and every one of them was blinking. I just knew that they were winking in secret at me as they had seen Patches wonderful gift. My brothers were asleep, and I had some peace all to myself. I just wished this time would never end. I huddled in my own special world, knowing now that the future would be better with Patches as my friend. I stole another glance out the back window. He was still following behind our car.

Daddy drove recklessly. The old car lurched as it hit a bump, and fishtailed as Daddy coaxed it to its top speed. The road rose when he reached the small bridge, and the wooden planks echoed as we clattered across. I bounced in the seat between my brothers, feeling like a jelly bean in a jar. My brothers were asleep, either in my lap or against my shoulder.

"So, have you fucked him, too?" Daddy hollered. "My God, do you fuck everybody?"

I scrunched back into the seat realizing that there was going to be a doozy of a fight. I felt the car slowing before it plowed through the wire fence. An uprooted fence post slammed across the hood of the car. Scotty began crying. I reached over and held his hand while the car bounced and jarred through the tall grass before coming to a rest down a steep embankment.

"Please, Melvin," Mama said.

"You'll fuckin' do as I say!" he exploded. "I'm the boss. From now on, I'll do the ordering. When I say hop, you'll hop!" He grabbed her by the hair, wrapping it around his fist.

Mama mumbled in a voice filled with fear. The words ran together without much sense. She pulled away and jumped, leaving her car door open. Daddy scrambled in pursuit of her. I crept out being careful not to be seen.

Stepped in her way, Daddy blocked her escape. His dark eyes icy, the madness carved his face into an ugly mask—hard and deep lines were slashes around his screaming mouth. He pushed Mama backward down the hill. Every other step, he struck her in the face with his fists, then grabbed her by the hair and shoved her into the rough bark of a tree. His eyes were crazed with violence. He held onto her hair with one hand, grabbed the back of her neck with the other, and pounded her face into the tree. Mama's head kept hitting the side of the tree with a thud.

"You stupid, rotten bitch." He kept pushing her into the big tree. "I should kick your stupid face in."

Mama's skin was wet with blood, and I was terrified at the sight of all that blood. I knew Mama could get away from him. Why didn't she?

But if she did get away, all Daddy had to do was motion with his finger and say, "Come here, Winnie, come here."

She would always go to him. I wondered why? Why didn't she run away, like me?

Daddy's syrupy, whispering voice made goose bumps on my arms. I didn't know what it did to Mama.

"Please, Melvin, oh Melvin. Oh Melvin, you broke my tooth." I had never heard her cry so pleadingly. She shuddered and sobbed in the shadows of the blood-stained tree.

Daddy pinned her up against it with his hand at her throat. Her face was twisted, a pronounced fear in her eyes. He choked her with one hand and beat her in the face with his fist. Blood covered Mama's face and ran down her faded print house dress. Daddy held one big hand around Mama's throat, and in the other he now brandished his pocket knife. The shiny blade popped out. He drew it back and forth across Mama's throat, his eyes glazed. All the while, he grinned and talked to her softly in that sarcastically sweet tone of voice.

Mama squirmed, trying to get away. She put both hands to her head for just an instant. Then Daddy picked up a stick and hit her backside, knocking her down. Crab-like, she scrambled along the side of the hill. When Daddy caught up with her, she broke away again. Mama let loose with a howl, her voice fading away to an echo of pain.

Then I heard an awful thump, and all was quiet.

A minute later, they came back into view. Daddy was dragging Mama by the ankles. She was battered horribly; blood oozed between the strings of her unkempt brown hair. Her face was a mass of red pulp.

As fast as I could, I ran back to the car and crawled into one corner of the floorboard. Covering my ears, I clenched my eyes tightly shut, when suddenly I realized I was sitting on the crank Daddy used to start the car. I picked it up, jumped from the car, and started down the hill. I heard thrashing in the brush, and caught a glimpse of Patches' shining eyes.

I took a stance in front of Daddy. Hate, not blood, ran through my veins. "Let go of Mama," I screamed, swinging the crank.

Daddy ducked.

The bar was a square-cornered "S" shape, an awkward shape for a weapon. It didn't go the way I aimed it. It was top-heavy, cumbersome, and made a swishing sound, but I kept swinging it just trying to keep him from getting close to me. Staggering backward, I tripped and fell, jolting the crank out of my hands.

With a stinging thwack, Daddy kicked me in the chin. Then he grabbed the crank and started beating Mama with it. I saw the big muscles of his arms moving; the skin twitched and strained. Those big tendons in his neck tightened like knotting ropes. His words were muffled by the swishing sound of the big crank.

Mama lurched once. Grunting and moaning, she grasped the big tree. Blood smeared two trails when her sticky, wet hands slid down the rough bark. Thick droplets of blood spotted her dress. Then, my Mama fell limply to the ground. Dark blood oozed around her head. She looked much smaller now—almost childlike.

I knew she had to be dead. Daddy circled her like a coyote and stood laughing, with the bloody crank hanging at his side. His laughter turned into a hacking cough. Laughing and coughing, he climbed back up the hill to the car.

I listened to the car grinding, then the roar of the motor. Mud sucked at the tires as Daddy revved the engine and spun the wheels.

I huddled in the brush under clumps of dried loose leaves, and dead branches for most of the night. I was terrified. I knew to stay hidden as he most certainly would come back for me. Fearful thoughts of coming consequences pounded at me. Would I ever be able to go home? My eyes darted from side to side. I knew I'd have to stay out of his sight for a time until this passed. My thoughts raced as I huddled in the darkness. I wanted to run to my Mama, but I was deathly frightened of blood. What if she were still alive and touched me when she was covered with all that blood? I crouched in the darkness and watched her. Where was this Jesus everybody talked about who was supposed to help people?

I began exploring my situation. Why did Daddy hate me so? Why are Mama and I the only one he hates so much? I didn't want to go home, but where would I go? If I didn't go home he might start beating one of my brothers. What would my brothers do without me? My Daddy always said when he got another breath, he would whip my brothers, but he never did. I would do anything to keep him from beating my brothers. I knew by wearing him out that I could keep him from doing that.

I slept off and on. I don't know how long I'd been hiding in the brush before I came out and saw Mama. Covered in dried blood and reeking of the sweet sickening smell, she hadn't moved from where Daddy had left her. I hugged myself, determined not to faint, and clenched my teeth. I was aware of a dark emptiness inside me. She's dead! The thought brought hot tears.

I stayed with Mama for many days. She never moved. Cold shivers passed through me as I knelt on the ground beside her and stared into her open eyes. Blood ran out her mouth and down her chin, and there was a gaping wound at the side of her head, matting her hair. The eyes were open and staring, and I could scarcely bear to look at her.

"Mama? Mama!" I pleaded.

She didn't answer. I couldn't touch her, or I'd be dead too. My fear of blood told me strange myths. In a daze, I moved deeper into the woods and started for home. I had to make sure my brothers were safe. Then I saw Patches standing in the path just in front of me. He ran ahead of me, stopped long enough to lift his leg to pee. I knew I was safe with him to guard me.

Moving faster, searching for a path, I knew Patches would stay close by. The cool, moist ground squashed between my toes. The leaves and needles from the trees felt soft.

I turned back, trying to retrace my steps, but everywhere I turned, everything looked the same. I knew I had to climb the mountain. I ran on through the woods. The trails I found were hunting paths and logging trails, uneven and rutted. I could feel eyes watching me...eyes that belonged to the creatures of the night. They fled in fear at the sight of Patches. I was used to those eyes. Some of those animals of the night were my friends. When I was much younger, I'd sit in darkness and stare out through the brush, watching the bright eyes glimmer in the moonlight—larger animals, bigger than the opossums and raccoons, watched me. I was never sure just how big they were, but I knew they were there. Lots of coyotes roamed the hills.

Lights came on in the houses dotting the hillside. The sun would soon be coming up. I peeked in through the windows and saw people moving about. I caught glimpses of homey warmth and a peace I'd never known.

I stood in the shadows and watched Mary Lou sitting at a table with her Daddy. Her Mama, wearing a bright red robe, cuddly and warm as toast, was busy pouring coffee for Mary Lou's Daddy. She set the pot at the back of the stove. Hanging from a rack over the stove were dozens of large pots and pans, bottoms shining. An enormous old table sat in the middle of the room, and three places were set at it.

She poured three glasses of juice and sat down across the table from her husband.

I watched them speaking to one another, although I couldn't hear a word they said. Mary Lou's father patted her hand.

I wondered, why doesn't my house look like this? My Daddy hates me. He likes my brothers better, especially Scotty. The only thing I do is take care of my brothers. And my father is a murderer—he's just killed my mother.

I sat at a vantage point high on the hill and waited until I saw Daddy drive off, knowing that he was going into town to gamble.

Before he came home early the next morning, I went back up the hill and watched over Mama. There were no changes in her.

I stayed out of Daddy's sight for several days. I had no way of knowing if my brothers searched for their own food.

By the time I did see my Daddy, I hoped he would have forgotten about beating me for trying to protect Mama.

I kept going back to see Mama, then one day she wasn't there. Had a bear or wild animal dragged her body back to its den?

Several days later, Daddy took us to the county hospital in Tulare. We waited in the car while Daddy went inside. He was gone a long time. Kids weren't allowed in the hospitals unless they were sick. When he came out, we drove around to another side of the hospital. He took us to a window, where we stood on our tiptoes and peeked inside. And there was Mama! She was asleep.

Bottles hung above her head, with clear tubes going down to her arms. I'd never seen anything like this. I felt strange, and didn't want to look at her. Mama's face was purple and yellow, and her head was bandaged. A tube ran into her mouth and was taped to her face; another went into the back of her hand.

I was relieved she was alive, but I really wasn't sure if it was Mama or not. She didn't look exactly like her. I looked at Daddy, who was holding Scotty up so he could see. Then he put Scotty on the ground, "You kids play while I go in and talk to Mama," he told us.

Scotty and my brothers flew off to play on the green lawn. I stood on my tiptoes wanting to get one more look at her to be sure she really was alive before I ran off to play too. Daddy went into the room and stood at the foot of the green iron bed. Looking past my Daddy, I saw another person in the room who also had those funny-looking bottles and tubes going into her nose and mouth.

I went out to play with my brothers. We were fascinated by an elderly man pushing a lawn mower across the lawn.

He paused for a moment and wiped his forehead with a bright red rag, then stuffed it back into his pocket. We watched a black man unload his heavy mower from the bed of an old truck. "THE COUNTY OF TULARE" was painted in black letters on the truck. The truck itself was brown, faded to a rusty orange.

The sun was directly overhead and very hot. The man rolled up the sleeves of his work shirt and took off his hat to wipe his forehead with one arm. He waved at Scotty. The old man hunched over, trimming the grass to all the same height. His shirt collar was stained a darker color than his skin.

People walked slowly, enjoying the bright summer sun and the surroundings. One man stood at a large double door, furiously puffing one cigarette after another, sending up clouds of smoke. Another stubbed out his cigarette in a potted plant as he walked hurriedly into the front door of the hospital.

I turned the other way and saw the mailman all dressed in blue, wheeling a big brown, leather bag on wheels. He left his cart on the sidewalk and carried the big stack of mail up the steps into the hospital.

My three brothers ran to the mail cart. Brian pushed it back and forth to see how it worked. Mickey took it away—he wanted a turn. The two of them got into a fight over the cart.

"I found it first," Brian insisted. "It's mine!"

"I don't care," whined Mickey. "I want to see it, too. Just let me look at it."

"No!" Brian yanked it away hard. He sprawled onto the ground with the cart on top of him. Mail scattered all over the sidewalk.

Scotty ran and picked up the little white envelopes, ripping them open. He was going from envelope to envelope, just ripping them all apart. He wadded up all the papers and threw them all over the hospital grounds. Some papers he took out of the envelopes, and some he didn't, but he opened them all. There were several small boxes. He dug his tiny fingers under the tape. The boxes were filled with separate small white envelopes, which he took out and left scattered all over the lawn.

We ran off to the other end of the big hospital. We knew enough not to let the mailman catch us. Or we'd be in for it. "This is a good place," Scotty said. With a wide grin, he counted off his steps in a loud voice. "One, two, five, nine..." His eyes were bright during these happy moments. He patted his pockets, as if he was looking for something. He pulled a wadded-up dollar bill from his overalls, along with a pretty card he'd taken from the mailman's cart. "It's mine now!" He stuffed it back into his pocket. "Let me see it, please, Scotty?" I asked. "No," he yelled back. "It's mine."

"Please let Sissy see it. I'll give it right back. I just want to read the card. I'll read it to you."

Grudgingly, he handed it to me.

"Listen, Scotty. It says, 'Hope your birthday is a happy one for a grandson as special as you.'"

"What's a "grandson", Sissy?"

"A grandson is...you know, like a good boy, good son. Grandson is greater than a good son. But listen.'Grandma is sorry you have to spend your birthday in the hospital. Here is a dollar to spend when you get home. Love, Grandma.'"

I wondered, what's a birthday? I'll ask Mama when she comes home...if she comes home.

Scotty left all the pretty little pieces of paper scattered all over the sidewalk. I ran around and picked them up. Some were pictures of animals—ducks, rabbits, and dogs. Others had bouquets of pretty flowers of every shape in bright reds, pinks, greens, and yellows. These tiny slips of paper with their beautiful pictures would later become very precious to me. I hid them under the seat of our car and treasured them for years. I copied the pictures and learned to draw from them.

I ran back to the hospital window and pulled myself up on the ledge to get one last look at Mama. Her dark, coffee-colored hair lay limp and stringy against the white of the pillow. Her eyes were closed, but the eyelids moved as if she were having a bad dream. I watched her chest lift up and down in time with a big machine that was attached to her body by tubes and wires. The bed was crumpled and brown with dried blood and splatter marks.

Daddy took hold of the curtain and those big rings on the metal track swung it around the bed. I couldn't see the other patient that was on the other side of Mama. My Daddy unbuckled his pants and dropped them. He crawled up onto the bed with Mama, and he got on top of her. He shut his eyes for a moment. Then he blinked, and his eyes opened slightly. There was a chilling, glazed look in them. Crystals of sharp ice seemed to go through my heart. I dropped down off the ledge. Standing with my back against the hospital wall, I felt like an angry bomb of realization had exploded inside me. Oh, not that again! Everywhere... everyone! Mama with Daddy, Mama with other men, in the hotel, at home, it seemed everyone had to "DO IT."

Another time when I visited Mama, the bandage was off and her head had a big scar like an ugly monster doll I'd seen once. I don't know how long she was in the hospital, but it was a long time. She didn't have any hair, and she wore a kerchief over her head. Many of her teeth were gone. The very day Mama was discharged from the hospital, on our way home she and Daddy stopped off in Porterville.

The two of them were right back at the bar.

The weather was turning cold. How I hated the winter. I could bear the summers, but the winters were hard for me and my brothers.

The trash barrels were piled high. Cardboard boxes were scattered everywhere. It looked like someone had gone through everything and just left it all lying in the streets.

I spent most of the night taking the boxes apart and stacking them on the ground behind the trash barrels. I kept the biggest one for myself and lay it on top of all the others I'd taken apart and flattened. I made sure it was big enough for me to crawl into. This way, I could stay warmer. I took a bag of clean food, mostly leftover sandwiches, to the car and left it in the front seat for my brothers. I made sure there were plenty of scraps left for Patches.

It was early evening, icy cold. Hurrying on, I crept to the back of the bar. I wanted to make sure one more time that Mama and Daddy weren't about to leave.

A man stood against the back door, tapping his foot and bobbing his head in time with the music. The leather in his boots was all wrinkled. I watched the big man's feet tapping up and down. He turned and spat, wiping his mouth with his shirt sleeve. I wasn't able to see much because of all the smoke.

Another man came outside and gave me a dollar to see my "little naked body". I grabbed the dollar before taking off my raincoat and dress. I shivered with the cold while he had his look, then I grabbed my clothes and ran away before putting them back on.

I went back to the trash pile and slid feet first into the big cardboard box. With some other pieces of cardboard, I covered myself to keep the wind off. Just the top of my head poked out of the box. I was warmer than I'd been in a long time. The warmth lulled me to sleep.

Patches scrounging in the trash wakened me. Noisily he wolfed down his food, swallowing it whole. "Come here, Patches," I whispered. "Come, boy."

He stopped. Everything was quiet. I knew he was still there, because I hadn't heard him run. Generally, he sounded like thunder as he ran.

I continued to talk to him and felt his movement, like raising his head up and down, or side to side. I kept quiet, not wanting to alarm him. I wanted him to get used to me being around.

"What's the matter, Patches?" He growled as if to answer me.

He came around to the back and peered at me lying under all the cardboard. He turned his head at an angle apparently confused. Without getting out of the box, I stuck my hand out. He came right over, smelled me and then jumped backward. Slowly he came forward again and licked my hand, then nuzzled it. I raised it slowly to the top of his head, and he moved away.

Patches sat down on his hind legs and watched me carefully; he put his head between his paws. We were eye-to-eye. I reached out and tried to stroke him, and again he moved, not letting me touch him.

My eyes filled with tears. If he only could know how happy this made me! I wanted to jump up and give him a big hug, but I knew that would frighten him. I tried to be gentle and quiet.

When Patches licked my hand the second time, I reached up and tried to touch him. He moved away. "Okay boy, I won't pat you."

He steadily gazed at me. The yellow-gray eyes spoke words of compassion with some strong cord of a newly-awakened devotion. I somehow sensed he seemed to feel responsible for me, just like I felt responsible for my brothers. There was love in those eyes, but still an occasional flicker of wild independence. Yes, we were so much alike, and I finally, for the first time in my life, had a friend.

The nurses in the hospital had told Mickey and me about Santa, but they also had told us that children have guardian angels. I wondered if angels could have fur instead of wings.

Patches' eyes blinked wisely as if in acknowledgment of my thoughts. I was to find out in the near future that furry angels can perform a rescue.

CHAPTER ELEVEN

Crossing through the school yard, I took time out to slide down the slide. Patches followed, scaling the ladder on three legs and then slid down after me. I skipped behind him into a park, following winding trails and tromping over and through thick underbrush for what seemed like hours. I had to stop often to pick sharp, tearing thorns from the bottoms of my feet. When I did, Patches sat and watched me, cocking his head to one side.

Though he limped along on three legs, he had the speed of a mountain lion. No bones seemed broken, but he was still badly injured. I kept up with him. Patches and me... pals...friends...we both had the same fortitude.

When I decided it was time to go back to the car, I rounded the corner and was shocked. The parking lot was empty, the street shadowy and deserted. Nobody stirred. The dark velvet of the night hung low, hugging me as if to protect. Everything was dead and still.

Standing in the shadow of the building, I didn't know which way to go, but I wasn't really frightened. My Daddy had said many times in the past that he was going to leave me. Now he finally had.

I peered around the empty parking lot where dozens of cars parked every night. Newspapers blew across the blacktop, scuttling along like wounded birds. Should I hide and wait for Daddy to come back tonight, or should I start out for home? I wondered.

Once I caught my breath, I crawled along the railroad track embankment to the road. I sat down putting my bare feet on the hard cold ground. With Patches at my side hopping Mama and Daddy would come back for me. Somehow the action of planting my feet was like a slap of the teacher's ruler to pay attention. My mind began presenting thoughts like lessons on a blackboard. Mama and Daddy might not know that I was even missing. Pictures of how my family lived: the gnawing hunger of my brothers; the strangling fear of beatings which hung over my head and Mama's, threatening to drop on either of us at Daddy's cruel whim.

Being left alone in the spooky parking lot seemed to seal the fact that I was different. Chin in hand, I bit my lip—not in intimidation, but in hardened resolve. I'd just take one step at a time...one step. Nobody cared about me except Patches. Nobody cared about him except me.

The night wind had iced its breath and was now freezing cold. "Let's go," I murmured to Patches. "Let's go, boy."

I sensed Patches would stay close by. I kept quiet, with my ears cocked, just like my furry friend. His newly-found devotion blew back and forth like the wind so that I wasn't honest-to-God sure about Patches. He'd come up and sniff me, but still wouldn't let me touch him.

Darkness surrounded us as I stumbled up the mountainside toward home. The muddy ground beneath my feet began to ooze up through my toes. With every step they became colder, but I went on to the next step, and the next, and the next, and the next, just like my heart had told me to do earlier. My feet turned red, and my legs ached then turned numb from the cold. I thought my toes would crack. Thick dampness surrounded me. On occasion, Patches showed himself circling, round-and-round. I knew I couldn't go any farther. The strength in my legs left me like the dirty water swirling through the cracks in the floor when Mickey and I dumped the bathtub. I frantically looked for a spot to get warm and sleep, looked for a spot to spend the night.

As I slipped through a back yard, I took a blanket from someone's clothesline. The neighborhood was silent, and I could hear the hum of traffic going up the mountain a few miles from me. I wondered if one of the cars carried my Mama, Daddy, and my brothers. If I ran fast enough or took a shortcut over the hill, I might catch up with them. Then I realized, if I did, I'd get a beating.

With a steady pace, I tramped upward, the blanket wrapped tightly around me. Patches circled me, leading me toward the hills, guiding me down one trail, then going in another direction entirely. The road became narrow, changing from gravel to dirt. He took me through a maze of paths as if we were playing a game of hide and seek.

I found myself following him through thick underbrush into a part of the mountains where I'd never been before. The forest grew snarled and knotted together. We headed up a twisted trail, going left, then turning back again sharply. I followed him through a deserted campground, past picnic tables and rusty trash cans. Ducking under a barbed wire fence, I stopped in the middle of a grassy cow pasture.

I turned north and then south, following closely behind Patches. I had completely lost my sense of direction and had no idea where I was. I couldn't have found my way back if I had wanted to!

I began to feel a little frightened. What if these dark hills twisted on forever? I imagined myself walking and walking for the rest of my life, unable to find my way out.

"Peggy, stop scaring yourself," I said aloud.

As I turned another corner, I heard a strange thumping sound. I spun around. Was something behind me? A cold chill ran down my back.

"I'm really lost," I murmured.

I walked on, accompanied by the shrill ringing of singing insects on all sides. After a short while, I pushed my way through a clump of tall, stiff weeds.

"Hey, boy!" I hollered at Patches. "I'm no dog. Don't lead me through brush!"

He stared at me as if he understood my every word. He tilted his head and stared at me. His ears quivered, then he took off again.

"Don't get too far ahead, boy!" I shouted.

The dog took me higher up the mountain than I'd ever been. Far above the valley floor, I hiked along the cattle trails until they turned into the trails of wild animals and logging roads. I scrambled over fallen trees, their jagged limbs slashing at my clothes and chest. Hurt and bleeding, I ran on blindly, mindlessly, through the black, dark night. Vines reached out for me like cunning snakes. I imagined the limbs that brushed my clothes were the savage arms of monsters of the night. My heart thumped madly.

Then Patches stopped.

"What are you looking at?" I whispered, scarcely able to catch my breath.

Patches darted off, rounding a corner and skidding on his side. A rabbit cowered in the tall brush. Patches swatted it as if to say, "Not this time," before scurrying on.

I tried to keep up with him, but he was soon out of sight. When I finally caught up with the big, tattered dog, he looked like he was laughing at me again. Quickly, he dug in a hole at the base of an old tree trunk. He pulled out a small ground squirrel, then went back for another and another. Each one was so tiny it slipped right down his throat in a gulp. I wondered fleetingly if they squirmed inside him.

The moon slid out from behind the black, heavy clouds. I reached out and touched the bark of a big oak tree with gnarled roots buckling the dirt. Patches stood behind the tree in the light from the cobwebbed clouded moon. He was watching me.

I followed him down a slight hill to the creek. Thick clumps of willow trees grew along the bank for miles in both directions. At the end of the trail, I stumbled onto a cabin with rotted wooden walls. Its rusty tin roof shyly curled under at the corners. It was little more than a hovel. Inside, it was so dark I could barely see a chair turned over on its side, and a plywood table with a splintering top.

Crumpled papers, yellowed with age, piled and huddled in a corner.

I settled myself near a wall with the blanket wrapped around me. Patches thumped his tail and lolled out his tongue, giving me a dog grin. Turning around many times, he finally curled up near the door. He gave me a sense of love and security I'd never felt before.

I dozed, but kept waking up with nightmares of Daddy beating me for not being where he'd told me to be. I knew I'd get it for sure when I got home. I hoped Daddy didn't hit my brothers because I wasn't in the car. I prayed he'd never beat my brothers like he beat me.

I didn't sleep much that night. Every time I woke, Patches was watching me.

"Hey, boy. Have you slept at all?"

He wiggled his ears. He put his matted head down between his paws, ears lowered, but kept his eyes fixed on me. It was like a current of love that flowed toward me from those eyes.

A pale pink streak over the treetops signaled the new day coming. The moon went off its watch.

I tensed and listened. Patches arched his neck. Pressing his ears against his head, he drew back his lips and snarled. That scared me. I knew he was smart and clever. I could see it in his eyes, and in his actions. The hackles on his back that had risen slowly came to rest. Perhaps he had heard a small animal.

I heard the sound of water as it noisily trickled down the hillside. I listened to the music of hidden fountains...all things thawing, bending, limbs snapping from the weight of moisture. It was time to go.

Patches circled around me, sniffing the wind as he went. The sounds made by wildlife in the woods dictated his moods and directed his actions. He was there to protect me. Instead of barking, he now howled like a wolf.

The sun appeared and blazed down on the trees. A woodpecker stuck his head around the side of a tree. I hurled a rock at a squirrel. It ran with silly scattering fear, chattering and shaking its tail in anger.

Patches dodged behind a clump of brush. I ran after him, then found myself teetering and groping for a handhold. I grabbed at thin air and fell a very long way down with a smashing thump. After a bruising bang, I found I had landed in a hole on my back. The breath was knocked out of me. When I opened my eyes, it was dark, as though I were blind. I heard Patches panting noisily nearby, his tail beating the ground as though to encourage me.

I called to him softly. "Patches, where are we? Where are we, boy?"

He thumped his tail again.

I could have died. I put my hand to my pounding heart. "I'm still breathing."

I realized I'd fallen into an enormous hole. My fall had been cushioned by the damp, spongy floor. I raked my fingers across it. The smell was enough to turn my stomach. It smelled of damp hair or fur.

I heard Patches get up and shake himself. Daylight outlined him as he stood near the opening of the hole. Brush was piled high all around the opening. Patches' body blocked most of the light. His form bobbed in the opening for a moment, then he scooted through the hole and was gone, leaving a streak of sky. Would he lead me into this trouble and then just abandon me?

I began to see more clearly. Thick green moss grew on the walls of the big hole. The tangled, dry vines seemed to be reaching and grabbing for me. The huge rocks that lined the walls came to life like spooky diamonds.

Then I heard noises. I was trapped. I couldn't move, couldn't breathe. Creatures were coming for me, closer and closer. I heard something moving in the earth, the sound of claws scratching, teeth grinding and gnawing. The scratching grew louder. Yellow eyes glowed in the darkness. I listened as creatures scrabbled over the dirt floor, and felt something warm and furry brush against my leg. Rats!

I was suddenly washed in sweat though it was still cold. I didn't want to even breathe the same air.

Another brushed against me, then many of them started to scrape around in the earth. They were restless. I'd really disturbed them. Now, they spoke to each other in shrill squeaks. They were getting braver.

Get out of here! Get out of here before they attack!

Where was Patches? Where was my guardian angel?

I slid over the damp, slimy floor. Please let me find my way out of here, I begged as I stumbled through the darkness. Fat bloated rats with thick coats of fur crawled about slowly. I squinted to see them, shivering. On my hands and knees, I crawled up to the opening, and sensed they followed, but I was afraid to look back. I felt the tree limbs and brush that covered the hole. It was cold, and slimy with moss. I tried again to pull myself out by holding onto brush, but my hands slipped on the damp moss covering the branches. I was covered with frigid mud that numbed my actions.

"Help me!" I screamed, struggling to crawl out of the hole. "Help! Help!" I called out again and again.

I heard Patches above me. He paced back and forth nervously. I had never heard him cry before, but soft whining sounds of concern hung in the morning air between us.

After a gulp of air, I reached up again and felt around until I finally found a dry thick branch. I had almost reached the opening when the earth beneath me gave way. I tumbled down, mud plopping on top of me. My face was buried in mud. I rolled free, and once again struggled to the top.

Finally, after many tries, I pulled myself through the hole. Sitting on the ground at the top of the hill, I examined my blistered hands. I couldn't rub them. They were covered with open blisters and hurt badly. I sobbed, until I looked around and suddenly gasped in utter surprise.

From where I sat, I could see the roof of my house! Had Patches known all along where I lived? Had he followed me home? Had Patches been living in this cave, or had he just now, this night, stumbled into it? I wished he could talk to me. There were a lot of questions I wanted to ask him. I wondered how many times I'd seen Patches on the hillside, but thought it was a wolf.

Nothing stirred; everything was quiet. It was still early. Most of the morning, I sat in the sun looking down the mountainside. I tried desperately to get warm and dry, to help recover from my horrible experience. But, deep down I knew that what had happened was far better than what was going to happen when Daddy got his hands on me.

Overhead, a hawk drew circles in the sky. He was flying low for that type of bird, and I thought he must have just left the nest for his first morning flight. As he passed over me, I saw the red of his tail, like a torch against the soft gray color of his underbody. Up, up, his circles grew wider as he drifted south over the hillside. He went high, higher with little movements of his wings. His circles seemed smaller as he went higher and higher, so high he became only a speck with wings in the sky. I almost lost him in the glare of the bright sunlight.

I blinked my eyes as he returned. The sun was bright… now I see him, now I don't. As the tiny speck passed over my head, he seemed to stop for an instant, and stayed there as if he were pasted against a cloud. He loomed, then dropped. I couldn't see his wings as he fell like a stone being dropped from the sky. I sat up in the prickly grass and watched him dive. For a moment, I thought he was coming down for me. Then he swooped, without touching ground, back up into the sky with a rabbit between his claws. The rabbit screamed as the hawk flew off. Bright blood dripped from the sky to the earth below, while the rabbit still squealed.

Later that morning, I watched as Daddy drove out our drive. It was what I'd been waiting for. I limped down the mountain and into the house. I was bombarded by my brothers' questions on where I'd been.

"We thought a mountain lion had gotcha'," Mickey smiled with a buck-tooth grin. But Mama just stared at the mountain in silence. I wondered, did she even know that I was gone?

By the time Daddy returned home, he'd forgotten everything about the night before.

A few days later, with my brothers in tow, I went back to the mountaintop. I wanted to show them the hole in the side of the mountain.

We headed into the clump of bushes, wandering deep into the thickets. The branches made sharp, snapping noises. Pushing the brush aside in the thickest part, the hole appeared.

Mickey jumped in first. It was much deeper than I'd remembered. With Mickey's help, I scrambled down. The two of us helped Brian and Scotty. We crawled along on our hands and knees until the hole just opened and became much bigger.

There was a deafening roar and air fanned our faces as bats by the hundreds flew blindly about. I heard them bump into the side of the cave. Some flew out, while others settled down again.

"We'll call this a cave!" Mickey shouted. His voice echoed many times, getting fainter and fainter. Suddenly the rats came squealing out, followed by sleepy skunks and fearless foxes. The scratching rats ran about sluggishly. I was scarcely strong enough to hold Patches as he wanted to chase the animals.

"Let him go Peggy, he'll chase them and they'll never come back," Mickey instructed me.

"No. He'll get bit by some diseased animal, then what'll we do?" I answered, holding tightly to his fur.

"Peggy, do you think Patches sleeps in here?" Mickey asked.

"How would I know?"

My eyes darted around. By now everything was so still, quiet, and dark. I made my brothers swear to keep this place a secret. We headed for our secret cave whenever Daddy came home. It was how I escaped many beatings.

Taking the wagon, we searched our neighbors' dumps, collecting anything we could salvage for our new home. We carried cardboard boxes to put on the cold ground, and collected old pots and pans, toys, wooden animals on strings, and old blankets because we knew we would be spending many nights in our secret cave. But would even our secret hideout and Patches be enough to protect us from Daddy? There were times I felt like the small rabbit in the sharp beak of the hawk—my blood falling, streaming to the ground... nowhere to go...no way to escape.

CHAPTER TWELVE

Daddy would beat me silly whenever he could get his hands on me. I kept a wary eye on him at all times, not giving him a chance. He really didn't like me and I never knew exactly why, unless it was because I'd fight back. Why couldn't Mama leave him? Why couldn't we all leave...just walk away? She could go to the end of the earth, and he'd find her. He'd hunt her down. I knew he would.

He'd kill our mother, and us kids too.

I knew Mama was scared. Just the sound of his voice painted her face into a mask of terror. At his approach, she'd whisper, "He's here." Her dark eyes would sink deeper into her skull, pupils dilated with fear.

"No," she would muttered. "It must be...must be a mistake. This can't be happening. Not again." Trying to get away, she would push through the door into the kitchen with Daddy right on her like an animal stalking its prey.

One night she crossed the porch and went down the steps. She barely managed to whisper, "Please... oh, please..." Daddy released her, and she slid away from him, up against the wall. She cowered there, not even trying to get up. Her eyes assumed a vacant stare. Her body was there, but Mama was gone. It was her only form of escape.

Mama and Daddy had only a few friends that I remember. Lulu Easley was Mama's friend. Her husband was Lois. My brothers loved to tease Lois about his name. Lois drove a big logging truck that was painted light purple. He was always hidden away under the big hood of his truck, and kept it shining like a huge eggplant. They had five or six kids and lived in Silver City, where Lois logged. Another friend was Pood McDaniels. Pood ran coon dogs on the mountainside where we lived. He drove around town in a big, white, dirty pickup. The back was filled with wire cages of all sizes. Pood lived in Springville, and he had many girls around our ages.

Pood always stopped by our house on his way coon hunting. Long before he arrived at our house, we knew he was coming. We could hear his dogs for miles. Patches also heard them. Pood's dogs bounced in their cages as he pulled into our driveway. With their ears tuned to the brush in the foothills, they barked and yapped and circled. His favorite dog always sat in front beside him.

Old Pood was short, leathery-skinned, squinty-eyed, chain-smoking, and good-humored. He looked like something out of the history books. He speed-talked to whomever happened to be within earshot.

He'd pull into our driveway, jump out with the motor still running, and start talking. Nobody ever knew what he said. He was just talking and mumbling aimlessly. Somehow Daddy seemed to make sense of the string of words.

"Why, that's a pack of lies," Daddy said. "It's nonsense, it's..." "Melvin, that's God's honest truth," Pood interrupted. Then he turned to the non-stop yapping dogs. "Shut up!"

Turning back to Daddy, he said, "My pup's the sweetest—shut up!" He was always interrupting himself that way, turning to yell at his dogs. "Someone shot some of my dogs over the past year, but that's okay," he said. "I'm raising pups faster than you can shoot'em. Shut up!"

Pulling a wrapper of chewing tobacco from his pocket, Pood bit off a chunk. He lowered his hand giving his dog a bite, then rewrapped the tobacco and put it back into his pocket.

When Daddy was home from the hospital, he and his friends played cards and drank. Cars came to our ramshackle, one-bedroom house all hours of the night. The men came in carrying their own table, chairs, and bags of liquor and food. Most drank from a brown bottle they passed around from table to table. Our shack reeked of their whiskey and sweat.

I liked this peculiar form of hospitality, because the gamblers always brought enough food for my brothers and me. A man on a motor scooter stayed at the end of the road, watching for the police. Our house was never searched by the police, but I heard the gamblers talk and joke about the possibility. I had no idea why the police would want to search our house.

Usually, the men would show up in the early hours of the morning, after the bars had closed and before the sun came up. Occasionally they stayed for several days. Sometimes several men left by morning, but at night they'd be back.

Sunday turned into Monday; Monday blurred into Tuesday, on and on into the next day. I didn't sleep much when the gamblers came.

I watched every move they made, keeping an eye open for anyone who might get too close. I listened to them talk and watched their lips, their sharp jaws with the dark shadows of beards. Their heads moved slowly on thick, muscular necks as they turned to glare at me or each other. Some looked grim and extremely strong.

One put his hands on his hip and tried to brush against me. He looked like an ape, with a deep, barrel chest, short, muscular neck, and massive legs. His eyes made contact with mine. From never taking my eyes off the man, I knew to stay out of his reach.

Another stood in the doorway, his shirt tail hanging out. I saw a patch of dirty skin near his navel. His open collar revealed a thick, hairy, neck with dirt caked in the creases.

Outside, another leaned against a tree. That was "Red." I could always recognized his sour, acrid smell. He was the biggest, most powerful man I'd ever seen. He looked like he had just grown right out of the ground like a redwood tree. A bright red beard covered his face, and his eyes were even more deadly than my Daddy's. The way he looked at me sparked an instant fear inside me. His look was different from anybody else's—except Daddy.

He stared at Mickey and me, but his flat, glazed eyes didn't seem to actually connect with us. When he unzipped his trousers and took out his big, hard purple thing, we ran. When we reached the house, he was still watching us.

Shorty was a short, square man who never removed his green jacket or his dirty cowboy hat. He coughed, hacked and spit, just like Daddy. Shorty was the first to start drinking when he woke up in the morning.

Jim had a leathery face and looked like he was the oldest. He would roll a cigarette and smoke it slowly while lingering over his bottle of whiskey.

Jake Moorhead, another one of Daddy's friends, came often. He was a real cowboy, a crazy ranch foreman who only had an occasional day off. He would arrive with an armload of food. When Jake came, Mama always began clattering pots and pans in the kitchen. She always gave him a delightful smile. By the way she greeted him, I knew he was special, not just another cowboy or gambler.

Jake was special to me too because he treated my brothers and me so well. He always brought us presents—cookies, coloring books, and comics. No one else ever did that.

Tall and thin, with white, wavy hair, cut short, Jake had those wonderful holes in his cheeks exactly like Brian and Scotty. One day I had a surprising thought: Had Daddy ever noticed that Brian and Scotty looked just like Jake?

Jake was the only man Mama ever talked with when Daddy was around. Daddy got mad if Mama talked with other men, but usually Jake helped Mama peel potatoes. He'd chop wood out back on the chopping stump, then he'd chuck up the fire, or whatever needed to be done. He'd sit at the rickety, metal top table and chat with Mama.

I secretly wished that Jake would come with his arms loaded with food every night. I liked it best when he was with us. Why doesn't Mama cook any other times except when Jake is here? I wondered.

Mama would slap the slab of pork into the frying pan. Grainy and iced with salt, the fat fried crisp with a very tough rind. The smell of burning wood and bacon would fill our tiny house. Mama made high, brown biscuits, dusted with flour. They tasted rich with soda. She also made thick, white gravy, specked with big specks of black pepper. The smell of strong coffee would come from the pot at the back of the stove, and a sizzle of angry grease usually spat from the black, crusted skillet. I loved all the wonderful food, but I'd become very sick, and puke. Mama said it was "too rich." I thought that was side-splitting funny. The ladies dressed for church were "too rich," not black-flecked gravy.

I loved these times best and wished they'd never end. Jake didn't drink. He said he couldn't drink and gamble. I didn't know what he really meant by that, but I was glad he didn't drink.

One morning, Mama poured Jake a big cup of dark brown coffee. I heard it sputter as she poured it into his cup. Then she set the pot of boiling coffee on the back of the cook stove.

It was funny the way Jake mixed his coffee. He made it white with milk, then added two or three heaping spoonsful of sugar. He would stir it slowly, almost lovingly for a long time, then carefully pour the coffee into a small saucer and slurp noisily.

Mama was thin and tall. She wore a loose, simple, gray house dress with faded flowers, and the color was all washed out, with the flower pattern only a hint of lighter gray than the background. The dress came down to her ankles, and her broad, bare feet moved quickly with a flapping noise over the floor. She wore her thin, fine hair gathered into a sparse, wispy knot at the back of her head. Her freckled arms were bare from her shoulders down.

Jake strolled to the edge of the porch, thumbs stuck in his front pockets. Sitting on the mattress, he stretched his long legs out before him and studied his boots. He leaned back with hands locked behind his head. Scotty straddled his lap, and Brian sat beside him. Brian rubbed Jake's leg, up and down, and listened to him tell stories.

Jake reached out gently and poked the tip of Scotty's nose. He got Scotty's nose between his fingers, and acted like he was trying to pull. Somehow, he had his own thumb between his two fingers and made it look just like Scotty's nose. He said, "See, I got your nose. I tore it off."

Scotty put his scrawny hand to his face, feeling his nose, and shook his head. "No you didn't, Jake. It's still there. I can still feel it." Scotty's bright little eyes danced. He looked at Jake with utter delight. He adored Jake. We all loved him.

Jake then reached up behind Scotty's ear and brought his hand back with a big, shiny quarter. "See what I found hidden behind your ear, son."

With his dirty hands, Scotty felt behind his ear. "Do it again, Jake! Get me 'nother one!"

"No, that's all I have tonight." He handed the quarter to Scotty.

"Jake, you know what? You sound just like my Daddy."

"What do you mean, son?"

"You know, Jake. You talk like my Daddy."

"Your Daddy and I have known each other a long, long time. We came from the same town in Texas, way before you were ever born."

"Well, where was I, Jake?" Scotty asked.

Jake laughed. "Where do all these questions come from? I can't keep up with you. No more questions now. You ask questions that even I can't answer."

I watched Scotty's bright eyes.

Once while Jake was there, an old bear-sized man with a round face and small, squinty eyes strolled to the door and flipped a cigarette out ahead of him. I watched it explode in a shower of sparks. A feeling of dread came over me as he stared down at me. I thought he looked like a toad. He stood with the screen door open, and unbuttoned his pants to take a pee. "Go on out to the yard," Jake said. "Don't you give a hoot in hell that there are kids around?"

The old man drew in a long, shaky breath. His eyes squinted, lower lip curled belligerently and he meandered on out into the yard.

The next morning, beer bottles were everywhere and ground-out cigarette butts littered the wooden floor of our old house. Jar lids overflowed with ashes. One gambler stuck his butts through the cracks in the floor. The room stank of whiskey and cigar smoke long after the gamblers were gone, lingering like ghosts left to haunt our shabby house. Once, when we hadn't had anything to eat in a long time, one of the men handed me half a sandwich. I held onto the half sandwich, not knowing who to give a bite to first, because we were all starving. I hurried outside and gave everyone a bite: a bite for Scotty; a bite for Brian, and a bite for Mickey. The last bite was for me.

Later, Mama said, "I'm really proud of you, Peggy. When that man handed you part of his sandwich, I thought you'd be so hungry you'd fight over it. I'm proud you didn't let on how hungry you were."

The loud laughter and cursing awakened us during many nights.

Patches barked in harmony with the neighbors' dogs up and down the mountainside. How ordinary he sounded. It was strange that Patches barked when he was at home, but when he was in the hills alone with me, he howled like a wolf. One night as Mickey sat on the floor next to the stove, taking in every word our drunken Daddy said, he reached up with one hand, fingers still little-boy dimpled, and gently stroked Daddy's pant leg.

When Daddy glanced down at him, his eyes held a dull stare that made me swallow hard. My body stiffened for two or three minutes, and I got a very strange feeling in the pit of my stomach. With all his sweetness toward us when others were around, Daddy was vicious. He never looked for a fight, but when involved in one, he fought to win.

Daddy told my brothers not to be sissies. "No overhand jabs, no slaps or scratches," he'd tell them.

Daddy was never known to lose a fight, even though he sometimes looked worse than the other man when it was over. He went in to win, with dropkicks and eye gouging, and all the other tricks he could use.

Daddy remained at a low boiling point most of the time. The smallest incident caused him to explode. He'd hurl something or someone against the wall, busting a hole clear through the wall or knocking a door off the hinges. With both his hands at a man's throat and his knee in his crotch, Daddy was sure to win.

The gamblers laughed a lot and used foul language. Standing on the steps, they took their things out of their britches and peed on the ground right in front of me. The frozen earth crunched under their feet. Arm-in-arm, they joked and laughed their way back into the house, as though peeing together was some kind of clubhouse ritual.

If Jake was around, he'd holler, "You go out into the dark to piss. Don't do it in front of that girl!" I really wished Daddy was like Jake.

Daddy sat on an orange crate, leaning back along the edge of the crate, his back touched against the wall. His arms stretched high over his head, fingers laced behind his neck. He reached and fumbled in his shirt pocket for a pack of Camels. He took one out of the package and tapped it on the table top several times, then finally stuck it in his mouth and lit it. I could hear slight sucking sounds as he drew on the cigarette.

Daddy kept glancing at Mickey from the corner of his eye, and I had a terrible feeling that Mickey had done or said something under his breath to set Daddy off in a drunken rage. I should have known better, because Daddy never caused a scene if someone was around. He winked and gave Mickey's small shoulder a squeeze. "You're almost a big boy."

"I am a big boy," Mickey replied.

"Me too," piped Scotty. Indignantly, he jumped up and slid between Daddy's knees. "I'm four!"

But as I studied his face next to Daddy's, it was like looking at a small version of Daddy's friend, Jake.

CHAPTER THIRTEEN

Christmas Eve I was seven we were again left alone in the car, parked behind the hotel and bar in Porterville, while Mama and Daddy drank and gambled. Crusted with dirt, we wore the same tattered clothing we'd worn for weeks. We had no shoes, coats, or blankets. We never had shoes. Our soles were as thick as cowhide. I could walk on nails or hot coals, whichever came first.

At Christmas, the kids from school got wagons and bikes, colors and books, trains that puffed, oranges and nuts. When I asked Mama why old Santa always forgot us, she'd just look at me and cry.

There was much excitement in town, and the streets of downtown Porterville were crowded. In the clubs and bars, another night of escape had begun. It was early evening, and the stores were still open. Cars filled the parking lots and hurried through the streets. Townspeople mingled on the sidewalks talking, shouting, waving, and hugging one another. All were dressed in brightly colored coats, carrying dazzlingly colored packages, all wrapped with big sparkling bows of silver, golds, reds, and greens. They went from one store to another, swinging big bags over their shoulders.

Some made several trips to their cars as they carried more packages.

Children whispered and giggled to one another along the way, while fathers pulled wagons loaded with gifts. One pushed a scooter. Several walked along with both tricycles and bicycles, putting them in the backs of bright, new pickups. Some pushed small, pink doll carriers. I sure wished one of those could be for me.

I determined that when I got back to school, I was gonna' tell all those stupid kids that there really isn't a Santa Claus, because I had watched all their mothers and fathers hide presents in their cars.

Wiggling down into my seat, I gawked, wondering, Why do they have so much, when my family has nothing? I told Scotty Christmas stories I'd heard from the other children in school. I tried to guess what was in the packages the people carried, and whom they were for. I made a game of it for Scotty. I told him there would be a big surprise package for him, and it made him grin from ear-to-ear. "Scotty, you'll get a big, fuzzy teddy bear, so big you won't be able to carry it."

"No! No, Sissy! I don't want the teddy bear. I want a big truck...this big." He held his little arms wide to show me what size truck he wanted.

Mickey jumped out of the car and walked around pretending he had a large, heavy bag of toys on his back, all for Scotty.

"I want red trucks and a yellow one too. I want one with real rubber tires. And a big one with pedals that I can ride."

Mickey and I knew there would be no packages for us in the morning. We knew this was just a game of fun and imagination. Santa never visited us.

"Scotty, it's only a game," I sighed. "There isn't really a Santa."

"Why, Sissy?"

"I don't know why. It's just a Christmas game." "Okay, Sissy, let's play the Christmas game."

The kids at school tell me Santa doesn't visit me because I'm mean and dirty. They say that my Mama and Daddy don't have any money. I couldn't ever figure out what money had to do with Santa's visit.

Caroler's merrily sang "Jingle Bells" and "Away in a Manger," followed by "Sleigh Bells Ring." The music rang into the night. Louder and louder they sang in harmony proclaiming Christmas from a big, gaily decorated wagon pulled by four strong horses. Clouds of steam came from their nostrils. The carolers were wrapped snugly in blankets, with colored scarves, muffs, and mittens. Many sat on bales of hay. Some stood in a row like wooden soldiers. All smiled happily.

As the big wagon went by, the caroler's smirked at me. I watched them make crazy circles by their heads, laughing. The voices lulled for a moment, then resumed with "Deck the Halls" as they rounded the corner and disappeared.

I listened intently until their voices faded, and then I could no longer hear them. I shifted, putting my ear closer to the car door to hear the last whisp of their merry voices.

Children called out, "Grandma! Hi, Grandma!" "Where's my grandma?" I wondered.

Hatred suddenly boiled inside me, and then just as quickly it festered into guilt.

With the arrival of darkness, the temperature plunged below freezing. I hunkered down deeper in the car, just peering out the window. I didn't want to be seen by the children I went to school with. I kept my eyes level with the window so I could watch them. The other kids had teased me because Santa didn't visit me. They told me it was because I was bad.

The darkened streets became quiet. The Christmas lights still shone brightly—red, green, yellow, and blue. Here and there, one was broken or missing. The lights blinked on and off like stars in the sky.

"Tell me a story, Sissy," Scotty pleaded. "Tell me the story about 'The Night before Christmas,' Sissy. Hurry, Sissy, tell me."

I told what I could remember of the story, then we sang scraps of songs in tuneless voices. I invented games for my brothers. We counted the stars to fill the void. Cars waited for their masters in the parking lots and along the sides of the streets. Everybody had their motors running to keep warm. Folks searched for loved ones. Many waited patiently. Bright lights flooded the parking lot.

One by one, store employees left through the back entrances with their arms full of packages. A few chatted for a moment or two before getting into their waiting cars. I knew their cars were warm. I'd hear them shout merrily, "Merry Christmas" or "Have a Merry Christmas!"

I watched a mother hug her children as she got into her waiting car. She put a protective, loving arm around her daughter. One woman made a fuss over the baby she was seeing for the first time. Families reunited.

It was Christmas Eve, and we were parked behind a bar without food or warmth. Anger lit a fire within me. We should have been in a good home with our very own Christmas tree with presents underneath, waiting for Santa, just like all the other children in the town.

It would be nice to have someone hug me, too. "God, I hate Christmas!" I said aloud. I hated all those stupid, happy people and I hated my Mama and my Daddy. My thoughts seemed to suffocate me: It's god-awful to be a kid at Christmas and not know any love at all. It's awful to be a kid at any time and not be loved. Well, at least my brothers know that I love them.

Rubbing my eyes with the backs of my hands to keep from crying, I jerked up off the seat and out of my cloud of anger. I looked around. For a moment, I had forgotten where I was.

"Sissy, I need to go! Hurry, Sissy!" Scotty held himself between his legs.

I waited until the traffic was gone before opening the car door. I took Scotty by the hand, breathing the pure, icy air. Walking rapidly, we headed behind the nearest tree. My breath steamed when I looked up at the twinkling stars. A pale three-quarter moon leered down, looking as it always did, so low you could almost touch it. All the stores were deserted now. Only a few folks staggered in and out of the bars.

Scotty splattered wet mud on my bare feet as he peed on the ground. Wiping the tops of my feet off on the back of each leg, I felt hard stares from people leaving the bar. I stuck my tongue out at them.

"I'm hungry, Sissy."

"Gawd," I said, looking down at Scotty. "Don't you know I can't get you any food yet? We have to wait until later." I made my way back to the car. "I'm sick and tired of you nagging and whining about being hungry all the time."

"But Sissy, I'm starving!" Scotty cried as I dragged him back to the car and shoved him in. Sniffling, Scotty wiped the snot on the back of his sleeve. His lower lip quivered as he tried to keep from crying.

Knots twisted in my insides. It wasn't his fault but the fire of hot resentment spread through me at our situation The sky was faintly lit. Christmas lights glowed from the windows. I crept along the alley to the back door of the bar, being careful not to be seen. The bar smelled like pee outside. The ground was wet and muddy; cold mud squished between my toes. The door was open to the outside toilet—the smell of blood mingled with vomit, and mucus.

I watched a drunk stumbled out to use the toilet. He didn't close the door, and peed on the walls, floor, and toilet seat. Others, not knowing where they were, stumbled into the ladies' rest room. Another leaned over the toilet bowl, gagging and puking. Yet another barely made it to the filthy toilet before falling to his knees, pressing his face into the big hole. On his knees like that, he reminded me of the pictures I'd seen in the hospital, of children praying.

A man blew his nose onto the ground outside the door, and another cleared his nose by blowing it into his hand and wiping it on his pant leg. That made me gag.

A man stumbled toward me. Chills rippled up my spine as I watched him in a wide-legged stance with his fists resting on the wall, his jeans hanging wide open. A sudden shiver went through me as I eyed his stubborn chin and his go-to-hell eyes.

He pointed his finger at me and cruel laughter knifed the air. I knew by the look in his eyes that he was going to try something fierce! His eyes were like glass, staring at me. Letting out a shuddering breath, I ran off.

I was crouched down in the shadows, hiding behind a pile of boxes, when I heard a man's footsteps coming across the parking lot. As the stranger approached, he carefully checked behind the trash cans on both sides of the alley. He moved in a half crouch. His crisp footsteps echoed in the cold night.

My own ragged heartbeat performed a muffled drum roll. The man slipped behind a row of five enormous trash barrels and hunkered down. I heard him call out my name in a whisper: "Peggy. Peggy, are you there?"

Cornered and in an extreme state of helplessness, I could do nothing but keep my eyes closed and listen.

He waited a minute, calling out my name again. Then I heard him turn and walk away from me back into the bar.

I huddled there, frozen.

When the door opened, I could see inside the bar. Though ugly, it somehow fascinated me. I wanted to watch myself in the mirror behind the bar. I wanted to spin on the high stools. There was a certain magical feeling: the smoky air, the mirrored walls, and the spinning stools. The hum of conversation and loud laughter could be heard over the western music that came from a jukebox.

More than once, a cowboy would come flying out the back door, followed by another, swinging and fighting. When that happened, I scurried back to the car.

Sometimes it was my Daddy swinging, pushing a man backward out the door. They'd shuffle about, circling, measuring each other. Two men stood next to a car, staring at the others fighting. A man squatted on his muscular haunches with his back against the wall, brown beady eyes watching like a rat. The yelling and screaming scared the crap right out of me.

Walking way down the main street of Porterville, I passed in front of a big building with a sign that said "FREE LIBRARY". I didn't know what a library was, but the "free" part caught my interest. Running around the building, I tried to look in, but I wasn't tall enough.

Crossing the street, I went by another bar, and peeking inside I could see only the bartender and six people. The people laughed as a couple picked themselves off the floor. I watched for awhile.

Trashcans overflowed, and I knew I would find all kinds of good things to eat. I also knew I wouldn't have to wait as late tonight. Most everyone would be home with families doing special things. I wouldn't have to worry about Daddy finding me out of the car.

When we thought it was safe, we jumped out of the old car, Scotty's tiny hand in my mittened one. I moved quickly, keeping myself in the shadows. We were all very excited. This scavenger hunt would be our Christmas. We moved about swiftly, the excitement keeping us warm.

I ran to the trash cans. Right on top of the heap was the biggest Christmas tree I'd ever seen. It was so big I couldn't pull it off the heap of trash. When my brothers caught up, the four of us pulled the tree down. We tugged and tugged until we got the lower part, and the biggest limb severed from the rest of the tree.

"My fingers are broken, Sissy," Scotty cried. "I can't feel'em!"

"Hush."

"Warm'em like this," Mickey said, rubbing his hands together rapidly.

"They still broken!" Scotty continued to cry.

"If you don't stop crying, Santa won't visit you," Mickey shouted.

"Damn it, Mickey! Don't tell him that, damn you. We all know Santa isn't going to visit us. Now he'll think it's because he cried. Damn you, Mickey!"

He shook his head, not looking at me. "Come on, let's take this limb."

This big limb was going to be our very own Christmas tree. We took all the tinsel from the rest of the tree to decorate our tree limb. We really thought we were special to have our own Christmas tree, even one with decorations. We worked through the rest of the trash. Our excitement blotted out the rotting smell. Trash littered the streets, blown from the abandoned sidewalks. We thought it was wonderful. We were just like other kids having their Christmas.

We found plenty of fruitcakes and cookies in the shapes of Christmas trees, bells and Santa with white icing and colored candies on top. We found Christmas candies, soft fudge with a bite missing, and hard, striped, ribbon candies. I even wrapped up the candy in bright red crackling paper I found.

Scotty found some white tissue paper with little colored, speckled, stars all over it. He wanted to take it home so he could have his very own stars. He asked me if he could plant them at our house. The grin on his little face was brighter than the stars on the paper.

With our tummies full, we climbed into the car with our Christmas tree and spent the rest of the night singing Christmas songs and eating cookies and candies. Scotty played with his stars before falling fast asleep.

In no time, Mickey and Brian were sound asleep, too. The Christmas tree limb took up most of the room. It was on the floorboard of the car and filled the back seat with the pungent aroma.

We were really proud of our Christmas tree. I thought about how pretty it would look in our house. I would put it between my room and my brothers' room. That way, we could all look at the pretty tree. When I got back to school, I could tell all those stupid old kids (who didn't know nothing anyway) that we did too have a Christmas tree.

I was awakened for just a moment when Daddy cranked the car. The motor rattled to a stop. He cranked again and again until the car jumped up and down, finally warming up. Things were quiet with Mama and Daddy. They weren't doing their usual fighting. The old car swerved down the road, crossing the middle line most of the way through town. I felt the car hit the side of the road. As I looked out the window, I saw the back tire rolling along lined up right at the edge of the country mountain road. The cliff fell off away from it, and all I could see was blackness down below.

We were really close to the edge.

A flick of the car's headlights caught the small, red eyes of an opossum at the side of the road. At the last moment, it twitched and dove back into the ditch.

Scotty and Brian were asleep with their heads in my lap, and Mickey was asleep on the floorboard of the car. I sat straight up in the seat and pushed my brothers off me. All my brothers moved a little from the car bumping around. I watched out the window to make sure we weren't going over the cliff.

"Get off me, Sissy." "Shh…I'm not on you."

"Peggy, be quiet," Mickey groaned. "You woke me up."

"Peggy, move that limb out of my face."

With all that excitement, everyone woke up and Scotty started crying. I pulled him onto my lap. He was sleepy and limp in my arms. I rocked him gently and sang softly.

"Hush little boy, don't say a word, Sissy's gonna buy you a mockingbird." I held him close. "If the mockingbird don't sing, Sissy's gonna buy you a diamond ring…"

Scotty sat straight up, screaming, "No! No Sissy! I want a truck, 'member? Don't you forget, now!"

I sang in soft whispers to get him back to sleep. I didn't want to disturb Daddy.

"Shut up, Peggy, I want to sleep," screamed Mickey.

"Shh. I'm trying to get Scotty back to sleep. Can't you see?"

Suddenly, the car pulled to the side of the road and screeched to a stop, the motor idling. Daddy sat there with both hands squeezing the steering wheel. His knuckles were white. He seemed to be in a daze for a moment before slowly turning in his seat. With his arm up on the back of the seat, he hollered, "Who put that damn tree branch in this car?"

In perfect unison, my three brothers said, "Peggy did."

Daddy's dark, cold eyes looked straight at me. I knew what was going to happen.

Daddy got out of the car, came around to the back, and opened my door. His eyes fixed on mine; he didn't utter a word.

I stared up at him, a thousand thoughts chasing through my mind. I just didn't understand what I had done to land myself in so much trouble. After all, it was Christmas, and all I wanted to do was to have a good Christmas for my little brothers. I kept searching my mind to understand what I had done. Every way I tried to get it together, it just didn't make sense to me.

He reached in with those hands as big as shovel blades and grabbed me by my hair. He shouted curses at me that curdled my blood. I became numb with fear and wasn't sly and quick enough. The breath snagged in my throat, but flew free in a feeble cry. I scooted across to the other side of the car and gripped a leather door strap with both hands, curling all my fingers tightly around it until my knuckles ached. I sweated and gasped for breath.

Daddy's jaw muscles twitched as he kept pulling me by my hair. He tugged and tugged until I finally tumbled across all my brothers, being dragged by my hair. He pulled me around the back of the car to the side of the road. I wrapped both my arms and legs around the tree limb.

Daddy finally peeled my arms and legs away from the tree. He no sooner peeled one off, than I had it locked tightly around the tree again. Over and over, Daddy kicked me in the head and ribs, finally pulling me free, "I'm gonna' beat the living shit out of you girl!" he screamed.

He glared at me with darting, ferocious eyes and gave me that sickening smile with his head flung back. He backhanded me across my mouth, and I tasted blood and could feel the blood run from my lip into my mouth. I touched my tongue to my lips and could taste the warm, salty blood. I hated him more than I ever imagined I could hate anybody.

With his arm high in the air, he came down hard, beating me with the Christmas tree branch in his free hand. He seemed so full of madness that he was unable to stop. His lips were white.

My three brothers jumped from the car and tried to pull him off me while Mama sat in the car with the door open, wringing her hands. "Oh, Melvin, stop! Please stop!"

Daddy snorted and groaned as he peered down at me lying on the ground.

As my tear-blurred vision slowly cleared, I turned my face toward Daddy and dared him with my eyes. Inches from my head was the toe of his shiny, polished shoe. I looked up past his starched, creased khaki trousers to his cruel face and dark eyes. It seemed like he was twelve feet tall, his head just a mere speck high above me. Muscular arms hung at his side, and the huge Christmas tree limb was held limply now in one hand. He resembled a huge grizzly bear. His thick and powerful head jutted toward me, eyes shifted back and forth like a madman.

I shut my eyes, waiting to be killed. Tugging at my mind again were the questions, What have I done to make my Daddy so mad? All I wanted to do was have a good Christmas for my brothers. Why doesn't my Daddy want me to do that? A sudden deep guttural growl came from the bushes.

Patches! Patches had caught up to the car. He looked twice as large in the darkness, hair standing on end. He snarled threateningly at Daddy. But just then, a light switched on from the house across the street, and I saw an elderly couple watching from their front porch. I was ashamed that I'd caused all this heartache and the humiliation for my Daddy. People had been watching while my three brothers cried and begged Daddy to let go of me. I knew I'd made a spectacle of myself and my family.

I heard our old car start up, and Patches evaporated into the night. Jumping up I ran to catch the car, dragging the Christmas tree limb behind me. Just as I climbed into the car, Daddy drove off with my door still open. I barely got inside, but I managed to drag our Christmas tree inside.

Still shivering and wheezing, I snuggled between my brothers. I couldn't stop sobbing—gasping and shaking. Suddenly, I was aware of a weight on my chest, collapsing and pressing down, squeezing the air out of me. The funny little tickle came, followed by the cough that I always got just before a breathing attack. I wheezed and gasped for breath, slumping over the tree limb.

Scotty cried, "Sissy's having her breathing trouble, Mama! Mama! Sissy can't breathe."

"Shut up, Scotty!" Mickey hissed nervously. "You know Sissy always gets in trouble when she can't breathe."

The spasms came rhythmically in great heaves, with mucous rattling in my throat. Daddy sat silently in the front seat. Everyone was quiet, except for me, in my struggle for air.

Every time Daddy beat me, I had a breathing attack. He thought I was mocking the way he breathed. I tried to be still, but it was impossible. I knew he would beat me again for mocking him.

Long after Christmas we watched the dumps and collected all the decorations that we could find. We decorated our house and waited for a tardy Santa. But he never came. Finally, in March, we pulled tinsel from the rafters.

The truth smacked hard. I'd knocked on the door of the church trying to find the man, Jesus, everyone said could help. He wasn't there, and Santa Claus didn't exist either.

The only one I could count on was Patches.

CHAPTER FOURTEEN

I was eight years old when one morning I stood at the back screen door watching Patches, my dog. He'd just caught a squirrel and was rolling it down the hillside with his nose. I watched as he picked it up in his teeth and with a sudden jerk of his head, threw it high in the air. I looked at the chewed, meaty flesh where he had rubbed off the fur. A sudden realization made my eyes widen with shock—Oh! Oh my God! Could it be? It wasn't a squirrel.

Running under it, Patches made another catch and tossed it high in the air again. This time it went off at an angle, and he chased down the hill after it. It bounced and landed in the tall grass. He picked it up and threw it high into the air again.

Giant black and purple flies swarmed around him. Some clung to the screen door. I knew Mama'd be mighty mad at me if I didn't get Patches, and all those ugly flies away from the door. She always screamed at me when Patches brought his kill too close to the house.

She was really sick, and had been in bed for many days. Mama, looking weak and pale, trembled as she shuffled across the floor, as though it was all she could do to lift one foot after the other. She screamed at me more when she didn't feel good, and always complained about all the noise Patches and I made.

I kept watching Patches. I knew I had to get him away from the house, and certainly didn't want him to bring that rotten, smelly thing any closer. Is it a baby? My mind probed the macabre idea, If it is, I sure don't want my brothers seeing it.

I ran out, slamming the ragged screen door behind me. Ducking under the sagging tin roof, I took care not to scrape my head where the tin sheet curled under at the corners. I couldn't take a chance to gash my head open, like I'd done so many other times. I took a big leap over the missing back steps, which were filled with garbage that had been thrown out the back door, then stumbled over the gaping holes, but caught myself.

The smell was god-awful. The back yard was swarming with gnats and flies, and the entire back of the house was black with flyspecks. Even in my terror, I picked a few flies off me, one by one. As usual, I scrunched one between my fingers just to feel it pop. Even with my hearing problem, I could hear the flies pop. Then I ran on. I had to get Patches away from the door and find out what he had in his mouth before Mama saw it.

The grass was waist high where I chased Patches down the hill. He dropped his catch and barked playfully. He was up and away before I could catch up with him, but he'd left his kill behind. As I approached it, I wondered why Patches always had to bring his kill home. Bending over, I reached down for the object. In the silence, I could hear the pounding of my heart.

Suddenly, I froze from fear. What Patches had was definitely not a dead animal. It was an arm from a dead baby—a human baby—Mama's baby...the one she'd made me bury.

Chills ran up the back of my arms and neck and lifted the hair off my scalp. My heart pounded, and I realized I was trembling violently. I bent over in the tall grass and buried my face in my knees. For a moment, I stared into space, not seeing anything. When my eyes focused my mouth dropped open, my knees gave out, and I fell to the ground.

Tears ran down my cheeks and dropped onto my arm, and I had to bite my lip to keep from sobbing out loud. My whole body shook, and I knew I was going to puke. Sometimes it seemed like I was always nauseous. I puked when I ate, and I was sick if I didn't eat.

But something was different about the wave that swept over me this time. I broke out in a cold sweat, then everything came up in a rush. It spattered everywhere—into the grass and all over me.

I wiped my arm on my dress. Patches came back, and his warm tongue washed my arm. For a few moments, I just cringed there in the tall grass, and after a while I began to calm down and think.

If he had the arm, maybe Patches had dug up the rest of the baby. If Mama found out, I'd be in big trouble. She'd know that I hadn't buried it deep enough last night. That dirt was too hard and dry for me to dig, but she wouldn't want to hear any excuses. I knew I had to get the arm away from Patches before one of my brothers saw it. And I had to find the rest of the dead baby before anyone else did—especially Mama.

I bent down to pick up the baby's arm, but with lightning speed, Patches snatched it away to play again. Everything was a game to Patches. Down through the tall grass he bounded, with me running right on his heels, chasing him along the fence to the hog pen.

On the other side, the huge hogs ran along beside me, making their usual grunts. My breathing sounded almost like theirs. My throat was dry and tight, and I was wheezing something awful. I had that funny tickle that I always got just before I had that breathing trouble. Whenever I ran or got into tall grasses or when Daddy beat me, I'd have one of those breathing attacks.

Noticing I was no longer chasing him, Patches skidded to a halt. He watched me for a minute, then decided to come back for a friendly pat. He could always count on me for a pat. Nudging and pushing with his nose, he laid his head in my hand. Satisfied, he ambled away.

I still had to get that arm. A chunk of ice lay in the pit of my stomach as I thought about what would happen if I didn't. I watched Patches from the corner of my eye, moving my head one way, then the other. I didn't want him to know I was really watching him. I was afraid he'd run off again with the arm.

A flash of movement caught my eye up near the house.

My brothers! They were outside, playing tag.

Patches licked my face, then took my hand in his mouth and pulled on me, whimpering. He pulled harder, again and again. He wanted me up, and apparently right now. He wanted me to chase him again. But I still couldn't breathe well enough to get up.

I watched my two brothers up near the house. Mickey and Scotty jumped up and down on the ground. They stomped hard as they hit, seeing who could stir up the most dust. I stroked Patches' neck, then moved upward to his head, trying to figure out what to do next.

Patches wagged his tail against the ground. I rubbed gently with the palm of my hand for a while, more firmly in circular motions. By now he was getting sleepy. His eyelids were droopy.

I looked up toward the house again. Mickey ran behind the house and Scotty was scrambling down the slope, running to me. Oh, Lordy! My heart started pounding again. Hardly able to speak, I said, "Patches, leave me alone!"

I tried to sound stern, but I had to get him out of here. It didn't work. He lay down on his side in the grass and started grooming himself.

My heart sank. Scotty came running down the hill as fast as his little legs could take him, his long, yellow curls blowing behind him in the wind. Scotty was four years old. Halfway down the hill, he fell on his knees and skidded. He came to a rolling halt on top of me. Out of breath, he asked, "What are you doing, Sissy? Can I play with you and Patches?"

"You sure can," I said, desperately scanning all directions in order to find the baby's body.

My eyes darted from him to the spot where the tiny arm lay, back to Patches, back to Scotty. "Sure, you can play with Patches and me," I managed to wheeze.

Scotty stretched out two grimy little hands, his face was shining with perspiration and his dungarees were caked with mud. He kicked at the grass he was sitting on and fell forward with a faint thud.

I looked at the spot again, back to Patches and to Scotty. I nodded slightly to him and continued to suck in gulps of air. I always had a bad time in the tall weeds and grass of the meadow, but I didn't dare leave the area. I had to stay here and find the baby.

Scotty lay down quietly beside me and patted Patches.

Mama always said, "Peggy, if anyone ever finds out about this, we'll all be taken away to jail. You'll never see your little brothers again. You wouldn't like that, would you?" Her voice and those words had made something twist and struggle inside me. She'd whispered other things, too—many things that I didn't understand.

Breathing was becoming more difficult, and my panic was rising too. What if Patches brought the arm back while Scotty was here? Scotty was looking at me, and he seemed worried. But he knew not to get Mama, because she just made it worse for me.

I tried to stay quiet. That was always best when I got like this. After a while, Scotty and I fell asleep.

When I woke up, everything was still. My breathing problem was over. I peered around. Patches roused, but Scotty slept on. Quietly, I scrambled to my feet, keeping a hold on Patches. I had to move fast to keep him from running away with the tiny arm again. We went directly to the spot that I'd watched for so long. Flies were buzzing all around it. My heart started pounding again; beads of cold sweat stung my eyes.

I clenched my teeth, shut my eyes and fighting a wave of nausea, grabbed the tiny part and flung it into the hog pen, willing myself not to feel its weight or moistness.

I kept my eyes shut for a long time. This is just how it is! This is how it's supposed to be, 'cause Mama said so! I told myself. The hogs snorted. The teeny arm was so small among the big hogs, no one would recognize what I had thrown in with them. The hogs fought and ate until there was no sign of it left.

I still had to find the rest of the baby. "What was that, Sissy?"

Startled, I turned around and saw Scotty sitting up on the ground rubbing his eyes with his fists. Had he seen?

"Oh, nothing...just nothing."

I picked him up and put him on my lap, snuggling into his yellow curls. I kissed the top of his head as I continued to watch Patches. Hopefully, he would lead me to the rest of the dead baby. But what if other animals had dug it up? No. If they had, that little arm wouldn't have been here.

I watched Patches run, bark, and chase through the weeds, up and under the fences. What would we do without him? I put Scotty down, and he trailed along behind, following at my heels. I played a game with him so he wouldn't notice, when I stumbled on the baby parts. Patches barked his usual greeting to me as I whistled.

We ran through the tall, cool grasses, ducking under the big tree limbs with the large, yellow dog running ahead. As I went, I looked every which way for the baby. I whistled and clapped my hands to keep Patches' attention and to try to get him to wait for us.

I was vastly relieved when Scotty spotted his two older brothers playing, and decided to run along after them.

All that day, I combed the meadow and the hillside looking for the rest of the baby. Later, when I was sure nobody was looking, I even went back to where I'd buried the little body, hoping to find it in that area. I probed around in the ground until way after dark. My hand shook with terror every time I reached down for something that I thought might be a piece of flesh. I thought I knew the exact spot, but now I wasn't sure. There in the vineyard, the rows all looked the same. I didn't even know which ones I'd already gone down. By this time, I was crying in frustrated confusion.

I gave up once, but on my way back to the house, panic set in again. I spun around and ran back to the vineyard, sure that I'd buried it down still another row. Digging frantically again, I still couldn't find it. I ran down every row and began crying even harder, Oh, God! Where did I bury that baby?

Nearly blinded by tears, I dug deep in the brown soil, then ran to yet another row, only to find nothing. Not a sign of a grave...not even one disturbed spot where Patches might have dug in the earth.

That night as I lay in bed, thinking for hours about the baby, I wondered how I would ever be able to find it. I knew I could never bury another one.

Words made small circles in my mind, Why am I the one who has to do this? Why can't Mama do her own dirty work? She's the one who had the baby and she's the one who killed it. Where did she get it from anyway?

Late that night I was awakened, drenched in sweat, by a dream of flying. I wasn't high in the sky, just barely out of reach of hundreds of people who were reaching for me. I was in a long, white gown that blew in the breeze. Looking down from the sky, I watched myself running away from the crowd, dressed in my same tattered clothes. Then I was looking back up at myself high in the sky. It wasn't a scary dream, yet it was as though a blanket of fear covered me as my eyes opened.

When I awoke, my dress was twisted tight in Scotty's fist. I couldn't move. I didn't know why he always had to hold onto my dress at night while he slept.

I stared at the ceiling, tears slipping out of the corners of my eyes made a path through the forest of my stringy hair. Sometimes I had dreams about babies crying. I couldn't remember anything else about the dreams, except the crying babies. Those were the worst, and I always woke in terror. I was tired of crying, tired of nightmares, and tired of struggling to remember.

For weeks the dream clung to the corners of my mind, where conscious thought rarely took a breath. It walked with me, whispering of other tragedies to come.

CHAPTER FIFTEEN

It was the middle of the night about nine months later. I lay on my bed, which was nothing but a mattress thrown on the wooden floor of the living room. The cracks between the floor boards were big enough for mice to crawl through. Peeking through the hole in my blanket, I saw a stream of yellow light outlining the door to my Mama's room—an eerie glow. I could hear her crying. Her screams filled our old house like a brush fire gone out of control. The house echoed with cries, "Oh Jesus! Jesus…Oh, Jesus!"

Her shrieking made me want to hide. But where could I go? My brothers were quiet. Scotty, just a baby, huddled beside me under the tattered old blanket, sucking his thumb. He was fast asleep. His tiny arm curled tightly around his fuzzy bear, the stuffing long gone. He had his fist curled tightly around the hem of my dress.

I shuddered slightly, then shut my eyes, pulled the blanket over my head, and fell asleep. I wakened again to the sound of Mama's strange cries. Daddy wasn't home, so why was she crying? Her screams seemed worse to me than when Daddy beat her.

Still in my bed, I could see out into the yard through the screens. The sky was clear, and I could see the stars. I fought with myself about whether I should get up to check on my Mama or not. I'd seen so many terrible things, I wasn't anxious to see more. But her moans and screams grew even louder.

I turned on my tummy and wiggled down deep into the mattress with both my arms tucked underneath me. I pulled my dress from Scotty's tiny fist, and he searched for another corner. I wanted desperately to block out the eerie sounds of the cries.

Finally, trying to be brave, I got out of bed and crept toward her room. I concentrated on the ray of light coming from her room, making a streak on the floor. I pushed open the door, smelled the coal-oil lamp, and saw a yellow light making dancing phantoms behind her on the wall.

The doorknob felt damp and cold, but I clutched it tightly. Filled with panic, I hugged my chest and suddenly felt a sinking feeling. Something strange was happening. Gritting my teeth, I dug my fingernails into both hands. Blood! I smelled it right away, that familiar smell, powerful and sickening.

Mama was lying on her back, her face contorted. Sweat and tears glistened in the deep lines etched by obvious pain. Trembling, I stood by the door, unsure of what to do next. She stared at the ceiling, her eyes registered a defeated hopelessness. That haunting gaze begged for help.

Picking up a wooden apple crate, I carried it to the corner of the room. Quietly I climbed up on it so I could see her better over the foot of the iron bed. Leaning against the wall, I actually didn't want her to see me in the corner of the room.

Mama's titties hung down, long and thin. Her dress, frayed and worn, was wet and pulled up to her waist. She struggled to turn on one side, with her face to the wall. Her body shook, and the damp hair was matted into tangled strings.

Reaching up, Mama held onto the foot of the bed with white knuckles and strained in terrible pain. Her lips were pale, mouth open, eyes wide. She trembled, breathing in loud puffs as thick red blood slithered down the inside of her legs. She twisted around as if she were about to go into a fit. I stared in dumb terror watching her body doubled over in pain.

I watched another wave of pain strike her, and heard a terrible sound come from deep in her throat, followed by long silence. For a minute, she closed her eyes together as if that might shut away the pain. Another spasm of pain grabbed her, almost tearing her off the bed. Her face was wet with tears, and she looked pitiful. Mama's bed and hands were covered with a mass of bloody mucus.

My mind raced with the words, It's blood, it's blood! The muscles of my legs ached from stretching to see over the iron frame of the bed. I wanted to help somehow, but the smell, the sight of the blood paralyzed me.

Just when I thought the pain was leaving, it hit her again, and each time it got worse and worse. She got up and tried to squat or lean forward by holding onto the bed railings. There was blood—pools of blood everywhere.

Rolling back onto the bed on her side, she hunched her shoulders and drew up her knees, hugging herself. Then it came again, more quickly than before. Her nails dug deep into the side of the bed. The pain pulled her up off the bed again like some invisible enemy. When the pain hit her the hardest, Mama got up into a squatting position. On her knees, holding onto the foot of the bed, she grunted and pushed down.

My heart hammered like a wild thing inside my chest.

Mama continued to strain and push. I knew the pain was far worse than even a few minutes earlier. Tears zigzagged down her cheeks. I had seen Mama in pain before, but nothing like this. After a spasm passed her weary face would slacken into loose, tired, folds. Her shoulders remained hunched, her arms drawn in close. Drenched in sweat, she was intent on what she was doing.

Suddenly her voice rose in shrill terror, and her whole body lifted up off the bed. A large mass dropped from her body like some misshapen intruder, like a bubble, bloody and strange. She stopped crying abruptly. She panted just like Patches sometimes did, and relaxed again, grunting. She pushed at her belly, slower this time, and harder.

Mama kept doing this over and over. The bubble got larger. Then something slipped quickly from inside her body, and more stuff came out. A large, rubbery thing eased from between her legs, a little at a time. Underneath her bottom was a strange mess, like a lump of bloody clay.

The dying, rotting smell made me sick. I was as frightened as I had ever been. I shut my eyes, wishing I could run, disappear. I didn't dare let Mama know that I was there. It looked like her whole insides had just dropped right out on the bed. Blood! Blood everywhere. Surely she'd die.

I could feel the sourness that heralded vomiting run up and down my stomach. Was I bad to be here? I didn't want to leave. I wanted to watch and see what happened next, and I didn't want Mama to die. I wanted to help, but my dilemma was that I couldn't let her see me watching. Gushes of blood poured from Mama. Shaking with fear, I wanted to turn away, but couldn't.

I heard a sound, barely distinguishable. I listened, straining my ears. A minute passed. My pounding heart finally slowed. Was it real, or had I only imagined it? I heard it again, then again. I waited for it to come again...a tiny cry...the first cry of a baby.

I suddenly realized what had happened, suddenly tried to piece together what I'd just seen. How did that happen? How did that baby get in there? Where did that baby come from? Did Mama know that a baby was in there? In where? Was I blind, not to have known before? This was not what I had expected at all. I was so tired. My body was numb. I sat on the apple crate, huddling in fear and dismay. Then I remembered those pieces of meat I'd found wrapped in paper lying under her bed. I had thought they were liver, but now I knew what they really were. There's been other babies, lots of them. The realization practically knocked me off the apple crate.

The baby cried softly and wiggled a little. Mama ignored it and was busy doing all sorts of strange things—things I had never seen before. Using bloody pieces of towels and cloth, she wiped this and that. Wadded up newspaper was everywhere, mostly covered with blood. Everything dripped in blood. The pillows and blankets were piled on the floor. The baby began to fuss and whine.

Mama moved, and the baby fell from the bed. She never even looked at it, didn't reach down to pick it up. The tiny red baby was kicking and screaming. She let it stay on the cold, hard floor. Mama fell forward onto the bed like a falling tree and remained that way for what seemed like a long time. I thought that was really strange when there was a tiny baby that needed her help.

I couldn't see the baby on the floor on the other side of the bed. I quietly slipped down off the box and stretched out on my stomach on the floor, trying to see it, but it was just too dark.

Mama finally sat up in the middle of the bed and slowly swung her legs over the side. She reached down for the baby, with hands covered in blood like the hands of a butcher, she rolled it tightly in a piece of cloth. I could still hear the muffled sound of the baby's cry.

She stood and held onto the side of the bed, wobbling as she walked. With the baby still under her arm, she made her way to the kitchen. I couldn't hear the baby cry anymore and knew it was dead. I was overwhelmed with a deep sadness which mingled with terror. My throat felt choked. I opened my mouth to scream, but nothing came out. Water was still running in the kitchen sink. Being careful so Mama would not hear, I peeked through the crack in the kitchen door. Then I pulled back sensing that something dreadful was about to happen. I didn't want to see, but couldn't keep myself from looking.

I was surprised—Mama was apparently giving the baby a bath, washing off all that blood. I'd surely like to go in there and help. So the baby wasn't dead, maybe just asleep, but it wasn't kicking like it had been.

Mama leaned over the sink full of water, not moving. She held something in the water. I watched as she raised her arms. A bundle floated to the top, and Mama pushed it under again. Mama's arms were wet up to her elbows. She sloshed water out of the sink and onto the floor. I could hear her crying, mumbling to herself, saying how she loved the baby, how she had no other choice. She said the baby was better off. "I'm so sorry...I didn't mean to..." she repeated again and again.

My heart pounded harder, and I felt a cold sweat break out on my back. Nothing's there at all. That's not a baby, I told myself, I'm just like Mama, seeing and hearing things that aren't really there like when she hears those cars driving in and out of our driveway where there isn't really a car there at all. I'm going to be just like her. I'm just seeing things that aren't there. Is this what they call "crazy"? Mama says when people die, they don't go to heaven, that they stay here, around the place where they die. A litany of words bombarded my mind in an attempt to blot out the scene in front of my eyes.

Mama put the baby, still wrapped in the paper, on the table. She put her hands in her lap, and wept.

A creeping fear nagged that I didn't want to know what was happening, but I was afraid I did know. My heart stuttered—breath began to pinch off. I can't have one of my breathing attacks, not now!

My breathing became more difficult. The air felt like mud, clogging my lungs with each breath. I closed my eyes in a spasm, too late. The bottom dropped out of my stomach.

Leaning against the wall, I puked. I didn't know why I was getting sick. It was like my body knew something my head couldn't quite capture in understanding.

"Peggy, is that you?" Mama screamed. "Peggy, answer me! Peggy, is that you?"

I puked and puked. It went all over the wall, floor, and my feet. I almost choked on it. Shivering, I finally was able to suck in a deep, shaky breath.

"Peggy! Peggy! If you don't answer me, Sissy, I'll whip you within an inch of your life. Peggy! Damn it, Peggy, will you answer me?"

I peeked around the door into the kitchen. She looked awful.

"Peggy, come in here this minute!"

I stepped in my own vomit and almost slipped in it as Mama motioned for me to come sit with her. Her dress was open down the front, and her breasts hung on long, thin strands of flesh. She put her hands over mine and told me I must never tell anyone about the baby. She told me she'd be taken away, that I would be taken from my brothers. None of us would ever see each other again. "Do you understand?" she reached over and wiped the stringy, matted hair from my face. I just sat wide-eyed, nodding my head up and down.

"Don't concern yourself with what you see."

I tried to tell myself that everything would be okay. I couldn't ever be separated from my brothers; however, I felt like I'd been beaten by Daddy. The chilly air hovered and invaded the air between us, but we didn't speak. It was as if an evil spell had settled over us.

My wounded mind formed bruised thoughts, I wish Mama would hold me. Doesn't she know how badly I hurt inside? I had never had a hug or kiss from her. There seemed to be nobody to comfort me. I felt disgust, yet pity and wished I could crawl into a ball like Scotty did when I held him. I wished she would cuddle me like I did him—just one time.

For a couple of days, there was no mention of the baby. I didn't know what happened to it, although I thought about it constantly. I was uncertain about Mama, and I was scared of her. Would Mama do this to me? No, she'd never kill me. Did she kill that baby? No, it just died from all that blood. Mama wasn't able to wash the blood off and it died.

Late one night two days later, Mama woke me by shaking me. Startled, I saw her standing at the side of my bed, her finger to her puckered lips, signaling me to be quiet. She motioned for me to get out of bed and follow her.

She took me by the hand and led me outside. Dry leaves crunched under our feet as we went through the gate and walked on the path toward the outhouse. Away from the house, she started to talk quietly.

She told me the baby was wrapped in a bundle and was on the floor in the outhouse. She wanted me to take the shovel into the vineyard and bury the bundle.

I began to cry. I was terrified by the idea.

"Stop sniffling, damn you, Peggy! Do as I tell you." As Mama talked, I could hear a catch in her voice. She turned and went back toward our house, leaving me alone on the path. Patches stood close behind me.

In the distance, a mountain lion called until others answered. Through the breeze, I heard the howling of coyotes. Tonight I was terrified of the wild animals.

Were they after the dead baby? Were they going to chase me and take the baby away? Would the animals kill me for this dead baby?

In a daze, I walked to the outhouse. Darkness was all around, and the only sound I heard was my own heartbeat telling me I was alive.

I stared straight ahead, following the path leading into the vineyard. The trail was overgrown with weeds and brush. I gazed fearfully into the distance, bracing myself, and edged into the fearful blackness around me. I just knew the wild animals were going to attack me when I picked up the baby. I opened the door of the outhouse and stared at the bundle, then I looked back out into the night, waiting for a pack of wolves to jump me. My heart hammered in my chest. I was afraid to touch it. I'd reach for it, but then jerk my hand back each time. It was a time before I could finally bring myself to pick it up.

I began to breath with great difficulty. A long, shuddering cry broke from my throat. I panicked and went into one of my breathing attacks, crawling and pawing at the earth, unable to get a breath.

This one was the worst I'd ever had. I reached the gate stumbling, holding onto a fence post with trembling hands, still waiting for a pack of wolves to jump me. I wheezed, gasped for air and wasn't able to walk into the vineyard to bury the baby. Returning to the outhouse, I slumped onto the splintered wooden floor.

I tried to rationalize that I was helping Mama with this baby and she needed help, but there was no way I could make it to the vineyard when I couldn't breathe well enough to walk. I dropped the baby into the deep, smelly hole in the outhouse. My stomach was in a violent stage, but nothing would come up as I gagged. I stayed in there all night, until I was over my breathing attack.

Mickey woke me the next morning, hollering at me to get out of the toilet so he could go. I got up, took the shovel and covered the bundle with all the green slime and everything else that was in the hole.

"Hurry, Peggy hurry!" he screamed.

I threw papers down the hole, spreading them over the bundle. When I opened the screeching door, Mickey said, "What's all the noise?"

"I threw away a baby," I told him.

"What baby?" Mickey grinned as though it was some kind of joke.

"Mama had a baby, and it died. I threw it away." "Threw it away? Threw it away where, Peggy?"

"I threw it in the hole in the toilet. Mama told me to bury it, but I threw it away."

"Huh uh, you didn't." Mickey looked into the toilet. Days later Mama was doing a wash in the back yard.

Her galvanized tub was full, and she stirred and stirred. Gazing into the tub of bloody foam, watching those bloody rags swishing about I wretched and vomited. It was that same ugly, putrid smell from the baby and it gagged my conscience.

"Damn it Peggy! What makes you sick?" Mama asked. As time passed it seemed to follow the same pattern.

Mama would be getting fat again, although I couldn't figure out how. We were all so skinny because we never had enough to eat. Though her arms were long and skinny, she was fat around the middle.

When I was older and I watched Mama vomiting every day, I knew why she was getting fatter. Why did she keep having babies that she didn't want, babies she killed? Babies she made me get rid of?

She sat on the stoop at the back of the house with her head hanging down, puking. Mama was always sick. She would vomit until the baby was born.

In the spring of the year, late one night, she wakened me, giving me a sharp look. She opened her mouth, but closed it without speaking. I rose in shrill terror. I knew what was going to happen. I shuddered at the sound of her voice, and started to argue.

Mama put her fingers over my mouth and shushed me. At times, her voice changed as she spoke to me. Sometimes her words never made any sense.

"I'm serious, Peggy. Think of your brothers' feelings and mine, instead of your own." Mama's voice became low and indistinct. "This is something we have to do."

My skin prickled, and a tightness grabbed my throat. I felt a thick lump of fear force its way into my stomach. A crushing vise-like grip caught me in the chest, and I slumped to the floor in fear, coughing and spitting.

Mama screamed at me. "There you go again! Why do you always do this? I know you're pretending. Who do you think you are?"

I held myself tight, trying hard to keep from having trouble with my breathing. But how did I keep myself from doing this? The harder I tried, the worse it got. Pee ran down my legs when I coughed.

By the light of the moon I set out, shifting the heavy bundle she'd given me in my arms. My breath billowed in white smoke before my eyes. My heart felt as if it was going to jump right out of my skin.

Wheezing heavily now, I was unable to walk standing up. I was tired of carrying the heavy baby. Patches followed me, even though I tried to chase him back. It was hard for me to breathe and talk to Patches at the same time. "Go home, Patches. Go home!" I pleaded, fearing he'd dig up the baby.

Patches reappeared, bouncing and dancing around in front of me. Because of Patches, I had no other choice. I went directly toward the hog pen and kicked the gate with my foot. It fell open, squeaking on rusty hinges. The hogs came running. I dropped the bundle onto the ground and backed out of the pen. The gate closed with a cold clank of metal.

I collapsed against the fence covering my ears with my hands. I didn't want to listen to the hogs snorting. Their disgusting sounds overpowered me. They got louder and louder, but I couldn't move. There was a stillness to the warm night air. This isn't gonna' happen to me again, I vowed.

Never knowing where I got the strength or the breath, I turned and ran. Each foot burned when it slapped against the ground. Through the soles of my feet, I felt my heart beat.

The next morning, there wasn't even a scrap of paper left in the hog pen.

Every time I was alone with Mama, she'd say something to me about the babies. Her voice always sounded strange and distant.

"I...I want to talk to you...about those babies...I'm not really sure...It's just that..." Her fingers nervously twisted at a button on her dress. Finally, after a long time, she asked, "Peggy, have you ever told anyone about the babies?"

Looking down into my lap, I answered, "No."

"If you tell, you will never see your brothers again," she'd warn.

I had told my brothers, although I didn't know if they really understood me. I wasn't sure that even I understood.

The months passed and again, late one night, Mama came after me. Her hands dripped with water.

When she reached for me, I tried to get away. The baby lay in the kitchen sink, wrapped in paper. Mama told me she wanted me to drown the baby. She said she was afraid she'd get in trouble if she did it.

"Peggy, you won't get into trouble because you're so young."

Sitting at the kitchen table, she told me to take the rubber stopper, plug the sink, and turn the water on.

My instincts told me to run. When I tried to move, my legs refused. My feet were glued to the cold floor. I remained paralyzed, and just stared into the sink of running water. The baby wiggled inside the paper wrappings, crying faintly, gasping for breath.

The water flowed in full force, but I didn't put the stopper in. The soggy paper around the baby washed away. I was in a trance, watching the water swirl down the drain, around and around, with a noisy, pulling, slurping sound. I imagined the baby swirling around, down, down, down like a funnel, on down the drain.

The paper from the baby's lower body was all washed away. The tiny legs kicked as it bawled, louder and louder.

I realized with a start that this was a girl baby. "A sister!" I screamed, snatching her out of the sink. She was sopping wet, but I held her to my chest, turning defiantly to face Mama.

She came toward me, shoving me backward, her eyes threatened.

I held the tiny baby close to me. I could feel her infant heart pounding on my chest. My baby sister cried loudly in my arms. I walked backward out the door.

"No, Mama, I won't do it! I've always wanted a baby sister. She's mine. I'll take care of her." I turned and ran, jumping down the three steps, dashing on out into the yard with the baby tight in my arms.

The paper was stuck to her like glue. She was bloody and stained with some kind of sticky paste. Long, sticky strings clung to her small body. The strings wouldn't break loose from her. I wondered, Why did Mama glue paper on her? And where did she get the glue?

The paper stuck to the baby's eyelids tighter than any other place. She screamed something fierce when I tried to pull it loose. The more she cried, the more she shook.

Holding my new sister under the water hose, I finally soaked the paper off. The tiny baby was blue, and her hands were held in tight little fists so strong even I couldn't open them. I pulled one finger out, then another and another. She gripped my thumb and hung on with all her might.

Mama ran out of the house and tried to snatch the squalling baby away from me, but I ran away.

My baby sister had the teeniest feet I had ever seen, and a fat little body. Her legs kicked in a funny, jumpy motion. I ran my hands all over her little, sticky body and smelled her. She had a strange odor.

I felt her little heart—tiny beats, one after the other. It felt just like a tiny lizard I'd caught once. Its tiny heart thumped when I held it close to me. I started crying and couldn't stop. I was crying and laughing at the same time, laughing because I had a sister, and crying because Mama was going to kill her. She was all mine. My very own baby sister. I held her tight to my chest, feeling her tiny heart beat against mine, kissing her cold, wet neck. I held her tightly and snuggled my face against her dark head.

"Everything is going to be all right," I whispered. "Don't worry. Your big Sissy is here. You're mine, all mine and nobody else's. I'm gonna' take care of you. I won't let nobody get you, nobody. I promise." I peered down at my new baby sister and told her, "If you only knew how long I wanted you. A sister. I know you don't understand, and neither do I, but I love you."

At the same time, a voice inside me was saying, Peggy, you're just plain dumb. You don't even know what love is. It's just a word you heard somebody say.

"Yeah, but I know one thing," I told her as I hushed her screams. "I wanted you!"

She was as pink as she could be, with a patch of dark hair on her head, fine and soft. Her wrists and ankles were ringed with chubby fat, and her neck was nearly hidden by her chin. Her eyes shut tightly and she tried to eat her fist, making wet, slurpy noises; her crooked legs kicked out.

I reached for a tiny foot. It was swallowed up in my hand. I had never seen anything so small and so beautiful.

What will the future bring for her...for us? Would she be better off dead?

She shivered and whimpered.

Taking a dirty wool shirt that hung across the fence, I wrapped my new sister tightly. It wasn't long before she started crying from hunger and cold. I put her on my shoulder, patting her bottom to quiet her. As she lay against me so helplessly, I named her "Rita".

For the next several days, Mama tried to snatch her from me, but I made certain that neighbors saw her, paraded her in front of them so that Mama couldn't kill her. We spent several nights in the cave hideout so that Mama couldn't get her away from me while I slept. My mother finally had to accept that Rita was mine.

Daddy would reappear just long enough to plant another child. When Mama threw up at the back of the house, I knew that I'd have more children to either bury or take care of. But I knew deep down that Mama could never force me to dispose of another baby.

A little over a year later Kathy was born, the only reason she wasn't drowned by Mama was because she had been born in a parking lot in Springville. A man in a black Hudson delivered her and then Mama went to the TB hospital.

Every time I was awakened early in the morning by running water, my heart would jump into my throat. I was to be terrorized by the sound for the rest of my life.

CHAPTER SIXTEEN

Between the age of nine and eleven years old, I couldn't hear the trucks coming. I'd learned to depend on my other instincts and that compensated for my lack of hearing. As a truck drew nearer, I could feel the ground vibrate. Patches had taught me this and it was just one more thing I learned in order to survive.

We were left home alone for days at a time to fend for ourselves. Mama and Daddy no longer took us with them. If they were gone for days, I walked to town and hunted for them. Hunger was an accepted part of our lives. I rarely noticed my hunger until I ate too much. Then I got sick.

During the hot summer months, dump trucks picked up over-ripe fruit from all the local packing houses. They dumped the garbage in all the hog farms in the surrounding area. They came every other day, traveling miles from the packing houses and restaurants.

Unwinding my legs, I rose from the tall grass and ran along the fence. Huge limbs stretched in front of me, wild honeysuckle vines wove through them to form a green, lacy roof. Each leaf was fighting for its share of sunlight. It was so pretty. A deer jumped straight up out of the meadow in front of me. I wanted to stop and look for a fawn, but I had to beat the hogs to the barn, or we would be without our meal for the day.

My brothers knew that the garbage trucks were coming. We all came running. Scotty followed at my heels with his clean thumb in his mouth. It was always like that. His little arms and legs were caked with dirt. Streams ran down the backs of his arms and legs, and clean "polka dots" speckled the tops of his feet where water had dropped. He had those holes in his cheeks Mama called "dimples" which appeared when he smiled or laughed.

We stood along the side of the fence, waiting for the truck to dump the load of slop. Scotty had his thumb in his mouth, and in his tiny fist clutched the hem of my dress. He had it twisted, rubbing a part of my dress on his nose. With his other hand, he picked fuzz and hog hair off the barbed wire. Mickey sped toward us in great leaps, running like a rabbit. He paused to pull off his oversized boots, then ran on to join us. Brian trailed behind, bouncing up and down in oversized galoshes. Their voices were loud.

The minute the truck was out of the way—with the truck bed high in the air—we stepped into the pens with our dirty, crusted feet. We'd slosh into the feed bins and stand on the first rungs of the fence so we could look down at the mess. Sometimes, purple guts spilled over into the hog's trough.

Now, though, "finding" meant actually eating this ghastly mess. I didn't want to eat it because of the smell, which was so strong it made me step back. A rat dashed out. I stood there with my mouth open. My body growled with pain; my stomach was tight and sour. I was so hungry.

We didn't have much time before the hogs would arrive. In just a few minutes, we had to get enough food for all of us for that day, and perhaps for the next day. If we didn't get away fast enough, we might be missing a leg. Oh, did we hurry!

"Mickey, be quick!" I yelled. "The hogs are getting closer." He was up to his hips, lollygagging along, carefully pondering every piece of food. His nostrils bulged as they took in the smell of rotten eggs. It was overpowering, but we were hungry.

Scotty sat outside the fence on the ground that was hardened from the large tires of the trucks. Dried mud covered his legs to his knees, like stockings. He was gloved to his elbows as well, in the stuff. His eyes sparkled. If I looked closely, I might find a patch of clean skin somewhere. The ground around the fence had a polished look. Scotty sucked his thumb, looking over the food as we threw it out.

We used sticks or broken handles from tools to comb through the garbage. The strong smell burned our eyes. It was so bad at times it took our breath away. If we were careless and stepped on a broken bottle, cutting a foot in our haste, we didn't slow down. No matter what, we had to beat the hogs to the food. We dug deep for a sandwich, preferably one with meat.

I gagged at the smell of rats—the worst of the filthy horrors. Climbing out of the hog pen just in time to keep from being attacked by the hog, I sat on the ground with sweat and sticky liquids dribbling down my face.

I took one baby on my lap while the other sat on the ground in front of me. With my fingers, I'd feed them each a bite at a time until they could hold no more. It never took much to fill them, but their hunger was back much sooner than I could get food.

Sometimes, all we had were just bites left over from sandwiches. That was all right with us. We never complained about what we had to eat. In the summer months, we had plenty of food. It wasn't always that way. In the winter, we went days without food. Each day, we faced starvation. I believe we would have killed for food.

Scotty picked up a wet, dead kitty from the slop we'd thrown out. I ducked in and slapped it out of his hand, and withdrew where it was safe. I knew Scotty would fight me for that kitty.

The kitty tumbled to the ground. As it did, I saw it move. We all leaped for the little kitten, drying it off with the hem of my dress. It was alive.

Mickey hollered from the distance, "Here's another one, Peggy." He continued digging and came out with three more kittens. One didn't move at all, so Mickey heaved it back into the slop with the hogs.

The six of us sat outside the fence most of the morning, eating all we could hold and playing with the kittens. On the other side of the fence, the hogs cleaned up all the slop. We made sure we saved food for the next day. There wouldn't be one thing left in the hog pen—not even the tiny, dead kittens.

Outside the fence, dried slop was covered with flies. They swarmed everywhere, sticking to the ground, eating the last of the thick liquids. A thick, sour, oozing, sickening, smell hovered about us. The flies made it hard to get the food. We worked hard, eating bit by bit, talking and laughing.

The remaining food fried on the hot, barren ground, and was soon covered by the flies. We were surrounded by the smell from the hogs and hog slop, and lulled by the buzzing of the flies.

Insects bred in the garbage. It was filled with soggy newspapers. At times it held open cans of spoiled fish, pieces of clothing, old greasy rags. Once we found an old cast-iron skillet with the handle broken off, but still crusted with food. Smells of rotted garbage mingled with other strong smells.

Over a period of time, we found shoes, although we never found shoes that matched. We saved them all, hoping someday to find a match. Our favorite pastime was trying to make shoes, cutting off the curled-up toes to make them shorter, punching extra holes to make them fit.

I walked around in high heels that were stiff and pinched at my instep. I wobbled and fell, almost breaking my ankle. All my brothers ran toward me, taking their turns trying on the high heels. They couldn't conquer them any better than I could. Mickey was certain he could do a better job as he wobbled in front of me. He shifted his weight from one foot to the other while Brian and Scotty rolled with laughter.

We managed to make sandals. We didn't care if they matched, since they fit and kept our feet warm, what the heck did we care? We wanted so much to be just like other kids.

The hogs mashed their tender pink snouts down into the slop, rooting and grunting their satisfaction. Mickey grunted a reply only half in jest. He was as grateful as the hogs.

Brian was gaunt and dirty with dried food on his face, but his hair, finely matted, looked white as snow in a ray of sunlight. He wiped his dirty hands on his shirt, wrapped one kitten tightly in his arms and, without meaning to, he killed it. Carrying it for days, refusing to believe what he'd done, he wouldn't let go of the kitten until it stank. Flies followed him and the dead kitten.

Once, we managed to keep a kitten alive. It was great having this small ball of fur. It slept with us and followed us everywhere we went. As it got older, we watched it catch its own food of rats and birds.

After the hogs finished eating, the pen looked like a deserted dump. Daily, the dump grew with old car tires, broken glass, and metal of all sorts. We had piles of scrap metal from wagons, bicycles, and tricycles. We tried to put together bicycles and wagons to play with, and finally managed to construct one bicycle that we all shared.

We pulled the babies to town in the wagon. We combed the dumps of the nearby ranches looking for shoes, but also for anything else one of us could wear, even if it didn't fit.

We also robbed and raided neighbors' gardens, and took apples and oranges from the growers. We stole chickens and rabbits when we could—preferably rabbits, since the chickens were too noisy.

It was a miracle we weren't arrested, but perhaps God looks the other way when children are starving. Prison was in the future, but not for stealing...

CHAPTER SEVENTEEN

If Mama didn't come home for a long time, I'd go looking for her. Sometimes I'd find her, sometimes I wouldn't. I'd go from bar to bar. Sometimes I'd take my brothers, and occasionally they'd stay at home. In the summer when it was warm, we'd all go. But in the winter, they'd stay home with the babies, and just Patches and I would make the trip to town.

I'd stand at the back door of the bar. A lady—not beautiful like my Mama, just ordinary, dowdy, but still a lady—would see me and tell me if she knew where my Mama might be. Her eyes were heavily made-up, and her slim fingers had long, painted nails.

Sometimes Mama was in the bar next door. Other times, she was upstairs in a room in the hotel, or I would learn that she had gone to Porterville with somebody else. Other times, I was told that she'd gone to the nearby city of Visalia. If I stayed in town long enough Mama usually showed up.

I liked to go to town by myself. The people were nicer to me. Men would buy me Coca Cola in a glass bottle or give me a nickel, and sometimes they'd give me their pocket change...maybe even a dollar. They teased me, saying I was cute, or that I had a baby-doll look. I liked that.

Once Mama took me on the elevator to a room she had in the hotel. The room was small and well-scrubbed, with shiny waxed floors. On the floor was what she called a pretty "rug." It had fringe all around. On top of the bed was a beautiful bedspread that was bright pink, white, yellow, and green. I rubbed it on my face. It was cleaner than anything I'd ever seen. In fact, I'd never seen such a bed.

The bathroom was down a long, dark hall. I watched men and women grope for the chain hanging from the bare overhead light bulb. When the light came on, the bathroom was bright as could be. The light bounced off the small, white, ceramic tiles on the walls. The ceiling was painted a soft, sky blue. The floor was glossy white tile, freshly scrubbed, and cold on my bare feet. I liked the sound of my bare feet slapping on the cold tile. The cold room smelled faintly of pine. I'd smelled the same scent often in the sanitorium.

All night long, I watched people going back and forth to the bathroom. Some men pulled their pants on as they went; others had their pants and belts open and loose.

Mama never told me the room was hers. Men came to her room day and night. Every time a man came, if she knew I was there, I'd have to leave. If she didn't see me, I'd just turn my back and huddle in the corner, feeling sick—sick and all mixed up, with a desire to please my Mama and a hatred for her when she did those things with the men. I'd make myself just slip into a dream until they finished.

On many cold, rainy nights, I slept on the floor of the elevator with my head resting on the seat. Every time the elevator door opened, I'd freeze when the cold air hit me.

If I was sleeping, the awful clanging of the door startled me awake.

The ladies and men were always drunk; some fought, and some laughed. The men carried large sums of money rolled in their fists. The women would laugh and snatch the money. I liked the way the ladies smelled, all clean and pretty.

One night, a drunk man sat on the bench in the elevator. He pulled a lady down on his lap while her dress and petticoats covered my head. His arms went under her dress while he searched for the hooks on her brassiere.

Gawd! I told myself, I don't ever want to wear one of those. I'd have to have hinges on my elbows to unfasten'em! The lady fumbled with his belt buckle. She wiggled and squirmed, and kicked off her high heels. I stared at the dark patch between her pink, pink legs as she kicked off a pair of light blue panties with "Monday" written on the hip. I couldn't figure that out. It wasn't Monday.

The man put the lady's hand on his big, swelling trousers—she mumbled words I didn't understand—something about a terrific "boner."

Then the elevator went back down to the ground floor. Another man sat down hard on the seat of the elevator and pulled his enormous thing out of his trousers. It stood way up past his navel, like a flagpole. The man's eyes rolled back in his head, and I thought he was going to faint or something.

I felt strangely excited myself, as if something good was happening to the lady. From the way she laughed and giggled, her eyes rolling and fluttering, I could tell she felt good.

At times men pulled down the ladies' panties, and I'd have their bare butts in my face. I became quite familiar with the sounds and lurches. When it was finished, I could always tell the men were drained.

Sometimes the men gave me a nickel. If they were drunk enough, they might give me a dollar. More than once, a man would try to touch my little titties. I didn't even have any.

I heard the bed springs squeaking in every room in the hotel. I waited for them to stop squeaking, and listened for the next. I tried to keep count in my head for each room. I learned the familiar moans and groans that signaled when they were through "doing it."

Through a crack in the door, I watched a naked woman on a bed. With her pink thighs spread, she squirmed and quivered. She reminded me of a squirrel that Patches had just caught. The man stood up and stretched, then rushed into the bathroom, not closing the door. Then he quickly left, still buttoning his trousers. His boots echoed on the wooden floor. If I was sleeping, the moans coming from the adjoining rooms and from Mama would waken me. I heard muffled screams and laughter, and more moans. Mama pressed her naked body against each man. Their bodies came together, kissing, nibbling, groaning. Within a few minutes, they would have their clothes off. It all seemed so stupid to take off all their clothes for such a short length of time.

One night in Porterville, I slipped into Mama's room because it was so cold and miserable in the elevator. Mama's room was much warmer. Hiding, I watched the rhythm of Mama and the men from my safe place, being careful not to be seen. I stayed very still and listened. Sometimes I'd sleep off and on. Men came and went most of the night.

I wondered why each man came into the room for just a short time, just to take their pants off. How stupid! After a few grunts and moans, the man would leave.

For a while, I thought it was a game they played. I watched the men's hands moving along Mama's body. It made me squirm. I watched the men touch her, feeling inside all her secret places.

Once, a drunk, seedy man spotted me sleeping in the corner of the room. He fumbled blindly in the dark, whispering, "Little girl, come'ere, little girl." He patted here and there on the floor.

I scampered across the floor, pressing into the corner with my hands over my mouth. I tried to be quiet so he wouldn't know where I was. A long cry escaped from my lips. The man turned in my direction, and I cried out again. He made a high, horrible animal sound.

On my hands and feet, I scrambled across the room. I couldn't see where I was going, but I ducked under a table and rolled myself into a tight ball. I tucked my head between my knees and pressed them tightly against my ears. The man came so close I could hear him breathing, grunting, and slobbering in the dark of the room. Even with my bad hearing, I could hear him. I smelled his sour whiskey breath as he stumbled around searching for me in the dark. He mumbled and cursed. Most of what he said, I couldn't understand.

When I peeked out from under the tablecloth, I saw Mama sleeping. Her eyes fluttered open for a second.

The hotel was still. The wood floor creaked as I scurried out the door, down the hallway, and onto the street. I remember wishing I could leap up and fly away like I did in my dreams...just high enough to be out of reach of anyone pursuing me. As young as I was at the time, somehow I knew I would be running from trouble for most of my life.

CHAPTER EIGHTEEN

When Daddy came home and Mama wasn't there, it wasn't usually long before Mama showed up. Someone in town would tell her Daddy was out of the hospital, so she'd find someone to bring her home. They'd let her out of the car at the side of the road. No one ever brought her all the way to the house.

One time Daddy lay across the mattress on the front porch with the rifle in his hands. It was always loaded. He stood and paced the floor. He always moved with a rugged force, coiled like a rattlesnake ready to strike and wore a desperate, angry expression on his face. Pure hatred oozed from him when he moved about. He'd check the gun, flipping the cylinder open, flipping it shut again. He did the same thing over and over.

Did he forget he'd just done that? I wondered.

Then he'd flop back down on the mattress, lean his head back and inhale deeply, as if to regain his control.

It scared me when I saw that intensity in his eyes. Just a tiny part of me died when I looked into those eyes. Our eyes met, eye-to-eye, but Daddy didn't seem to see me.

The minute Mama got out of the car, Daddy started yelling. "Hey! Winnie! You bitch! I understand from the men in town that you can dance! Let me see you do the two-step!"

He aimed the gun and fired. The bullet hit the dirt road right in front of her feet. "Now hop, you bitch, and turn. That's right! Yeah, baby, on two feet." Another bullet kicked up dirt at her feet. "Yep, you really know what I mean. Now, turn around again for your old man. Hop, two, three…turn, Winnie. Is that the way it's done? Swing under my arm. Is that the way? Winnie! Winnie! Answer me. Cross the left foot over the right. Is that the step they call the Varsuvianne, or is it the two-step?"

Mama dodged the bullets, jumping all the way up the drive, doing all the steps exactly as Daddy called them out. As time went by, Mama realized he was only trying to scare her. She soon quit dodging the bullets and would deliberately walk slowly up the drive.

Why does she even bother coming home? I wondered.

But I knew why. Daddy would go to the end of the world looking for her. That's what he said he'd do. There was no place where she could go. He'd kill her, and probably some of us too, to let her know that he was serious. It was his way of keeping Mama in line.

Daddy was rarely home, but when he was, he was angry, mean, jealous, and always drunk. The day after a mean streak, Daddy would promise perpetually it would never happen again. He'd say, "I promise it won't happen again Winnie. Just lost my temper." At the time, he could be quite persuasive, and I believe he was sincere.

For a day or so after Daddy came home, everything would be calm. It was obvious though that Mama was edgy.

She always tried to keep us quiet. She kept saying, "Shhh, now don't upset Daddy."

Strange and frightening noises came from the old house. I knew how my Mama sounded when she was afraid. Once again, she would be in a battle with the beast.

It started abruptly one night. "Oh, great you slut!" His face was within inches of her face. The door clattered open, and he backed her out of the house, down the steps into the yard. Daddy panted as he sweated and swung. With his shoulders hunched and his hands in fists, he looked like a bull lumbering out into the yard. His eyes flashed icy, hard and cold. Sweat streamed down his face. "I'll blow your goddamn head off."

His fists whitened at the knuckles while he ground them in the palm of his other hand. That hard and mean mask took over his face. I went cold as I watched my Daddy change, right before my eyes. In just minutes, his neck swelled and the veins stuck out. His eyes grew narrow and cold, icy cold, and his mouth was a firm, cruel slash.

Mama and Daddy were silhouetted against the dreary, gray sky. I dreaded what I knew was about to happen as I listened to the anger in his voice. I knew it was coming. It was just minutes and then...he would laugh. If Daddy had a gun, he would hold it to the side of Mama's head and say, "I oughta blow your goddamn brains out, you bitch."

In seconds, he went through the same process all over again.

But my more serious problem was trying to feed two babies. We older ones could take care of each other, and we had managed with one baby, but it was extremely difficult with two. I had to force them to take clabbered milk. Neither of them liked it. I didn't understand why, because I loved clabbered milk.

I stole a milk cow, which we hid in the house during the day and tethered out in the yard at night. The milk cow helped, but it wasn't long before Mr. Hart came looking for her.

After that, we prowled the neighbors' yards at night and milked their cows. At times, we could steal milk already in a pitcher from the neighbors' iceboxes on their back porches. The cream was thick on top, and we didn't have the tool to skim it off.

The townspeople were getting tired of us, and they weren't as patient as they'd been before. The fruit season was over, and trucks hadn't started coming in to feed the hogs. It was off-season for everything.

Both babies screamed constantly from hunger. Night and day, they gave me no rest. They wouldn't stop crying.

Every day, I put my baby sisters in the wagon and pulled them to the river. The motion of the wagon rocked them to sleep, but the minute I stopped, they started screaming again. I sat on the rocks crying, watching the roaring, whirling, waters below. Sometimes I felt like throwing the babies into the rapids, since there was no hope for them. I wanted to jump in with them both, but for some reason I couldn't. Why? The churning, gray-green water swirled below, while I cried and watched my baby sisters.

I didn't know if I could go to anyone for help. I didn't know whom I could trust. I didn't want to be taken away from my brothers. Mama said that I'd never see my brothers if I told anything. I had faith in no one, except my brothers, and Patches.

Every time I went down to the river with the babies in the wagon, I always pulled them back up the hill. I would scarcely get back home before they would scream again. I'd repeat the same thing all over again—down to the river and back home. But it was terrible to see them always hungry, cold, and sick.

Each time I took them back home, I just brought them back to agony and starvation. Now I know why Mama killed her babies, my mind reproached me.

As summer approached my body also began to blossom, but so did all my fears and my concerns about "being different." They were growing right along with me. My problems were getting bigger, too. A loneliness gnawed at me like a cancer.

Neither Rita or Kathy belonged to Daddy. He knew it, and talked about them not being his kids.

One morning Rita was sitting on a blanket out back. Behind her was the old well, with a wooden cover over it. One of us was always taking the cover off the old well.

The only kid I ever heard Daddy talk to, or show any affection to, was Scotty. Was it because Jake was his friend? Mickey and I were the only two kids that Daddy fathered, and I knew he hated me. I think it was because I was so ornery. I fought him when he beat Mama.

Suddenly, Mama screamed at me, "Peggy! Peggy! Hurry and get Rita!"

Turning, Daddy had a rock and was about to bash Rita's head. I ran for her just in time, scooping her up as the rock hit the ground.

"That little bastard baby ain't mine," Daddy said. "She should be killed. You better keep her out of my sight and away from me."

After that, no one ever left any of the babies alone when Daddy was around.

From inside the house, I could hear the never-ending arguing. I heard a loud slap, as though Daddy had backhanded Mama. She cried, and Daddy cursed her. They were cooped up together in the hot house amid all that growing hatred. Mama was screaming. It seemed as if that's all she ever did.

"Stop that screaming!" Daddy yelled. "Stop it right now." I heard the crushing sound of his fist hitting her.

Mama came backward out of the house, Daddy trailing behind. With his fists, he hit her first on one side of the face, and then the other. She stumbled backward down the three steps and fell to the ground. Blood was everywhere. Mama tried to get up, but Daddy kept kicking her, over and over, cursing her all the while.

Using my fist, I hit my Daddy right in the eye as hard as I could. He didn't even flinch.

Daddy's hand tangled in my hair. He snapped my head backward. Everything changed, as if time suddenly had shifted into slow motion. Daddy's mouth gaped wide open. I fought back with all my might, with everything in me. I didn't give an inch, and I didn't care if he killed me.

I knew how to wear him out so he didn't have the energy to beat anyone else. If he caught me, he'd make it doubly hard on me. That was all right, because at least for a while I'd be safe, and so would Mickey and Brian.

I always knew by the sound of Daddy's belt buckle hitting the floor k-plunk, when he was going to beat me.

He'd whip that belt dramatically out of his pants, pulling it out in slow-motion which always punctuated the action. I was wiry, skinny, and strong, and as fast as a fox. Out in the open, I could get away from him if he didn't get me in a confined area.

I fought back. Even though I was beaten badly, I didn't stop. Every time he knocked me down, I came back for more. I wasn't about to give up, especially to him. I was going to fight him until he dropped, and I knew that wouldn't take long.

Daddy was shocked. I'd never fought him like this before. Now he was furious. He was so mad he seemed to have the strength of a mule. I had never seen him last this long.

Finally he couldn't breathe, and collapsed to the ground, out of breath. He sat in the dirt for a long time, staring at me with those mean, dark eyes. How I hated that look. How I hated my father. I wish someone would kill him. I wish I could.

Daddy glared at me, and I wouldn't let my eyes move from his. "Oh, shit!"

My whole insides quivered. I was tired and weak; the muscles of my arms felt bloodless—limp and helpless. I was stunned by what I'd done. My brothers stood at a distance with their hands over their mouths, snickering. I could tell they were surprised. Mama was on her feet now, and then crouched over Daddy.

"Winnie, I'm gonna kill that girl," he said.

I limped to my brothers and dropped to my knees.

Feeling dizzy, I had one of my breathing attacks. "Good for you, Peggy," Mickey whispered.

Scotty echoed, "Good for you, Sissy."

By now, Daddy had regained his strength. "I'll get you, girl," he snarled.

From my position on the ground, I slowly raised up and glared at him. His expression changed to baffled disbelief. I knew I was in deep shit.

"Head for the hills!" Mickey yelled. "He's at it again!

He's mighty pissed, and he'll blow us to smithereens!" We darted off, running up the side of the mountain.

My brothers followed close behind. Mickey's knees almost reached his nose with each step. He glanced back over his shoulder now and then to make sure we were together. In the background, I heard Daddy yelling, "You'd better get your ass moving, girl. I'm gonna kill you when I get my hands on you."

Small birds circled a slice of the sky as we raced through the thick leaves covering the mountain. The loud flutter of quail scattering in the brush accompanied us as we headed into the clump of bushes. A hawk skimmed over the trees, searching for mice. From the busy fluttering of feathers, I could tell the bird was working hard and was excited. Then it flew on, after a faint cry.

We'd entered the secret world of our cave-hideout.

Patches came bounding out, tail wagging a welcome.

We huddled together for the rest of the night, and for several days, hoping that Mama would take care of the two babies. We only came out long enough to see if Daddy had left. Only when Daddy went back in the hospital, did we go home. Within minutes after our return, Mama left again. We were left to fend for ourselves, alone again. We knew the day would come when Daddy would show up. He'd walk in with his arms full of sacks packed with whiskey, beer, and cigarettes, but no food.

About a month had passed, when early one evening dark clouds hung low in the sky. The wind was strong. Orange and brown leaves weakened by age, snapped off and began their slow, singsong descent to the ground.

From the house, Daddy hollered, "Sissy, come here."

I should have known something was up, as he never called me Sissy.

"Come here, Sissy. I want you to try this jacket on. I found it at the hospital."

I looked at the jacket. I really didn't like the looks of it. Puke khaki wasn't my favorite color. But it would keep me warm, so why should I care?

Icy shivers went through my heart as Daddy crept toward me, holding the jacket. Something told me I shouldn't let him put this jacket on me. Daddy would never do something nice for me. But maybe he was changing. Maybe he was sorry for all the bad things he'd done to me.

The jacket seemed large, but I thought I'd grow into it by winter. For some reason though, I had a hard time getting into it. My arms were crossed. Daddy said it would straighten out when I got it on. I had never seen a jacket that belted in the back.

I saw Mama standing in the door with her hands over her mouth. Between clenched teeth, she said, "Oh, Melvin, don't do that. Please don't do that."

I strongly sensed now that something was wrong, but the realization came too late. Daddy was already buckling the jacket behind me. My arms were crossed over my chest. I was tied in, with no way out.

He leaned forward, his face bright red. Pointing a finger at me, he snarled, "Now, you little fucker, let's see how strong you are. Do you think you can get out of this?" His finger waggled at me.

Daddy yanked me up by the back of the jacket and shoved me ahead of him. I went down head first, landing on my face in the dirt. With my arms bound to my chest, I had no way of catching myself. I heard the bones in my neck crack. I couldn't get up.

Yanking me up by the back of the jacket he dragged me to the back of the house, where he chained me to a big fig tree with my feet dangling above the ground. The chain lay heavy against my scrawny body. Most of it was wrapped around the trunk of the tree.

Hanging from the tree, I screamed hysterically. I tore at the inside of the jacket until my fingers bled. My head bobbed from side-to-side as I kicked wildly. I couldn't touch the ground. Stretching my feet, I was able to touch the gnarled root of the big tree.

Using a piece of green water hose, Daddy beat me on my legs. Red whelps, blisters, and bleeding cuts soon covered my legs.

During the night, Patches stretched out on top of the roots of the tree. With my feet resting on his back, I wept until I finally fell into a fitful sleep.

Every day, Daddy came out and beat me with the broken piece of hose. It seemed like he had just beat me, and I was getting settled down, when he was back beating me again. I couldn't rest for listening to his footsteps when he banged the back screen door closed. I could tell by the hesitation in his footsteps when he leaned down to pick up the piece of water hose.

He always slapped it against his own leg as he jumped down the back steps, then over to me. I don't know which was worse, the beatings or waiting for him to beat me again. I don't know how long I hung from the fig tree. I was cold and wet, and a hazy fog swirled around me. Through the misty, thick air, I could see a faint light coming from our house.

One night, after Daddy had gone back to the hospital, Mickey cut the jacket off. As long as we lived in that house the jacket hung there. Nobody ever bothered to take down the slashed strait jacket which served as a constant reminder of the savage cruelty which lived in this house.

CHAPTER NINETEEN

We always left long before the sun was up to go to the bus stop. On our way, we'd raid somebody's icebox before our neighbors were up. Some of them had locked cabinets or wooden boxes where they kept other things like canned items, flour, and sugar. We'd steal milk, putting it in the river to keep cold until we returned late in the afternoon.

Each day, as I got on the bus and started down the long, endless aisle, each student sitting alone would edge to the aisle side of his seat, saying something like, "It's saved for Mary."

The next one would repeat almost the same thing. On down the aisle I'd go to the taunts of "Ugh! You can't sit with me."

On and on, it never changed.

I didn't attend school much—I didn't always reach school, even though I knew I could get plenty of food there. It seemed that I could often find other things to do.

When I did show up, the students held their noses and complained that I stank. My slightest movement seemed to send me into the cloakroom.

The cloakroom was long and narrow, with high ceilings. The coats hung on big hooks, high over my head. There was a long, narrow, wooden bench that went the length of the coat-racks. The kids had to jump up onto the bench to get their coats down. All their lunches were lined up on the back of the bench.

I crawled onto the bench, slid way to the back, and buried myself among the long coats. That was where I spent most of my school time. Day after day, I stretched my legs out along the back of the wall. If someone came in, they couldn't see me.

I liked it in the cloakroom. If I hadn't slept the night before, I'd sleep there.. I didn't have to listen to the other kids snickering at me, or watch them hold their noses.

Clinging to the bench, unable to see anything at all, I held my breath and listened to the hum of voices coming from my classroom behind the wall.

I opened the sack lunches, one at a time, eating what I liked best first, and putting the rest aside for later. I rolled the wax paper into a ball in my hands, then threw it against the wall.

Food was so foreign to me that the instant I put food into my stomach, I'd throw up. I'd eat and puke, eat and puke some more. I spent the whole morning in the cloakroom, and nobody ever checked on me. By the time lunch time rolled around, I'd eaten all the lunches. The cloakroom was a disaster—orange peelings, apple cores, papers, and lunch bags thrown all over the room. Not to mention the vomit. When it was discovered I thought the teacher was going to faint.

The janitor, who was also the bus driver, took to calling me "Cootie." The students quickly picked up that nickname, too.

The next day when I boarded the yellow school bus, I panicked. I stood in the aisle of the bus, immobilized while the other students poked fun at me. The bus driver jammed down the accelerator and took off sending me sprawling.

The kids screamed and shouted that I didn't have on any panties, and said I didn't have a brain.

Everybody—the teachers, the janitor, the other students—they all told me, "You're no good. You're a creep. You're nothing but slime." On and on. They all said the same thing, day after day.

Their taunts always swirled around in my brain. I understood fully that I was different, yet I just didn't know why.

The teacher put me into the cloakroom again the next day, even though she knew what I was going to do. Subsequently, they sent me to another classroom as punishment, and that teacher also put me in the cloakroom. The teachers finally made me promise that I wouldn't eat the other students' lunches. I promised I wouldn't, and I really tried not to. I held my hands in my lap, my fingers entwined and red from trying not to open the lunches. But I couldn't keep myself from eating their lunches, no matter how hard I tried. My stomach rumbled with hunger pains. Once I knocked loudly on the cloakroom door. Knock, knock, knock. No one answered. I kept knocking.

Finally, Miss Barley yanked the door open and screamed, "What do you want?"

I told her I was trying hard not to eat the lunches, but I couldn't help myself. I was going to eat them, if she didn't take me out. She told me to use self-control and slammed the door in my face.

I stood there with my hand on the doorknob and my ear against the door. I raised my voice so she could hear, "Miss Barley, what is self-control?" She didn't answer me.

I couldn't understand why no one wanted me to eat. It was okay for the other students to eat, but not me. They called me a thief because I wanted to eat. They ate. Did that make them thieves, too? I just couldn't understand.

I could make myself vomit right in the middle of the classroom or on the school ground. All I had to do was just say to myself, "Puke," and I'd puke. If the kids teased me too much when I was out on the school grounds, I'd puke. That was one way to keep them away from me.

I liked to play on the monkey bars. When I pulled myself up on the bars, the other kids were always right there. They laughed and teased me. It took all my concentration to ignore them. A smaller boy beside me jumped down and went to another swing, away from me and all the laughing kids.

Hand-over-hand, I continued high up the rungs of the monkey bars. My arms and legs were like invisible spun threads between the metal poles. I moved with great speed. After reaching the top, I jumped, screaming like a hawk all the way down, and landed with a thud. The kids all scattered. My scream was so piercing, all the kids on the slide and nearby swings also brought their playing to a halt. Sometimes when I screamed like that, the teachers would stop and turn to see if someone had gotten hurt. When they saw that it was only me, they'd return to their conversations. If one of the other children screamed, the teacher's ran from every direction.

When I darted for the merry-go-round, the other kids tried to get it spinning too fast for me to get on. But I was always able to catch it. As it slowed, the other kids slipped off one by one.

At the edge of the playground, two or three kids pointed at me and laughed. I burned with anger, making the merry-go-round go faster and faster to get away from the snickering crowd. As I came back around on the merry- go-round, I realized that the crowd had grown. Each time I came around, there were more kids. Some fell down and rolled in the grass with laughter.

From the corner of my eye, I saw the teachers running toward me. As they got closer, the students hollered, "Miss Barley, Peggy doesn't have any panties on."

Everyone howled with laughter as I continued. Going around me in circles, they chanted, "Lully, lully, lully. Stinky, stinky, Peggy."

I simply shut out their noise.

I knew I was different, but I also knew that someday I would fly high above them—just like in my dreams. They couldn't touch or catch me up there.

CHAPTER TWENTY

Everytime Daddy passed out, we stole the change from his pockets. We just scrounged up the coins here and there. If a man dropped a coin on the floor at our house during a poker game, I'd put my foot over it. When no one was looking, I'd scoot it through a crack. The next day when nobody was around, I'd crawl under the house and get it. We kept the change tucked inside a squirrel hole in an old oak tree down by the bridge.

The counter in Mr. Hull's store ran the length of the big room. On it was a large paper holder and a ball of string for wrapping and tying purchases, plus a plug tobacco cutter, a coffee grinder, a wheel of bright yellow cheese under a glass dome, and a big brass cash register. Mr. Hull would take a fat black pencil from behind his ear and write prices of items on a brown paper, then add up the total. I watched him intently. I could add the prices upside down faster than he could right side up, and I was only eleven-years-old.

My brothers and I always took enough money to show Mr. Hull that we actually had some to purchase things.. If he knew we had money, we didn't have any trouble getting into the store, even though we left his store with most of the money we came in with.

Mr. Hull had a round little face, outlined with lots of curly hair the color of metal. It was fuzzy and seemed to stand on end. He wore strange glasses with square corners. He and his wife, Ciddy, talked funny—their accents made them hard to understand them.

Most times we'd sit in behind the store up on the hillside. We knew the precise time to enter the store, and waited until the time was ripe. First thing in the morning and noon were the right times—the busier the better.

Brian would always stay on the hillside with the two babies and Patches. At times, Brian would wander away and leave the babies alone with Patches, who sometimes found himself doubling as angel and babysitter.

Before we attacked the store, we'd schedule our entry for early morning. We always made sure Mr. Hull was busy with customers. Most farmers and ranchers would stop into the store early every morning for supplies, again at noon, and again late in the afternoon. We were long gone by late afternoon.

The store was my favorite place to be though I dreaded entering the store just as much as Mr. Hull dreaded us. He'd meet us at the door with that "hog's breath," as Mickey called it.

Mr. Hull regularly shouted at us in his peculiar voice, practically foaming at the mouth. "You slimy little thieves. You can't come in. If you stay here bothering around me for half a minute longer, you'll get something you don't want. You're nothing but damn beggars." He would punctuate the statement by hammering one fist on the counter. "Why do you come here and make trouble? Your Daddy never earned a cent in his life, and he owes me money now. Money that I'll never see." Mr. Hull always went on and on, jabbering about our father.

"But, Mr. Hull," I would say, in a shy, mischievous voice, holding out my hand, "I have money, and I want to buy one of those ice cream cones."

"All right, all right. Since you have money, I'll let you in. Just this time. I promise you, I'm going to be watching every move you dirty little pigs make. If I catch you thieving from me, I'm gonna' hang you scrawny little turds by the ears."

At times, Mr. Hull would ask a customer to keep watch on us. The customer generally got busy chatting with other farmers, and he'd forget about us.

The store was my favorite place to be, once I got up enough courage to go inside. Easing myself alongside the massive shelves, I walked slowly up and down each row, taking everything in, with my eyes as big as marbles. I'd touch the bright red, blue, and yellow labels, tightly wrapped around each of the shiny cans. I moved them first this way to the right, then back in the other directions.

Now and then, as I shoved something aside, I'd find myself eye-to-eye with Mr. Hull. He'd be glaring at me from the other side with a mean scowl painted on his face. Sometimes, as I went up and down the aisles, I'd catch Mr. Hull on his toes peeking around the end of an aisle at one of my brothers.

As I continued, looking at everything, I heard the hollow sound of men's boots on the planked floor. I always knew exactly where Mr. Hull was, but because I was barefoot, he never knew where I was.

At one end of the counter were towering columns of flour in their brightly printed sacks. They were stacked from the floor to the ceiling. I heard one of the girls say her Mama had made her a dress from the printed sack. A fat gray barrel sat in front of the big wooden cash register. It was filled to the brim with crispy crackers. I loved them, but rarely got one because the barrel was in plain view.

After taking a bite of pickle I'd snatched from the pickle crock, I tossed it back. I looked at the items on display. Everything looked so good when I was trying to decide what my haul was going to be. There were crates of big oranges and bright red and green apples. Up along the other side of the counter were the big clear jars full of tobacco. Chewing tobacco filled other shelves.

Glass jars lined up in a row were filled with big, fat jawbreakers—the ones that were so big they hurt my jaw when I sucked on them and spit would fill my mouth dripping down onto my chin. Other jars held long, black, twisted licorice, jelly beans, and yellow and orange caramel corn. How I longed for a Sugar Daddy wrapped in bright orange and yellow wrappers. I loved them more than anything. Every day, I stole one on my way to school.

When I grew up, I planned to buy everything in the store. I'd even buy something for my brothers—anything they wanted. I couldn't wait until I grew up, then I'd show that dumb ol' Mr. Hull.

Nobody paid any attention to Scotty because he was so little. He'd crawl around behind the crates of vegetables, oranges, and apples to hide behind the pickle barrel. Oh, how he loved those pickles! He'd dip into the barrel with the dipper and fill his pants with pickles. He'd crawl out the front or back door of the store and hide until the rest of us came out. Sometimes he made two, three, or more trips in and out of the store. If it was summer and he had short pants on, the pickle juice etched clean stripes down his legs.

When I came out, his little eyes would be dancing as if they were saying, "How'd I do, Sissy?" He was so proud of himself for helping us. I called him my "little sourpuss."

One-by-one, we'd finally leave Mr. Hull's store with our stash. Sometimes we would come back for another bunch of stuff. Finally, we'd get our ice-cream and pay for it, then leave the store for good. To make Mr. Hull happy, we always paid for something. But we always left with most of our change still in our pockets.

On our way from the store, I scrounged through all the trash cans, looking for food for Patches.

In the early days, I hid Patches when we entered the store. He was so skittish. After I left the store, I would head straight up the steep hill where Patches would be waiting for me. He'd been kicked and even shot at so often that he didn't mind hiding.

When I returned, I always found him in the same spot where I'd left him. "Patches?" I would whisper. "Is that you?" I always said that, even though I knew it was my fuzzy guardian angel. I would crawl up to where he sat on the ground, and kneel in front of him, hugging his neck. He always responded by licking my face, neck, and forehead with his big, warm, wet tongue. He loved all my affection and caresses.

"Time for breakfast, boy," I whispered one morning after a particularly big haul from the store. Taking a big, greasy sack out from my jacket, I let Patches smell it. "Are you hungry, Patches? I sure am!" I took out two cold hamburgers, one for Patches and a smaller one for me. He also got french fries and would respond by licking my face, then wagging his tail. He looked at me with bright, intelligent eyes, and seemed to nod at the right times, as if he were saying "thank you." He always expressed gratitude by kissing my face with rough-tongued dog licks.

After Patches was with us a while and he got used to the stores, he'd slither into the store on his belly. He'd always come back out quickly with something in his mouth for us. Patches knew a Coca-Cola bottle. He liked Coke, and usually came out of the store with one.

I'd open it and take a sip, then give Patches a sip. "Hurry, boy, it's dripping down your chin." He was so excited, but he never missed a drop. Patches watched as I drank the rest, cocking his head from side-to-side.

Sometimes, as we walked the flume toward home with our bellies full, Patches would catch his daily meal—usually a ground squirrel—even though I had already brought him his breakfast. He'd get a rabbit, occasionally. There were lots of rabbits, but Patches didn't like to catch wild rabbits. We stole tame rabbits.

Sometimes we headed for home along the river, and other times we'd climb over the hills. We'd roll in the grass, laughing as we relived our adventures, talking about how we "really put one over on old Mr. Hull."

As we made our way, we'd snoop around all the old barns or dig in the trash for a pair of shoes or boots that might fit. We found quilts, clothes, and all sorts of other things.

I always looked for nipples for my two baby sisters. We could use different kinds of bottles, but we had to have nipples.

We thought we were so rich when we found such treasures. We'd play all afternoon in the woods. Sometimes we went home, and sometimes we camped out. We might sleep under an old tree down by the river or in someone's barn. The moon shined brightly, making it light everywhere except in the shadows. We poked along while everyone else was still sound asleep. We sat on rocks and watched the moon go off watch. After a while, a pale streak would come over the mountaintops, and we knew that day was coming. The Tule River looked miles and miles across, but it wasn't. In the winter it would sometimes freeze over, and in the spring it was swift and dangerous. I could never tell how deep it was, but the river was fast. Nobody could last long in that current, no matter how good a swimmer you were. We were in the river summer and winter. It didn't matter.

We had to cross. Sometimes we slipped off a stone and fell in, even before we'd learned to swim. In seconds, we'd be spinning downstream a mile or two.

I always tried to tell my brothers to relax and float, to let themselves go where the current took them. But they never listened, and constantly got into trouble. Patches always managed to rescued them.

One day we learned that Aunt Anne, Mama's sister, was riding the train coming from Texas to visit. Mama hadn't seen any of her family in over nine years she said. Relatives never came, and Mama and Daddy both had left all their family in Texas and Oklahoma a long time ago.

Mama whistled and yodeled when she was happy, so hearing her always cheered me up. Not even a bird could whistle like my Mama. She yodeled clear and sweet, sometimes dropping the notes one by one. It had been a long, long time since I'd seen her happy. I picked back through my memories. When had I last seen Mama laugh and giggle? I couldn't remember.

She cooked "goodies," as she called them, for a week. She had plenty of chicken she'd canned and stored away. Mama cooked greens and fried okra, chicken 'n' dumplings, a big pot of beans, biscuits and corn bread, and cakes. That's what I liked best...cakes, brown on their bottoms.

Mama said she was preparing a good southern feast. Where had Mama gotten all that food, I wondered? Was it just for Aunt Anne? Mama never got food for us.

Mama found someone to take her to Tulare to meet Aunt Anne at the train station. Aunt Anne would stay in town in the hotel, Mama had said, since we didn't have room for her to stay with us. Not to mention the fact that she probably wouldn't want to stay in that house with us, anyway.

We waited all afternoon for Mama to return with our honored visitor. We were about as excited as we had ever been. Mama had talked about nothing else since she found out Aunt Anne was coming to visit.

In the late afternoon, Mickey came running into the house. "He's here!"

Brian echoed, "Sissy, he's here."

Then Scotty was yelling, "He's here, Sissy! Daddy's coming! Sissy, are you listening to me?"

They all huddled around me, not knowing what to expect. None of us ever knew what kind of mood Daddy would be in.

Daddy arrived with his arm full of big brown paper bags, overflowing with the usual things. He took the bottle of whiskey, along with his beer and cigarettes, to the front porch. He shuffled to the bed on the porch and sat down on the old mattress. Holding his rifle between his legs, he loaded it. He had his hand tight on the trigger. I watched his cold, dark eyes, and listened to his voice full of rage and a promise of death as he mumbled something I couldn't understand. I knew it was bad, just by watching him.

Daddy propped the rifle against the wall, then lay down on the boys' bed, stretching out his legs and crossing his ankles.

"This is the day you're gonna' die for sure," he muttered. He said it over and over. I'll never forget the way he looked that day. With the rifle in his hands, something sinister happened to him. Jumping up, knuckles white, gun muzzle weaving, Daddy hollered, "I'll blow you into tiny pieces, you bitch. No one will know who you are!"

He cocked the hammer and slouched back down on the bed. I watched with mounting horror as he jacked the slide with a click, clack. Within minutes, he would be back up on his feet, checking out the gun again, staring down the barrel. He'd heft it as if he was getting himself used to the feel and weight, testing the action of the hammer. I watched his finger curl tightly around the trigger, tugging slowly.

I was so frightened I thought my heart had stopped. Daddy cracked open the rifle and studied it carefully.

He kept talking to himself.

Over and over, he repeated the scenario. Slowly, he lowered the rifle to the floor and lay there with his eyes closed. His face was bright red.

He fought to control his breathing...he wheezed, coughed, and waited. A real bad case of jitters seemed to give him a hard time catching his breath. His chest heaved, and I could see that he was working hard to control his breathing.

Scared, I peered out at him from the cracks in the apple crates which separated me from him. Kathy was asleep, and Rita played quietly with the stuffed animals.

I knew I must get my brothers and the babies... leave for the hills. But, I wanted to see my Aunt Anne too. An internal voice screamed that something bad was about to happen. I didn't move, because I didn't want Daddy to know that I was close by.

Along toward early evening, a car pulled into our driveway. I grabbed Rita, scooted past Daddy and ran from the porch. Snatching Kathy, Mickey followed, each with a baby on our hips.

When the car came to a stop, Mama and Aunt Anne got out. The driver stayed in the car, driving to the end of the driveway where he waited.

Daddy started shooting. The first blast seemed to shred the sky above Mama's and Aunt Anne's heads. Aunt Anne dropped to the ground. Daddy started to shoot at their feet, hitting the ground in front of them. His sweaty, naked chest bulged with muscles that rippled and gleamed in the sun as he pointed the rifle and fired again, making the sand fly up.

Mama just stood there, but Aunt Anne screamed frantically. She jumped, shaking and trembling, yelling "No! No! No!," in ear-piercing screams.

Daddy ran down the dusty old drive to meet them, waving his rifle and cursing. He grabbed Mama by her hair and dragged her into the house.

"Who was that man who brought you home?" he snarled. "Who was he, bitch? Answer me right now!" He reached over and slapped her. "You fucking whore," the savage words came like gunshots.

Daddy lunged forward, grabbing her again. He put the muzzle of the gun against her forehead and cocked it. I saw her face which was a mask of terror. My Aunt Anne seemed horrified and remained outside with us. She didn't know our Daddy, and had no idea what was going on.

Finally she ran into the house, to help her sister. We ran inside close behind her.

"I'm going to make you pay," Daddy yelled. "Damn! I'm going to make you feel some pain."

Mickey and I jumped on Daddy's back, hitting him with our fists. He flung us off and threw us on the floor, then kicked me hard in the stomach and side. The room started to spin. I tried to get up, but fell forward. Mickey screamed and pulled at me. He wasn't big enough to pull me up, but he kept tugging.

"Easy," I heard Mickey say. "We're almost there." "Almost there...almost where?" My eyes wouldn't stay open.

When I was finally able to keep them open, I saw that Mickey and Brian were pulling me up the mountain, where it was safe. I must have been in a semi-conscious state for them to have led me out of the house toward safety.

We sat for the longest time, looking down on our house. We wanted to help Mama, but we knew we couldn't. I worried about Aunt Anne.

We watched as Mama and Aunt Anne ran from the house with Daddy right behind, shooting at them. The hog-shed was all splintered from being shot at. More shots were fired, and more screams echoed up the mountainside. It was as if the air were heavy with Aunt Anne's fear—Mama's hopelessness. I finally couldn't stand to watch anymore and buried my head in my hands. Patches nuzzled his head against me and began to cry softly. Even he seemed touched by the tragedy below. I wished that he'd been a vicious as I thought he was when I first found him.

Mama and Aunt Anne ran to the waiting car, which drove off quickly. Daddy stood at the end of the driveway, waving the rifle and cursing after them. Taking aim, he shot repeatedly. Finally, he crouched down on his heels. His face reflected a snarling hatred and dark evil.

We stayed there in the safety of the blue-black, rocky mountains until night fall. I continued to watch the house, knowing Daddy would be gone soon to some bar.

Mama stayed in town at the hotel with Aunt Anne. Every day, we went to see them. I sat on the floor of the hotel room and went through Aunt Anne's suitcase. I loved her things. I had never seen such beautiful things. They were so pretty, and they all matched. I felt her pretty, soft, silky things, rubbing them on my face and smelling them. One of her suitcases was small. It was full of tiny bottles of all sorts of lotions and perfumes.

One night, all of us got to sleep in the hotel all night. I slept on the rug on the floor with my brothers and my two baby sisters.

The next night Mama and Aunt Anne went to Camp Nelson to a dance. Mama wore some of Aunt Anne's clothes and she looked so pretty. I'd never seen my Mama all dressed up. I wished she could always look that way. If she did, maybe I could too someday I reasoned.

When they came home, there were two men with them... men I'd never seen before.

Daddy was in and out of town. When Scotty saw him, he'd take off to be with him. Sometimes he stayed with Daddy and other times he stayed in the hotel with us. A few days later, Daddy took Scotty and left town. Mama told me Daddy called her at the bar saying Scotty was really sick and in a hospital in Fresno. The doctor thought he was going to die. Daddy said he wanted her to ride the bus to Fresno, to see Scotty, before he died.

Mama told me she was going to see what was wrong with him. I know Mama had an unholy fear of what Daddy might do to Scotty.

Mama and Aunt Anne got on the bus for Visalia. Mama explained that Aunt Anne would catch another bus that would take her back to Texas.

All of us kids set out for home. It was a long walk, but had we known what lay ahead, we would never have gone back.

CHAPTER TWENTY-ONE

I don't know how much time passed, but school was still in progress when Mama left home.

I had just turned eleven, and school had recessed for the year when we heard a car coming early one summer evening. The ground was dry and cracked. The hard, cracked road to the house was covered with two or three inches of soft, fine dust.

Mickey bounded up the road. His legs reached out in front of him, stirring up great clouds of dust as if he were in a foot race. At the old gate, he hollered at the top of his lungs, "A car is coming, Peggy! Maybe Mama's back!"

Moving slowly behind him was the shiniest, brightest car I had ever seen. It was long and white, with wooden sides. I shaded my eyes, blinded by the bright sunlight reflecting from the hood of the car. A car hadn't been up our drive since Mama had left. Who was it? What did they want?

One woman drove and another sat in the seat next to her. They pulled up to the front of the house and got out of the car.

The young one said, "Hi there, young lady. Is your Mama home?"

Mickey had Rita on his hip, her little legs wrapped tight around his waist as she hung on for dear life. Kathy dangled in front of me with my arms holding her tight.

I answered cautiously, "No." "Is your Daddy home?"

"No. My Mama went to get him."

"Where did she have to go to get your Daddy.?" the older woman asked.

"How would I know?" I screamed. "My baby brother is in the hospital somewhere and about to die. Mama went to see him." Who are these stupid people, anyway?

The woman whose hands fluttered like wounded birds walked toward me, pushing me backward. Her eyes looked huge behind the thick, black-rimmed glasses. They moved rapidly from me, to each of my brothers, and scanned our house. She talked fast, shaking her head back and forth.

My lips trembled. I was afraid. With each backward step, I felt her strong determination, her power. Words of warning jumped into my mind. I felt trouble was about to erupt.

I moved between Mickey and Brian and slipped my hand into Mickey's. My heart thumped like a drum. I was sure my brothers could hear it. Something horrible was happening.

I listened as the woman's fast, heavy steps crossed the wooden floor of our house. She appeared again at the front door, motioning for the other lady to come in. The younger women, walked through the door.

She said, "It's clean enough. Look at the baby's bed." "But look, it's nothing but a crate. An ordinary apple crate!"

They peered and probed at everything in and out of the house, mumbling in low voices.

"It's a case of abandonment, pure and simple," one lady said.

The words sounded like we had a bad disease.

We waited in the yard, watching and listening. Patches had growled threateningly at the woman when she had pushed me. Now, he began to nudge me in the direction of the mountain. He began to move in circles around us as though herding us away from the house. We started walking backward, watching the women, who were busy snapping pictures, while we quietly made our way to the side of our mountain.

Once we were behind the pig shed, where we couldn't be seen, we ran with Patches behind us. We crossed the road and ducked under the barbed wire fence, and had disappeared from sight before they knew we were gone, or which direction we had taken. By the time they came out of the house, we had hidden in our secret hideout up on the mountain where we could watch them from high on the hill. The grass was dry and prickly on our legs and the bottoms of our feet. The hillside was brown from the scorching sun.

Finally, when the social worker's realized we were gone they walked around the house one way, and back the other, searching. They walked faster and faster. The older woman flapped her arms and hands as she talked. Their mouths moved, but we couldn't hear what they were saying. One woman went out to the car and honked the horn again and again. Standing with the car door open, she honked and searched the property with her eyes; however, she wasn't scanning the direction where we sat.

From high on the ridge, I watched as they got into their car and drove slowly out the drive. The car stopped and honked again. Red brake lights went off and on, until finally the car moved slowly down the mountain road. We watched their red tail lights blink on and off for miles as they descended.

While it was still dark early the following morning, I set out for food with Patches at my side. Cars were parked at our house. A sheriff's car was in the drive, along with that same black Hudson from the day before.

I wanted to get to Mr. Hull's store before he opened. As I made my way through the brush, I saw the eyes of wild animals peering out at me. I heard sounds of animals scampering out of my way. Patches stayed at my side, circling around me.

I arrived at the market long before Mr. Hull opened, and sat on a hill behind the store, watching the sun come up. I was his first customer. When I entered the store, he gave me a very unusual look, as though somehow he wasn't surprised to see me. A squirmy feeling persisted in telling me something was wrong.

Usually I begged or stole from him, but this time I came right out and asked for food. He didn't yell. He didn't call me a thief. But this time he gave me a whole bagful of food, and even closed and locked up his store to take me home. I let him, because I really was in a hurry, and was anxious to know what was going on at our house. Mr. Hull didn't say a word to me. That squirmy feeling told me something was horribly wrong.

The minute Mr. Hull pulled into our drive, I had my hand on the door handle. I grabbed the sack of groceries and jumped out of the car. I was under the fence and up the hill before he even knew what had happened.

My heart boomed with terror. Something deep inside told me this was the end of us—the end of our family. I fought to drive off a sudden smothering grief that overwhelmed me.

Now many cars were parked at our house. There was a huge, dark green truck with high wooden rails on the sides. It was full of men dressed in jeans, white T-shirts, and boots. I thought they were fire fighters. There were two smaller trucks exactly like the bigger one, with the same emblem painted on the side of the door. The sheriff's car was still in front of the house. I wondered if all these people had spent the night in our house.

We stood on the slope of the mountain under the shade of the oaks. Lizards skittered on the rocks, then sat pulsing, watching us curiously. A squirrel scurried in a tree. One hawk swooped low while another circled lazily overhead, scanning to pick up a meal.

Trucks and cars came and went most of the day. We heard their horns blow. A man spoke into a big, funny- looking thing that he held in his hands. We could hear his voice, but we were too far away to understand what he said. After dark, we felt safe enough to creep down the mountainside. We didn't get close enough to hear their words, but we heard many voices. The man picked up the horn again from the back of the truck and spoke into it. "Children! Children! If you hear me, please come down now. Your mother is hurt, she's asking for you. Please come down. Your mother needs you." He repeated this over and over.

Gazing at one another, Mickey and I picked up the babies, and headed down the side of the mountain. Brian followed, pee running down his leg.

Everybody hollered as we stepped into the clearing. The men jumped from the truck, and everyone charged our way. A group of the young men in boots began to dart toward us, stopping when the pushy woman called them back.

The two babies started screaming. We hid behind the barn. The man with the horn spoke again. All the others stayed behind him as he spoke to us.

"Don't be frightened, children. We're not here to harm you. Please come here." Again, he told us that our mother was hurt and had sent him to get us. The man said he was here to take us to our Mama.

Slowly we moved into the yard. A dozen or more people stood around, then came forward. I took a step backward.

The man spoke, gently now, "It's okay. Come here. We're here to help you, not harm you."

Kathy dug her tiny fingers into my neck.

"It's all right," I whispered, holding her tightly. I could tell that she was as frightened as I was.

Mickey said, "it's okay, Peggy. Come on."

A woman stepped forward, taking a small package from her bag. She handed us a piece of bubble gum. With my grubby hands, I snatched bag and all out of her hands. I distributed the contents of candy and bubble gum.

There was a lot of food, and huge metal jugs filled with water on the back of a flatbed truck. Stacks and stacks of big metal racks held bottled milk. They had sandwiches and fruit. We didn't wait for anybody to offer us food; we helped ourselves. The people watched us, and the crowd of young men laughed.

Something deep inside me tried to catch my attention, I didn't know what it was...then the word "orphan" rang loudly in my ears. Had I heard or imagined it?

"What's a orphan?" I asked between bites.

"Who said anything about an orphan, did you tell her they're orphans Mrs. Peliter?" the one social worker asked.

"No not me, I didn't say that word," she said.

"We're taking you to a foster home until we locate your parents," one of the men said as he herded us into the white station wagon.

"Shove over, Mickey," I said.

"No! You always get the window. Now it's my turn."

"I said shove over. This is all your fault. Get your skinny ass over, now!" I railed.

Mickey scooted over, and I climbed into the car. Brian, on the other side, cranked the window down, then up and down again.

"Stop it, Brian," I said.

"Make me, Sissy. Try'n make me."

Slapping him, I yelled, "Quit it now. I can't hear with that noisy thing!"

"Kids," the case worked said, "quit sniping at each other." "What's sniping?" I asked.

"Arguing with each other."

"Well, she started it," Mickey said. "I don't like her telling me what to do. And I ain't gonna' do what she says." The social worker turned around in her seat and glared.

She held Kathy on her lap. Mickey held Rita.

Kathy screamed non-stop.

"Give me my baby!" I demanded. "Not now," the lady said.

"I know she wants me. Can't you tell? If you'd give her to me, she'll shut up."

"Peggy, I think you have been a little mommy about long enough. Let me have her now and we'll just give you a rest."

"I don't want no rest!" I shouted. "Give her to me!"

The old bag just turned around in the front seat and ignored me while my baby squalled. "This is all your fault, Mickey! I didn't want to come down off the hill. Now see what you did." I tried to bury my fear by attacking my brother and realized I was drowning in the river of my emotions. I hated my mother, and I pitied her. I hated her for allowing Daddy to torment her so. But mostly, right now, I hated them both. I didn't know I could be so filled with hatred—hate for myself, my parents, and worst of all, the hate for the social workers. I just stared ahead, seething with bitterness.

Finally, I couldn't keep back the tears which had been burning behind my eyelids.

Mickey watched me as he ground his tears away with small fists. He straightened himself when he saw me watching him, pretending that he was all right, but I saw the anguish in his eyes. He sucked in his breath just before a sob escaped. I pulled myself together and sat up straight, trying to mentally shut out Mickey's pitiful sobs.

All our treasures were left behind. All the precious stuffed toys I'd collected and mended for my babies. I worked so hard so they could have toys like other children, now they had nothing. Why, why, why...

A whine came from Patches as he lunged toward the car. He put his front paws on the door, and his big head filled the window. He made the sound like a wolf and the plaintive howl sent shivers down my spine as it echoed from the mountain above.

The older woman cranked the steering wheel hard, making a U-turn. Slowly she drove out of the long, dusty driveway onto the narrow, paved, mountain road.

I stared back at our old house, knowing somehow that I'd never be here again. I saw the old strait jacket my Daddy had hung me in. It swayed slowly in the breeze—a banner which spoke of the abuse here, now nothing more than faded, rotting strips which dangled from the tree as if solemnly waving "goodbye".

Patches chased us out the long rutted drive. He was picking up speed now, but slowed to make the curve out onto the main highway; his ears stood at right angles to the large head, held aloft by the wind of his speed. Finally he stopped and watched us from the edge of the road. Within minutes he appeared in the road in front of us. He had run a shorter route to catch us.

He began the chase again. Mickey hollered from the window, "Way to go, boy!"

"Oh, please...my dog!" I begged the social workers. As the car continued to gain speed, they rigidly stared out the windshield, seemingly oblivious to the large mahogany dog who desperately tried to keep up with the children he'd loved and protected. I watched as he was soon completely swallowed up by the plume of swirling dust which spewed over the wild grape, Buckeye trees, and scrub brush alongside the road. Patches! My dog...my friend...my guardian angel—the only love I had ever known.

Soon he was completely out of sight. I would fix his image on my heart forever. I was to never see him again.

CHAPTER TWENTY-TWO

We hadn't been on the road long—maybe thirty minutes—when the social worker parked the station wagon in front of a house that looked not unlike the shack we'd just left in Springville. It surely wasn't any better. The tattered screens on the front porch had big rusty holes, patched from other rusty screens. The brown-shingled roof was patched with rows of corrugated tin. Bright yellow plastic hung on big black rings inside the screened porch like a drape.

Through the fly-specked screen door, I saw a huge rhino of a woman, her mammoth hips dragged behind as she came out the door. We all covered our mouths to keep from laughing.

"I knew I was getting a houseful of little darlings," she hollered. "Just look at you! You are about the sweetest things I've ever seen in all my years of taking in foster children."

Little darlings? Gawd! This woman is nuts. Little darlings my ass! She'll change her mind about little darlings before the sun goes down, I thought but didn't dare say aloud.

Turning around in her seat, the social worker told us to be good.

"But I'm not good," I said.

Under her breath, she murmured, "Yes, I can see that."

The big lady, still full of laughter, opened the door on my side of the car. "Come on out, you little darlings. I can just tell by looking at you that you're half starved. No meat on those arms. Look at these puny arms." She gave me a pinch.

I pinched her back. I hung onto a small portion of her skin and twisted, taking delight in seeing her flinch.

"I got plenty to eat," she said. "You'll soon feel better." How does this old hag know I'll feel better?

She shook one finger in my face and laughed. "I saw you cross your eyes at me." She crossed her eyes back. "See, I can do it too. I was a kid once, you know."

Her breasts were huge, but she managed to fold both arms over the mammoth bosom. Mickey called her "Old Hogsbreath." We all laughed. She didn't have many teeth, and the two front ones stuck out like a rabbit's. Mickey and I snickered.

She wore a print house dress with a dirty apron tied around her middle. A nasty, old brown rag dangled from one hand. She wiped her mouth with it, then spit. I never saw a woman spit that far—clear across the drive. "Hogsbreath" wiped her mouth again and stuffed the crumpled rag back in the pocket of her apron.

The house was as filthy as the rag. Dust balls and bits of scraps clung to the inside wall along the dirt-caked linoleum on the porch. A bed crouched in one corner, a dresser missing the top drawer stood beside it. Forgotten newspapers, yellow and tattered, littered both sides. Junk of all kinds filled the porch. The door to her shack stood open, allowing a view straight back to the kitchen. A shadowy figure stood at the open door of the icebox. Shadows like ghosts filled the house. It was dark, musty, and smelled dank like our secret cave.

This place they'd taken us to was actually worse than our own home. At least I kept our house clean for my babies. Stuffing leaked from the sofa. A scratched and chipped table forlornly showed its many painted layers of colors. An ugly lamp stood on a crooked pole in the corner, the shade had yellowed with age. A ratty hassock with horsehair dribbling out was patched with adhesive tape. Mickey and I played leap-frog over it.

Sitting on the sofa, I almost sank to the floor. Mickey sat next to me and tried to inch closer.

"Get off me!" I yelled. "This is all your fault. We'd still be home if it weren't for you!"

Kathy started crying.

Mickey jumped up fast. The springs screeched a noisy protest.

"Now see what you've gone and done," the old lady shouted at me.

Mickey rubbed his butt. Rita climbed onto the couch. She sat back, banging her head on its back while she watched us play with the worn out springs sticking through with the sharpness of ice picks.

The old lady laughed and said, "I should have warned you that them springs would poke you."

She made us bathe first before we could do anything. The water was only lukewarm. She stayed in the bathroom and washed each of us. She pulled my arms first this way and scrubbed, then raised them up and scrubbed some more. I thought she was going to scrub my skin right off me. It hurt. Checking through every strand of hair, Hogsbreath explained she was looking for bugs. She laughed and talked the whole time calling us "little darlings" and "ragamuffins." The tub was different from any tub I'd ever seen. White, funny, square things floated in the water, with "I-V-O-R-Y"

printed on them. "What's this?" I asked. "That's soap. Haven't you ever seen soap?"

"This is soap? Mickey, look! This is soap! I'm glad to have soap. Now I'll smell pretty like the girls at school in Springville."

I watched as she showed me how to rub the big block of soap between the palms of my hands. It made little dirty bubbles on my body. My brothers and I giggled and threw the foamy white stuff at one another. The bathroom was soon full of soapy foam. It clung to the walls and the floor; it melted, leaving puddles all over the floor. The woman stood at the door and watched us. She tried to get us to stop, but there wasn't any way she could seem to control us. We were beyond anyone's control.

Both babies screamed at the top of their lungs. I had to bathe them. Mrs. Hogsbreath didn't seem to know anything, much less how to bathe my sisters.

She pulled a large box from a shelf in the closet. When she flipped the top open, dust flew in every direction. It was filled with heaps of tattered clothing.

"These clothes are plain and practical," she said, "well cared for, but wearing thin. They're only dresses. I don't have any britches for boys."

"Not me! I ain't wearing no dress!" Mickey shouted. "It's only for today," she giggled. "A social worker will bring boys' clothes tomorrow. These are clean and something to wear."

"Not me!" Mickey proclaimed belligerently. "Brian can wear them, but I'm not!"

"Oh no, I won't," shouted Brian.

"Oh, yes you will, young man! It's all I have right now! And you're not about to put those filthy dungarees back on! I'm burning those!"

Grudgingly, they both put on the dresses and panties. Mickey looked at Brian and started to laugh, and Brian looked at Mickey and snorted with belly laughs. My two brothers would not leave the house.

She made me put on those dumb silk panties too. I didn't argue with her, but the minute she turned her back, I took them off and kept my knees pressed together.

Huddling together in the house we whispered about running away, knowing we could find our way home, we'd done it so often before. From the back of her house, we could almost see the mountain where our house was, but we knew they'd just go back and find us.

The only way Mrs. Hogsbreath got us to bed was to put a mattress on the floor and let us sleep together. I didn't want to, because I knew Brian would wet the bed. He always did. She put the mattress on the kitchen floor near the back door, right outside her bedroom.

Rita and Kathy bawled all night. Old Mrs. Hogsbreath finally came in and yanked Rita from my arms. Rita screamed even louder. They only stopped when I took them back into the bed with us.

Old Mrs. Hogsbreath returned to the door a dozen times during the night and asked me why I couldn't keep them quiet. Even then, she kept laughing at her own jokes. She tried again to take one baby, who shrieked loud enough to wake the dead. There was nothing a body could do to keep them quiet. I'd never seen them act this way. I shook all over as I held and rocked each one. Finally they both slept, exhausted.

But I couldn't sleep. In my mind I made all kinds of plans on how to get away from there. It kept me awake. The eerie threat of what was happening to us made me feel a part of me was missing, and I didn't know what to do.

It just ain't right, I told myself. Something happens and suddenly your life is turned upside down. Everything is gone, you've got nothing left but echoes, empty echoes, a big black hole where our lives used to be. I could hear the big clock high on the wall ticking...ticking our lives away. I felt as if a blanket of fear was smothering and choking, drowning me. I hugged my babies close. When I knew the others finally slept, I wept quietly in the darkness, letting my aching heart have its way. I wanted to put my arms around Patches, bury my face in the fur of his neck.

Late into the night, I heard crickets that sounded as if they were in bed with us, and the loud whistle of a train. I drew the blanket up under my chin and slipped deep down into the mattress. In the distance, dogs barked. I hoped Patches was taking care of our house. I vowed I'd find a way to get us back home tomorrow. When Mama gets back home, boy will she be mad! I reveled in the thought.

Mickey shook me. I sat straight up in bed. "What's the matter?"

"I'm scared to go to sleep." "Why?"

"If I do, I'm afraid you'll be gone in the morning, just like Mama." I could hear the fright in his voice.

"That's silly. I ain't going nowhere, and 'specially not without you. Go to sleep."

Later, when I knew Mickey thought I was asleep, I heard him softly crying.

I didn't have the strength to control my emotions myself. I felt helpless, powerless, and was suddenly seized by some shivering weakness. Then anger rumbled inside me like thunder. I clung more tightly to my baby sisters. Rita nuzzled her face into my neck as I held her tightly.

It didn't seem real. I rolled my fists round and round the mattress. I sniffed the musty odor, and traced my fingers around the tiny stitches that outlined the scraps of the cloth quilt. The colors faded into shades of brown, grays, and blue. The loud clock ticked on its small shelf above the mantle.

A picture hung high on the wall near the molding, a photograph of a smiling grandma. I played with the dial of a strange black thing on the table beside me. It was ugly, and seemed to have no purpose. It was a weird black thing. I touched it, feeling the smooth shiny surface. The house was without a sound, and I jumped as that ugly thing began to ring. Running to it, the old woman began talking to the stupid thing. I didn't understand when old Mrs. Hogsbreath told us to be quiet she was, "on the telephone."

I whispered to Mickey. "Telephone? What's that?" The fat lady held a part of the funny black thing in her hand. One end was stuck next to her ear while she talked into the other end. I'd never seen anything like that before.

"I have five little orphans here," she said into that ugly thing.

Orphans? There's that word again. Is she talking about us? I wondered.

"Just fine—their family lived a rather poor life. Someone will come later and take the girls. I'll keep the boys with me."

I questioned this mentally, they're gonna' take us away? Only us girls. That can't be. Our future together seemed to be slipping right through my hands. I listened to the rest of her conversation. When she'd finished, she put the thing on top of its black box. It looked like it was two separate pieces. As she turned and walked away, I asked, "What's that thing...that black thing?"

She turned and looked at me. "What thing are you talking about?"

I touched it. "That. What is it?"

Still looking at me very strangely, she said, "That's a telephone. Do you mean to tell me you've never seen a telephone? Well, I guess you haven't." She turned and left the room mumbling.

The minute she was gone, I grabbed for the telephone. Picking it up, I heard a voice say, "Number please, number please, number please, number please." I quietly put it back down.

Standing up I motioned for Mickey. He edged his way toward me. I picked up the telephone and put it to his ear. "Number please, number please, number please." We both started to giggle. Someone shouted, "You kids get off this telephone line, right now!"

Laughing harder, we put the telephone back and ran from the room just as Mrs. Hogsbreath entered the kitchen. At that very moment, that thing rang again. She picked it up, and both Mickey and I strained to listen.

"Yes, I do. I have five new little darlings." Grinning, she looked at Mickey and me. "I'll see to it that it doesn't happen again, Mildred. You can count on it." She put the thing down.

I pulled my knees against my chest to ease the pain. "Peggy?"

I took a deep breath. Somehow, I sensed what Mickey was going to say.

"What, Mickey?"

"Oh God, what are we going to do?"

"Don't worry, it's going to be all right. Just wait and see, Mama will be back. Probably today. And boy, will she be fighting mad. And besides, when Aunt Anne gets back to Texas she is going to tell all our relatives about this. You just wait and see, someone will be coming for us."

"Do you really think so?"

"Of course! Aunt Ann will tell the world and we'll have these grandma's coming. You just wait and see."

"Oh Gosh!...I sure hope so. You know Peggy I never thought of that. Golly Peggy, you are smart."

Rita was taking in every word we said while she held my dress twisted in her fingers.

It was a moment more before he cleared his throat and spoke again. "Someone's coming today, Peggy...that Mrs. Pelassier, or whatever her name is. She's coming again today...but only for you."

"You don't know what you're talking about, Mickey." Mrs. Hogsbreath called us to the table to "eat a bite."

We had burnt crunchy, dry bread, with yellow stuff smeared on it. There were bowls of steaming hot oatmeal. I'd had oatmeal before, but not like this. Her oatmeal had milk and sugar. About the same time, we all picked up the bowls and drank the oatmeal down in one gulp.

"My little darlings are hungry," she said. "Here, have some more. I have plenty. I'll get you fattened up, just give me time." She leaned over me to put more toast on the table. This time it wasn't as black as the other. I liked it burned the best.

I tried to feed the babies with my fingers, but this stuff was too thin. It ran through my fingers and down onto the floor. I asked her for oatmeal without the milk, so I could feed the babies. She told me to use a spoon. I tried to use the spoon like she showed me. I didn't like that, and neither did my babies.

She settled herself heavily in a chair beside me. She took one of my babies into her lap and commenced to show me how to feed them. With the other baby, I watched and tried to do what she showed me.

"Don't you know nothing?" I asked her. "These babies ain't like other babies."

The more she stuck that stupid spoon down their throats, the harder they screamed and kicked. Rita knocked the spoon clear out of her hand.

"See, I told you she don't like that thing. How would you like for me to stick that big thing down your throat?"

Rita picked up a bowl of oatmeal and dumped it on her head. Setting her down, Mrs. Hogsbreath ran for a rag. We screamed with laughter. Rita laughed harder. Brian laughed the hardest. A yellow trail of urine ran down his leg to a puddle on the floor.

I handed Kathy to Mickey, telling him to feed her. Picking up Rita, I sat on the chair. "Let me show you how." With our fingers, Mickey and I fed our babies. The old woman stood watching with her arms over her bosom, shaking her head back and forth, clucking like a brood hen. Later that morning, the case worker returned. I was sure surprised to see her again and my mind began to race: I bet our Mama's come home. Yep, I bet we'll be taken back to our home. My Mama's really mad that her kids are gone. This proves it. My Mama's told'em to bring her kids home.

Boy, I know she's just fuming. I bet this case worker is taking us back to our home. The words whirled like wind-blown leaves in my mind.

"She's come back for us, Mickey. Mama's home and she's come to take us back home." I jumped up and down.

That old Mrs. Hogsbreath just looked at me shaking her head sadly as the case worker put me, along with my two baby sisters, in the car.

"Aren't my brothers coming, too?" I asked. "Not this time."

"Are they coming later?" "I'm not sure."

I fought her as she put the three of us into the back seat, then closed and locked the door. She went to her side of the car, got in, and started the car.

On my knees in the seat, I watched out the back window. Mickey came barreling out the door almost knocking it off the hinges, with that ratty dress way up to his waist. It was the only time he had come outside with that dumb dress on. He chased the county car down the road, running as fast as he could. He stopped at the side of the road and picked up a handful of gravel throwing it defiantly at the car.

I watched him until he was just a dot and finally out of sight. Something had been cut out of me, and there was nothing I could do. There was a huge hole in my stomach, an emptiness like gnawing hunger. I tried not to think as the old social worker drove blindly, hitting the sides of the road like Daddy did when he'd been drinking. She swerved around an old truck. Its klaxon horn screamed as she drove randomly back into her own lane. Her reckless speeding spoke volumes—it was as though she couldn't get rid of us fast enough.

My mind scattered like marbles in some lunatic game wondering where she was taking us. Would I ever see my brothers again...my Mama? Why wasn't Mama here with me...us? Wait. It's a mistake.

Suddenly the back seat of the car began to swirl around me. Everything turned gray, and tiny pin pricks of light began to dance in front of my eyes. I gasped for air, inhaling large gulps. I couldn't breathe. Not now! Oh God...not now! I fought with myself. I could feel consciousness ebbing away as I struggled with the old breathing problem. I tried to picture Santa Claus...Jesus...good things...Patches. And when I focused on the love and sadness in my dog's eyes as we drove away, my breathing returned to normal, but I was filled with an overwhelming sensation of powerlessness. My eyes filled with tears which washed away the dots of light. I began to sob. Hot tears ran down my face.

The social worker maneuvered the car rapidly down the road. We flew by row after row of orange groves. She glanced in the rearview mirror, but continued to talk in her calm, unfeelingly professional voice telling me something about this next foster home she was taking us to.

"I hate you! I hate you! I hate everybody!" I screamed at her.

"Yes, I know. Everybody in your situation hates me. You'll understand some day." The manicured voice went on and on. "It is not the end of the world."

I didn't understand her, and I didn't want to listen to her jabbering. I closed my ears to her stupid babbling, wiped my tears on the hem of my ugly, clean dress and made monkey faces at her in the mirror.

We were taken to a home in Farmersville. The Marshalls were farmers. Mrs. Marshall was a school teacher in the Farmersville elementary school. They had two other children: Shelly my age; and Roger who was older. Both were adopted.

This house had one of those stupid telephones too, only someone was always talking on it, and when they weren't, it was always ringing, insisting demandingly that someone pick it up, just like a squalling child. I was fascinated by it. Shelly had the most beautiful room I had ever seen. The wallpaper was pink and white, and there was a fluffy ruffle around her bed. Everything matched, just like I'd heard the girls talk about in Springville.

Bookcases lined the wall, stuffed with books for all ages: BLACK BEAUTY; THE BOBSEY TWINS; LITTLE WOMEN. Tall Coke bottles stood in a soldierly line on the window sill. There were dolls of every sort dressed in native costumes, and some danced to music. A box overflowed with colored costume jewelry. In the corner there was a doll house filled with tiny, wee people and furniture. I'd never, ever seen anything like that. Gawd! My mind wouldn't stop tempting me. I wanted to touch this stuff, wanted her to leave the room so I could run my fingers over some of it.

"What are those dumb looking Coke bottles for?" I asked Shelly.

"Don't you know anything? Those are pressing my hair ribbons. Can't you see?" Various brightly colored ribbons circled round and round each bottle. She unrolled one to show me, and it had a slight curl to it.

Both beds were piled high with plush, fuzzy animals who watched us with big black eyes. I knew it was going to be almost impossible to keep Rita out of them.

The minute Rita headed for the stuffed animals, Shelly stepped to block her with arms outstretched. "These are mine. No one can play with them. I don't even play with them myself," she said in a haughty tone.

"How boring," I said. "Why have'em, if you don't play with them?" Why would anyone have toys and not play with them? This was the first time I'd ever seen toys that weren't tattered with all the stuffing falling out.

Shelly leaped through the air, singing. "On Tuesdays, I take ballet lessons. You can watch me. On Wednesdays, I have piano lessons. Did you see the piano in the living room? It's mine. And on Fridays, I have 4-H. I bet you don't even know about any of those things."

That night at the dinner table, I lifted up out of my seat and leaned one knee on the side of the table. Stretching over, with most of my body across the table, I grabbed a pork chop off the platter.

Mrs. Marshall, sitting tall and straight in her chair, gave me a strange look and almost choked on a mouthful of food. She politely told me to ask for what I wanted the next time. With the pork chop clutched in my fist, I took a tearing bite.

Mrs. Marshall tried to show me how to use the "utensils," as she called them. I didn't like that. I'd seen a spoon before. My Mama used them to stir with. I'd never seen those other funny looking things before.

I was so hungry and the food was the best I'd ever had. There was corn, creamed corn; I ate and ate thinking that I'd never get enough. I was so full I felt like I was about to pop. A few minutes later, I barfed up everything. It went all over me, the table, and the floor. Everyone in the Marshall family ran in different directions. I'd never seen people scatter over seeing vomit as though there was a wildfire coming. Mrs. Marshall cleared her throat and stood up quickly.

The next evening, Mrs. Marshall summoned me from the yard and gave me instructions about how to help her in the kitchen. She took me to the sink and helped me wash my hands with soap clear up to my elbows. "Scrub for three minutes straight, then rinse and dry yourself off," she instructed.

On the counter, she had a stack of dinner plates, drinking glasses, and utensils. Mrs. Marshall picked up a plate, folded a napkin, then set the utensils to the side.

"This is the way we set a table. I would like for you to carry all these dishes and utensils to the dining room. Put one at each chair, just like I have shown you here. When you are through, come back in here and help me." On a tray, she carried the napkins, salt and pepper shakers, and other things that I didn't recognize.

After carrying everything to the table, I went around and pulled out every chair. I lined up all the plates on the table. I put the utensils and the napkins into the center of the plates, deliberately setting them along with the drinking glasses in the seat of the chair while devilishly thinking, The old hag will be happy now! It didn't take me but just a minute, and I went back into the kitchen.

"Have you finished so soon?" She handed me other things to carry to the table—bread, out of the wrapper and on a plate, and butter with a stupid knife stuck in it. There was also a bowl of corn. I loved corn.

Stupid Shelly ran in, and Mrs. Marshall hugged her briefly, giving her a big smile. "Now run along and entertain Rita while we get dinner on the table."

Shelly stuck her tongue out as me as she went out. "Cootie," she whispered.

"Shut up!" I screamed back at her.

"Now Peggy, we don't talk that way in this house." "You may not talk like that, but I sure as hell do!"

Mrs. Marshall dragged me over and sat me down hard in a wooden kitchen chair. "Now, I'm telling you again, we do not talk like that in this house. Is that understood?"

Hanging my head, I answered, "yes" but my mind spun a defiant scenario, You don't know everything I know, you just wait and see. My Mama's coming for me, real soon. She's taking me and my sister. I know she's coming. The thoughts ricochetted around with the speed of bullets from Daddy's rifle.

Pulling the sides of my mouth down, I made a face at stuck-up Shelly.

"Mama! Mama! She made a face."

Mrs. Marshall looked away. "I know. Why don't you try to get along with Shelly. Please, Peggy?"

"Mama, come look at the way Peggy set the table," Shelly's sing-song voice tattled.

Mrs. Marshall ran out of the kitchen with a rag in her hand. She came back even faster and slapped the rag on the counter. It made a big crackling sound. "Can't you do anything the way I tell you?" With her elbows on the counter, she put her head into her hands. She held that position for a long time while I watched.

Finally, she raised up. "Come with me, Peggy. You are going to do this one thing, if you never do anything while you're here, you are going to do this the way I showed you."

"What's wrong with how I did it?"

"I want it done the way I showed you. Here, I'll set one place up again, and I want the others exactly like it. Do you understand? Move! I'm disgusted with you."

I took a plate off the chair and set it on the table. I went to the next plate and put it on the table.

Turning on her heel, Mrs. Marshall went back into the kitchen. "You'll have to hurry. This will delay our dinner."

In a few moments, she returned carrying a big platter of meat plus a bowl of vegetables and potatoes.

"No! No!" She set the food on the table. She held her head in both hands, standing silent for a long time. "You're going to have to try harder."

This time, she slammed a dinner plate down hard. She folded a napkin and put it to the left of the plate, then put the fork to the side of the napkin. "Not on top of, but to the side. Like this. Peggy, watch me. See! Now we put the knife to the right of the plate, with the blade facing into the plate and the spoon beside it. Got it? Then put the drinking glass over your knife. Okay? Do you think you can do it, now that I've shown you again? Do I dare turn my back? Do you think for once you can do this the way I have shown you?" Her voice grew louder with each sentence. Frown lines creased her forehead.

Mr. Marshall had now come into the dining room. Everyone was standing around waiting for me to get the table set right.

Shelly smirked at me and grinned. "Gee, Mom, I hate Peggy. Do we have to keep her?"

Mrs. Marshall bit her lip and looked away. "We have to try to get along for now."

Nobody had much to say during dinner—that is, until I puked again.

"Why do you do this?" she asked, her voice tinged with exasperation. Dragging me into the kitchen sink she made me clean myself up.

"Shelly, you show Peggy how we clean off the table," Mrs. Marshall said. "When everything is off the table, Shelly, you may play with Rita while I show Peggy how to clean the kitchen."

Mrs. Marshall washed the dishes while I dried them. The sopping rag dripped water on the floor. I went to work with the old sponge and scrubbing powder that was on the drainboard. After awhile, I had made little headway. My arms ached.

I was so absorbed in my thoughts that I didn't notice anything. I longed for my brothers, wondering it they were all right. The more I thought about them, the harder it was. A big part of me was missing.

My eyes filled with tears. I brushed the hair out of my face and wiped my eyes with the back of my hands. I didn't want anyone to see me cry. I had to try to change my thoughts, but I still saw images of Mickey chasing me down the road, wearing that dress...Patches chasing me down the road.

Mrs. Marshall began dumping several detergents, she called them, into a metal mop bucket. A string mop leaned against the cupboard.

"Do you always do this work?" I asked.

"This is good training," she told me. "I don't suppose you ever saw anyone mop a floor before."

"Oh yes I have. I mopped our floor at home every day. Sometimes two, three times a day."

"That wasn't what I was told. Mrs. Cunningham said you lived in filth."

"That isn't so. Our house was very clean. How in the world would you know if our house was clean or not? You weren't there."

"Well, I believe what Mrs. Cunningham told me."

I gaped at her. I put a wisp of hair in my mouth and began to suck on it. Ducking down, I scrubbed furiously at the floor with the mop.

Mrs. Marshall examined the floor, first one way, then the other. "Peggy, use some elbow grease," she scolded. "It's no wonder you thought your house was clean. You don't know how to clean."

I felt like laughing in her face. She was so weird. It seemed like every second, she came back and inspected what I'd done.

"You must learn what it is to work," she said.

Kathy was tied into a high chair with a wide towel. She banged on the metal tray with a spoon.

"Be quiet, Kathy," I told her.

"She's not your baby any more, she's ours," Shelly said. "She's my baby, you don't know nothing!"

Later when I went up to bed, I looked in Shelly's room. She was leaping through the air doing ballet steps. She mumbled something under her breath. The sing-song words sounded like, "My Mama doesn't like you. She's going to carry you off. We're keeping the babies, but we aren't keeping you."

"You don't know nothing. You're so stupid. They ain't carrying me off without my two sisters. Those are my sisters, not yours." I made a face to punctuate my statements.

"Oh, yes they are. My Mommie told me so." She executed another leap into the air.

With a stamp of my foot, I said, "My Mama is coming back for me and my sisters. When she comes back to our house and finds out someone has taken us away, she'll be here to get us. You just wait and see. Anyway, those are my sisters, not yours."

"They're mine, now. We're going to keep them, my Mommie said so, but we don't want you," the sing-song voice taunted as she followed me into my room.

I sat on the bed with my hands tight in my lap and kicked my feet back and forth, watching her. I wanted to get up and kick her, but I knew I'd be in for it if I did. When Shelly left the room, I shut the door tight and glared at my reflection in the mirror.

The following morning, just as I wakened, Mrs. Marshall came in with a small box and packed my few belongings. She told me I was going to Visalia with her.

"I'm coming back, ain't I?" I grabbed the foot of the bed and held on for one terrified second. I didn't want to hear her answer. "Do I have to stay there forever?"

She didn't say anything.

As I turned to pick up my box, I saw a couple of pictures of my sisters lying on the top of a table. I didn't know where they had come from, but I grabbed them and crammed them deep into the top of my box.

"Peggy!" Mrs. Marshall called. "What are you doing? Hurry along now. We don't have much time."

In a powerless daze, I waited on the steps of the front porch with the box at my feet while Mrs. Marshall went to get the car. Rita and Kathy watched from behind the screen door and blabbed to me. I just knew it would be a long time before I'd see them again. I wanted so badly to pull them both to me and tell them "goodbye." I knew that I'd break down if I did. Something wouldn't allow me to. I knew I'd break like one of those old stupid, China dolls of Shelly's.

A hatred boiled up inside me. I was filled with a bitter rage. I wanted to take my fists and beat those strangers' brains out. I wanted to scream, kick, and holler. It was all my fault. I could just hear them saying, "I don't know what's wrong with her."

Why, oh why did Mama walk away. Did she really not want us, like they said?

"Hurry on, Peggy," Mrs. Marshall directed. "Load your clothes into the car. Don't cause me to be late." She put me in the front seat beside her. I swung my legs as we started on the long stretch of road. Loudly, she said, "Don't do that. How many times do I have to tell you not to swing your legs?"

I wished I'd wake up and find out this was just a dream. I tasted the salt in my tears and saw them drip down onto my hands that were locked tight in my lap. I felt all my energy drain away like water running down a hole.

I could still feel the warmth of Rita and Kathy. I missed them already. In my head I talked to them in baby talk. The voice came from my heart and not my mouth. I had forgotten that I was no longer with them. I was numb. Will my sisters remember me? Sure they will. Nothing will ever take away those memories. I'm their big Sissy, and they'll always remember me.

My tears dropped like rain. They came with thunder, but unlike the thunder in the sky, there was no end.

"Peggy, are you awake?" Mrs. Marshall asked. "We're here now."

I had never been to "town." I had heard other kids speak about "town." The buildings were so tall they poked into the sky. The streets were lined with shiny new cars. We had arrived in Visalia. Mrs. Marshall parked behind a large building. Leaving the car motor running, she jumped out and said, "I'll be right back." She went up many steps and knocked on the back door.

The same woman who had taken us from our home in Springville opened the door. They spoke for a minute before both came back to the car. I paid no attention to their talk, but stared out the window, wishing my brothers were here too.

Mrs. Marshall opened the back door and took out the box. Right on top, with images shining, were the pictures I had taken of my sisters. They showed slightly from under the lid. "See?" she said to the case worker. "See what I mean? I can't trust her with anything. She stole these pictures, just common pictures." She took the pictures out of the box, and put them in her bag.

The case worker opened my door and told me to get into her car. She opened the back door of a brown car parked alongside. Putting a firm hand in the middle of my back, she pushed as she told me to hurry and get in. "Best to go now. No point in hanging about when there's a journey to make."

She slammed the back door, and I kicked on the back of her seat. She screamed at me.

"Why do I have to tell you not to kick the back of my seat while I'm driving? You're old enough to know better." Moving was better than thinking. It was like a nightmare.

I would wake up any moment and be back home with my brothers and baby sisters. Someone was going to come along and say, "Hey, hold everything. There has been a terrible mistake!"

When I was with Mickey, I was strong and not afraid of anything. Now I felt weak and helpless.

"I hope you will do better here in this next home, Peggy," the social worker said. "We aren't going to have enough homes for you, if you keep this up. Now, I don't want you to think it was anything you did. I know you didn't do it intentionally. Just be careful from now on, please. You know this will be the third foster home I've taken you to."

"It don't really matter," I said to her. "You know my Mama is coming for me soon. And anyway, I already don't like this next foster mother. I'm going to shove her right square in the mouth the minute I see her."

"Now, don't talk like that, young lady. Be nice."

"I'm not nice!" I yelled at her. "I don't want to be good! Do you hear me?"

She continued to mumble, and I continued to ignore every word. This was the longest journey I'd ever made. How I hated all grownups, even my Mama and Daddy.

I tried not to look back. It was hard. My mind wandered. I felt like a part of me was not there. I had to lock thoughts away in my heart so I wouldn't look back. I kept my eyes busy looking at the grape vineyards passing rapidly by, then the orange groves and the olive groves...grove-after-grove. My heart ached like never before.

Mama's coming any day now. We'll be together again.

The words circled to the tune of, "Yankee Doodle."

The social worker pulled the car into a paved driveway lined with trees all clipped like picture book cutouts. There were rose bushes by the hundreds, the earth under them freshly spaded. The lawn was mowed close to the ground, with not a weed in sight. I had never seen anything like it. It was right out of a story book, but I knew it wouldn't work for me. I just wanted to go back home.

"Now, remember what I told you, Peggy. Please behave yourself. This is a wonderful couple, and I'm sure you will be very happy here. This is just what you need."

"How in the hell do you know what I need?"

"Now, watch what you say. Where did a cute thing like you ever learn such language?"

"I know cuter language than that, if you'd like to hear."

"No, no. Come on, now. Get out, and don't forget your box."

The screen door opened just as we stepped up onto the steps, and a woman with thinning hair appeared. I saw her pink scalp between each strand of hair. She was short and as wide as she was tall. Standing behind her was a little, skinny, dried-up prune of a man.

"This is Mr. and Mrs. Barber," the social worker said. "Say 'hello', Peggy."

I gritted my teeth and took a deep breath, eyeing the distance between him and me. I could sense something strange...the way Mr. Barber looked at me. A feeling stirred deep down inside me remembering, he had the look of those men in Springville.

"Hello," I said.

Six girls peered out at me through the screen door, then scooted through it. They looked weird. One of them had her tongue hanging out of her mouth, looking as if she had chewed on it. Another held her hands up to her head, shaking them continually. Another walked funny. One, called Roberta, wore a bright shirt with huge flowers. She was as big as a moose, and looked part man. She had a hump on her back. The smallest of the bunch, with a cute, pixie face, got so close I could feel her breath, "That's Roberta. We call her Berta for short."

Another shouted, "Don't pay no attention to Berta. She never knows what she's talking about." They all laughed.

Berta screamed, "I do too know!" Her lips seemed to cover her whole face. In a booming voice, deeper than any man's, she screamed, "I do too know what I'm talking about. Mama, did you hear what Cora said?" She got right in my face with her big, booming voice. Spit flew everywhere when she talked. "Don't listen to them. You're going to be our new sister, huh? Huh? Aren't you?"

"Sister? Did I hear you say sister? I'm sure as hell not your sister! You look like a retard, or something."

Mrs. Barber leaped from the screen door. "Did I hear you call my girl a 'retard'? Listen, there's one thing we'd better get straight right now" she pointed a finger at me. "I will not have you making fun of my girls. Just 'cause they don't quite look like you and aren't quite as smart as you, don't give you the right to make fun of them!"

I stifled a laugh. This was the first person who had ever thought I was smart. "Well, look at them. They sure as hell look dumb to me. I never saw anybody who looked like them."

Mrs. Barber's eyes flashed. "Just because they look different doesn't give you any right to make fun of them. They have feelings too, just like you."

Mrs. Cunningham, the social worker, spoke under her breath. "You know, Peggy's mother left the home at the end of April. Here it is almost the end of July, and this is the third home I've put her in. I do hope you can work with her." "Well, you might as well take me with you, 'cause I'm not staying here. I want to be with my brothers and sisters, and I'm going to be."

"Peggy, dear. How often do I have to tell you, we don't have a home big enough right now to put all of you together." "Oh yes you do! Why don't you take all these retards away and bring my brothers and sisters here?"

"Oh no you don't!" Mrs. Barber screamed. "These are my darlings. I've had some of them since they were babies." "Well, I have two darling baby sisters to replace your babies."

"Now Peggy, we simply can't do that right now. We are looking for a home for all of you."

The girls led me to their room. It was one long room with eight single beds lined up along both sides of the room.

The "dormitory" they called it. The bath was down the hall. Two of the girls helped me unpack my box. They were being nice to me, acting thrilled to have a new sister. I didn't understand why they thought I was their sister, I wasn't a sister to anybody but Rita and Kathy.

Long after supper, I heard a strange noise outside the window. "What's that?"

One girl said, "Oh, it's just Daddy Barber. He watches us at night. He won't hurt you. He just likes to watch."

I didn't walk, and I didn't run—I leaped from that room, screaming as loud as my lungs could scream. Out into the backyard, I went. Sure enough, there was that old man, standing with his hands on the window sill, looking in.

Everyone came out into the yard, even Mrs. Barber. They all tried to coax me to go back into the house. Mrs. Barber didn't seem surprised at all. The girls begged and pleaded with me to go back into the house.

Mr. Barber, with his hands in his pockets, walked toward me. Bending down, he made his head level with mine. I looked him right in his eyes. The eyeballs moved from side to side and jumped up and down in the sockets. I'd never seen eyes like that before. His eyes were clear blue—clear, like the rivers.

I didn't take my eyes off his. I stared him down.

One of the girls said, "You won't peek no more, will ya', Daddy Barber, will ya?"

"Say you won't, Daddy Barber," pleaded another. "That's the only way we can get her back in the house."

"He won't hurt you, Peggy!" said another girl. "He just likes to watch us. Don't you, Daddy Barber?"

I sat in a hammock. I didn't sleep at all and never closed my eyes once.

Before daylight the next morning, Mrs. Barber drove me into town and left me on the steps of the welfare office. She didn't even wait for them to open. She drove away, leaving me on the steps in the dark, alone.

I really wasn't afraid when I'd been alone in the mountains in Springville, because Patches had been with me. He had been my guardian angles, protecting me from mountain lions, coyotes and creatures of the night. I was soon to find there were other kinds of predators who prayed on little girls, and there were no Patches to guard me.

CHAPTER TWENTY-THREE

The Visalia Welfare waiting room was enormous, with hundreds of waiting people. They turned and stared as the social worker told me to sit on the high bench. Gobs of small children with snotty noses hung onto their mommies crying. Others had sticky jam hands and a sandwich squashed in their fingers.

Something inside me seemed to stutter. My head filled to overflowing with the noise, and angry panic made me want to shove these people out a window. I hoped that I wouldn't have one of those breathing attacks while sitting on the hard bench.

My beautiful Mama is coming and I know she is, I kept telling myself.

The case worker at the window watched me intently with bird-like eyes. I jumped down off the bench and ran out the door and down the long stairway.

Clusters of people lined the steps, some talking, some smoking, and some just sitting quietly. Some were dressed ragged like me. Blacks and Mexicans mingled with men who swaggered around in leather jackets and jeans, dressed like cowboys. Winos sat on the pavement and stood in corners. Many reeked like the bars in Springville.

High on the building above were hundreds of pigeons. Their wings flapped noisily and their feet stretched out just before they touched the rooftop. I looked toward the mountains and could still see the mountains where I lived. I'm not far from home. I know that I can find my way.

My Mama is home now and she's coming for me. The internal words attempted to blot out the roar of chatter. A social worker ran to the door holding it open. "Peggy!" she called out. "Peggy, come back in here. Stay here until someone has time to take you elsewhere."

I followed her back. She pointed to the bench.

"Now sit here until I have time to find a place for you." She went back down the long corridor, her high heels clicking all the way.

My feet didn't touch the floor. I sat with my shoulders slumped, hands tightly clenched in my lap. I swung my legs back and forth and looked at the dirt in the cracks of the big, wooden floor...listening, waiting. Every time I thought about getting up from the bench, somebody with their arms stacked high to the ceiling with papers came out and called out names. I listened for mine.

In the distance, I heard names being called, and heard the loud echo of footsteps, fast and heavy. A woman behind the glass looked at me from behind a big stack of papers. Her voice sounded demanding and cruel.

A constant stream of people prowled the entrance, spilling containers of liquid and toting a diaper bag or lunches. Inside were rows of benches filled with people, bored, scampering children tripping over outstretched legs, and weary mothers pretending not to notice. Small groups laughed and joked, and seemed to know each other. Young mothers paraded with children trailing after, with outstretched hands. Children whooped through the halls and on the landing outside at the top of the stairway.

A man in a corner stubbed out his cigarette and examined his fingers. He frowned and rubbed at the rusty stains between his fingers. He lit another cigarette as he continued looking at his stained skin. Another huddled in the corner just outside the entrance. Slung over his arm was a tattered pea-green jacket with faded initials printed across the breast. I saw what was left of a half-eaten sandwich wrapped in paper, which poked out of one pocket for a breath of fresh air. I carefully watched everyone who entered the heavy doors, expecting my Mama or one of my brothers to step through at any moment.

This is it! This is the day I've been waiting for.

My Mama and my brothers are in one of those office. She's come after us, it's a surprise, yep! I can't wait. I'll show them stupid people. Mama will run for me with arms outstretched. She'll hug and kiss me, too. My Mama wants me. The thoughts comforted me.

The curiosity of the other children drove me nuts. Every one of them took turns coming over to ask me where my Mama was. One asked me if the social worker was my Mama.

"That is not my Mama, stupid," I snapped. "My Mama is beautiful."

They'd ask, "Is she coming back? Why did she go off and leave you?" The questions were never-ending. The hullabaloo was simply too much to tolerate much longer.

Jumping up with my hands on my hips, I yelled, "How in the hell do you think I know? Are you stupid or something?"

Or I'd say, "Why don't you mind your own damn business. I'm not a mind reader." I was full of hatred, anger, and rage because I longed for my brothers and sisters.

At long last, a social worker came out motioned for me to follow her. She walked at a steady pace. I had to run to keep up with her. Her head darted about rapidly, searching the doorways as we passed. She led me into a room full of old oak furniture, scarred with cigarette burns.

The office had gray walls, with a heavy oak desk and gray metal filing cabinets. There were worn, oak benches in a line behind me, battered and scarred like old wooden soldiers. There were no pictures or calendars on the bare walls, no pencils or tablets nor folders on the desk. The room looked like it was hardly ever used.

The woman put me at a desk and handed me a hamburger and a bottle of milk. She told me that when I finished my lunch, I was to remain in the room and wait for her. She said she'd be back for me and flounced off in a snit of annoyance. She reminded me of a rubber band—if I dared to ask one little question, she'd snap my head right off.

The room was so hot. My stomach began a rolling surge and felt like it was going down a fast elevator. The harder I tried to hold it in, the worse it was. I clamped my teeth together, thinking I could keep the food from coming up.

That didn't work, though. It spewed out between my teeth—big chunks of hamburger. The milk was still cold. It went everywhere, all over me, the desk, and the floor. I wished I hadn't eaten it all, but I loved hamburgers. I had never had many, and never a whole, warm one all to myself.

I wiped my mouth with the hem of my dress, then wiped the tops of my feet on the back of my dress. I ran to the door to get someone to help me, but saw no one as it was quiet out in the hall. Standing there for a long time, I finally went back to the desk and to dissipate the putrid odor, I left the door open. Also, I could yell if someone came by.

I went to the window. The windows were massive and way too high for me to see out. It was quiet everywhere. It had been so noisy before, but now there wasn't a sound. My mind took up the slack:

I wish I could make all this go away! If someone would just tell me how my brothers are. Are they still where I last saw them, or have they been moved to another foster home? I don't trust these stupid social workers. I'm going to find my brothers...I've got to...I know I can. I watched the directions carefully coming here so that I know I can find my way back to them.

I finally fell asleep on the big bench, waiting for someone to come. The scars on it had been caused by a passing parade of humanity caught in the clutches of "the system". More scars were about to be inflicted on me, but it all began in such an apparently innocent way.

CHAPTER TWENTY-FOUR

I loved her from the moment I first saw her. She was like a fairy princess, small, fine-boned, and porcelain-skinned—skin which was almost transparent. I'd never in my life seen anyone, anywhere, as pretty and graceful. Her hair was long and dark, pinned into a bun at the nape of her slender neck. She wore ruby-red lipstick and gobs of mascara. She looked fragile, with the suggestion of an oriental look about her.

She sat beside me on the bench in the Visalia Welfare Office. Long, fuzzy wisps of hair escaped her bun, caressing the back of her neck. Reaching, she took my hand. Her hands were soft, even softer than my baby sister's, I thought. Her nails were long and polished bright red.

Keeping my head down, not looking directly at her, I thought, this lady loves me, her hands tell me so. I'd never had anybody hold my hands. It was a wondrous moment. I felt accepted, loved as I'd never been. At that moment, I wanted to throw myself into her arms.

My fingernails! Hers were so pretty, I mustn't let her see mine. Trying to calm the wild knocking in my chest, I listened to her soft voice. I was embarrassed for her, convinced that she was crazy for wanting me.

Many rings circled her delicate fingers. One ring was large and heart-shaped with a big, green stone in the middle with tiny hinges on one side. She opened it so I could see. There was a puff of cotton with perfume inside. She put her ring to my nose so I could smell. The fragrance lingered in the air for a long time. I had never seen anything or smelled anything like that before, ever. It smelled so pretty, just like many women from the bars.

She wore a full-skirted, red and purple plaid sun dress with a matching bolero open in the front, and red high-heels. I'd never seen high heels like hers. They were perfect, without a scratch. Her legs were perfectly formed, with the seams of her stockings straight up the back.

I found myself wondering, why this lady would sit in a room and hold my hand. I had no idea what it all meant. I was an ugly little girl and not at all smart; therefore, I could scarcely believe why she fussed over me.

She said her name was Geraldine Crosby, but that everyone called her "Jeri" for short. She asked me about the mess I'd left in the room. I told her I had gotten sick to my stomach. She asked me if the hamburger made me sick, and I told her everything I ate made me sick.

Her bosom, rounded and pink, was nothing like my Mama's hanging titties. Jeri cradled my head against her chest. "There, there," she crooned, pressing my head tight against her soft, warm breasts. It reminded me of my very first day of school, when my classmates were being hugged by their Mommies. I had always longed for hugs and to bury my face against my Mama's warm belly while her arms protected me. I had a fleeting wish that those old stupid kids in Springville could see me now!

It was a hasty hug, but I loved it. It didn't deter me from hoping that the next time it would last longer. The putrid smell of vomit didn't seem to bother Jeri one tiny bit.

"It's going to be all right, you poor pitiful orphan," she said, patting my head. "We're going to make everything 'normal' for you."

"Orphan"...orphan—the word sounded so lonesome.

Normal? What is that... "normal?"

I gazed appreciatively at this lady as she bent over me, cleaning away the dried residue of my stomach's rebellion. I saw things that I hadn't noticed before: a tiny nose, sculptured and daintily sprinkled with freckles across it. Long fluttering eyelashes occasionally kissed her cheeks.

I inhaled her heady, sweet smell while my eyes fixed on the mesmerizing sight of her as she fidgeted and fussed over me. Jeri seemed to sparkle when she smiled while listening to me.

Stroking my head like some kind of fairy godmother she said, "I imagine you hate everybody. But now things are going to be okay." Her voice was silky smooth.

Arms folded, she stared at me with a piercing look. I couldn't read her mind, but in a way I felt sad, not able to look away. Her clear blue eyes probed mine.

"How would you like to go home with me and be my little girl?" she asked.

There must be something wrong with this woman. No one has ever wanted me. She just doesn't know what she's getting in for, my mind warned. Suddenly flying out the room, she told me she knew where to find clean clothes.

The social worker returned with her. Their arms were draped with clothes. Each of them held dresses against me to see which one would fit. We found one that was rumpled, but clean.

"Peggy, where are your shoes?" the social worker asked. "Oh, I don't have any," I rubbed one foot against the other. "But that's okay. I don't need none."

"Any," Jeri corrected. "Excuse me, I shouldn't have said that."

The social worker seemed surprised. "You mean you didn't have on any shoes when you came in?"

"No."

"You've been in three foster homes, and no one bought you shoes?"

"At the Marshall's, I wore Shelly's shoes. I had to give 'em back when I left."

Jeri said we'd go straight from the Welfare Office and buy shoes. "We're going to wipe that slate clean and start all over. That's what we're going to do with you, Peggy." She took my hand.

A warning flag seemed to flutter inside me. I liked being in control, which I normally was with my brothers, but I knew I wasn't in control here. I gave Jeri a studied look trying to see inside her. I just knew this woman was up to something else. She really didn't want me. No one had ever liked me, except my brothers and sisters…not even the social worker or Mrs. Marshall, especially not stupid Shelly.

Wipe the slate clean, what does that mean? I wanted a pair of shoes, my very own shoes. I just couldn't imagine how it felt to have my own shoes. I wondered, would they fit? Will they be too long, or too short so that my toes will scrunch up at the end and hurt? I can't wait to find out how they look. My heart thumped madly in keen excitement.

Walking proudly out of the Welfare Office and down the steps, I grinned as those kids stared at Jeri... beautiful Jeri holding my hand. It was July 27, 1948, and I was going to get my very first pair of shoes.

Walking down Main Street, she still had my hand. It didn't seem to matter to her one bit that I was barefooted and my dress was badly wrinkled.

Going into J.C. Penney's, she stopped in the bathing suit section and had me try on bathing suit after bathing suit.

"My brothers and me swim naked at home," I told Jeri. "Sometimes we swim in our clothes though. I don't need no bathing suit. Just the shoes."

Jeri looked down at me. A horrified look marred her beautiful face. "What did you say?"

I felt a chill seep deep down into my bones. "Mickey and me, we don't need no bathing suit. We swim naked."

"My brothers and I," Jeri said, in a tone that was chipped from ice. "Mickey and I. We do not need a bathing suit. Never say, 'Mickey and me.' It's not proper grammar. The correct way is, 'We don't need a bathing suit.' You'll learn all that with time."

Grammar, what was that? All these words that I've never heard before. Oh well, like she said, I'll learn all this dumb stuff. That's all it is, dumb stuff. I done just fine the way I talked before.

As for the nakedness, that's okay," Jeri said, smiling. "I'm an artist, and I see nothing wrong with the naked body. But I think we need a swim suit."

She bought me a knit two-piece bathing suit. She also purchased my first pair of sandals, white with buckles on the side, as well as a pair of shoes called "Oxfords." Two pairs of shoes of my very own! The words danced in my head.

We tried on dress after dress. I was tired, but I was so excited. She said that these clothes cost her a lot of money… money that she didn't have.

If she don't have money, how did she buy'em? Oh, I know how. Mickey, and me, oops, Mickey and I, don't need no money either.

Jeri embraced me. I giggled, and actually felt like crying at the same time We were both laden with shopping bags walking hand-in-hand back to Jeri's car. I walked with my head down as I just couldn't take my eyes off my new shoes. I asked her again if she was going to take the shoes away from me, and if they were really all mine. It felt so strange not to feel the pavement and not have my toes pinched. The shoes were so pretty and shiny.

Jeri kept telling me to walk tall, straight, with my head up.

"I can't," I said. "I want to watch my feet. I like my shoes." My very own shoes. My head was spinning in circles. I just couldn't imagine what I'd done to deserve not one, but two pairs of shoes.

We walked down the wide street lined with small parks. Hundreds of trees spread a leafy canopy over the walkway. Jeri helped me into the car. It was the first time I'd ever had someone help me. Usually, I was shoved or pushed. Even Mrs. Cunningham, with her hand on my back, shoved me into her car. Jeri had a station wagon with wooden doors, almost like the social worker's, only her's was dark red. It was new, and had that new smell. She helped me smooth out my dress so it wouldn't wrinkle more.

"It don't matter," I told her. "It's all wrinkled anyway."

"It doesn't matter," she corrected. "Never say 'don't.' You'll learn proper English. From here on, none of your dresses will ever be wrinkled. This little girl is going to shine." She smiled. "We're going to put all those problems behind you, Peggy."

Boy! Maybe I'll look like all those girls in Springville. I thought. I wished they could see me now.

I really didn't know what she was talking about, but for now, it didn't matter. All I wanted were my brothers and sisters back. I knew Mama was really mad by now.

Jeri pulled the car out onto the street, and we drove across the Santa Fe railroad tracks that ran alongside the Welfare Office. She drove around the block and headed toward the mountains.

As the crow flies, it is only a short trip from Springville to Visalia, then up the mountain and on to Three Rivers. But it was to be a long epic journey for me.

Visalia was an oasis dotted with oaks standing on tiptoe stretching out of a flat, brown landscape in the blistering summer's heat. On the way, Jeri told me about the little town of Three Rivers where she lived with her husband, Hunter.

"Why don't you like men? she asked. "Oh, I don't know. They hurt."

She told me I would like this man because he was nice. He was different, she said. She told me they were dancers. They traveled, working long days and nights with performance exhibitions and television shows. She told me they couldn't have children, and she'd always wanted a little girl just like me.

I looked at her warily. This was just about the strangest thing I'd ever heard. No one had ever wanted me. What was with this lady anyway? My mind taunted that she'd take me back to that stupid welfare place, just like everybody else did.

Jeri tried to question me about my family, but I just wanted to keep them locked in my heart. She told me that I'd have a fresh start.

My mind instantly rebelled. I don't want a fresh start! I don't want to forget! I want my Mama, brothers, and my sisters back. That's what I want...but I want to keep the shoes. I've waited so long for those sisters, and now they are both gone, just like that—with a snap of the fingers...gone. Just like a puff of smoke. Poof! Gone. Both of them! How could that be? This stupid lady doesn't know nothing. She never even had no kids. How does she know what I want?

Jeri drilled me on how a child should act and speak and behave in public. Every time I opened my mouth, Jeri corrected my grammar. It seemed as though I couldn't say one thing right. I'd never had anyone do that. I'd always gotten along just fine.

"Oh, there's plenty of time," Jeri said. "You'll learn. You're going to be like any other 'normal' kid."

Normal? That word again. My mind closed in on me. I wonder exactly what it means? I wish I wasn't so different. I feel like I'm in a deep, black hole and can't get out, with nothing to hold onto. Just like the first time I fell into that cave with Patches. Patches...where is he? My brothers. Where are they? Are they still at that stupid old snaggle- toothed woman's house?

Jeri drove up the winding mountain road. It was a long, slow drive. We went right by the mountain where I'd lived with my family, and right by Highway 65 where Mickey chased the social worker's car, wearing that dress. I didn't tell Jeri. Keeping that to myself might come in handy in case I decided to run away. After all, I might not like this lady.

Brown from the hot summer sun, the mountains looked like home, with huge trees and gnarled trunks. Oak trees grew thick at the edge of the road, along with white- trunked buckeyes with their tall, white plumes and green limbs blowing in the wind. Massive rocks nested amid the trees. A cowboy crawled under a barbed wire fence and waved as we passed.

I looked back at him and down the hill behind me. The valley floor spread out in a patchwork of colors. Highway 198 wound up the side of the mountain.

"Do you know that man?" I asked.

"No, but everybody waves to everyone else up here. You're going to live here where it's safe. Nobody locks their houses at night, or their cars."

"It was like that in Springville. My brothers and me went into the houses when no one was home and took food for our babies. We took only food...nuthin' else."

"You stole?" Her quick intake of breath showed she was startled.

"Sure we stole. How else would I feed my babies?"
"Well, I don't know, but I'd never steal from my neighbors."
"You might not, but I sure would and did, and I'm damn proud of it."

"Now, now, careful with your language. My dear, you have a lot to learn and I hope that I'll be able to teach you, with time I suppose." She murmured under her breath, "This will be a real challenge."

I gazed out the car window, barely noticing the scenery rushing by, as I wished I could be at home with Patches and my brothers. The images of Mickey wearing that stupid dress, chasing me down the street were still locked in my mind. The curtains of my family just wouldn't close. Memories hung in my mind like cobwebs.

Three Rivers, California, population under six hundred, including children, is an unincorporated town forty miles from Visalia at the gateway to Sequoia National Park. It has no mayor. There are three churches, two gas stations, one school, no library, and it's crime free.

Some people can't look past their noses. It's a tiny community, so when somebody does do something, it's blown out of proportion. Secrets are hard to keep. Everyone knows everyone else's business.

I studied the wood houses as we passed. All the houses on the side of the mountain were built high on the hills. On the other side were two markets, one with gas pumps out front. We passed the post office and a restaurant in a round building called the "Buckaroo". I could see the Keweah River rushing by. Another restaurant was on the river's side of the road, with windows all the way around.

Jeri pointed to the school as we drove by. It wasn't nearly as big as the Springville school. She drove slowly around horseshoe curves which wound up a hill, past the Presbyterian Church. Jeri said that she and Hunter were members, and that I'd go with them too. I'd always wanted to go to church.

"They threw me out of church in Springville," I told her. "I'll tell you something, Peggy. No one will throw you out here. I'll see to that. You are going to be a 'normal' kid."

Normal? There it is again! I wish she'd tell me what it is. I'm sure as hell not going to ask! NORMAL. I tried to spell it.

Along the way, we stopped to see Hunter, Jeri's husband, who was building their new home. He looked down from high on a ladder. His curly hair fell across his brow. He was holding nails between his lips and he would pause, let the hammer droop, and take one of the nails from his teeth as though it were a piece of food.

We stepped out of the car and walked toward Hunter. I watched the hammer rising and falling. The muscle in his arm tightened with the motion of the tool. Sometimes he'd stop to wipe the hair back with his knuckles, mumbling something around a mouthful of nails. He wore a dirty, khaki slouch hat, khaki work pants, and a blue work shirt rolled way up past his elbows and covered by a funny apron with big square brass buckles on a leather belt. His shoes were cracked, and the soles were swollen and boat-shaped from obvious years of sun, dust and being bathed in rain. His face was wrinkled, like the leather of his shoes. I'd never seen a man wear an apron before.

He dropped the hammer to his side and took the nails from his mouth. Dropping down two steps at a time, he came running toward us. He grinned at me, and all he said was, "Uh huh," grinning and shaking his head as though in approval.

After I'd gotten acquainted with Hunter, we were back on our way, going north. The Crosbys' house was a couple of miles off the main highway, on Dinely Road. Crossing over two cattle guards, the tires crunched over the gravel driveway down along the river. Both sides of the drive were overgrown with hanging vines, thick blackberry bushes, redbud, and manzanita. The undergrowth was thick with dark oak leaves. It reminded me of Springville.

The house was massive. Jeri said in the early 1900's, the house had been a youth hostel. She also told me that I could pick out my own colors of paint and wallpaper for my brand new bedroom, in the new house. I'd never slept in a room by myself.

The old hostel was brown-shingled like a chocolate iced cake, from the roof to the ground. As we pulled up to the house, I saw many cars parked nearby. Jeri told me they had a great swimming hole, and their friends swam there every day. As Jeri stopped the car in the driveway, dozens of people came running up from the river, wearing bathing suits with colorful towels wrapped around them.

Jeri was surprised. Everyone talked and laughed at the same time. I was frightened. No one had ever been happy to see me. After I got out of the car, I stood by watching shyly. All the young girls ran to my side, singing, "Playmate, come out and play with me."

Taking turns, the girls reached out and tried to hold my hand…just like the little girls did in Springville when someone was having a birthday party. My heart pounded in my chest, and I was filled with a terror I'd never felt before. I just knew one of these girls was going to call me, "Cootie." Maybe one would push me, pull my hair, or even pinch me. I knew it had to happen any minute now.

"Peggy, it's a surprise party—a baby shower, all for you".
"I don't want no goddamn baby shower. I'm not a baby!"

Horrified faces looked at me. There was a sudden intake of breath from Jeri.

"I know how that is! I remember how it was when I butted into parties at home they teased me and chased me away," I shouted.

"Nobody's going to chase you away here," Jeri said. "It's alright, you just wait and see."

I stood my ground. "And besides, in Springville the girls told me I had to be invited, and I never got an invitation." "In this case dear, you don't need an invitation. This party is for you, and it's a surprise."

I'd never had a girl hold my hand. My heart pounded with fear as I waited to be shoved or kicked.

Everybody went down to the river while Jeri took me inside to put on my new bathing suit.

"First of all Peggy, we must watch our mouth. I understand that there is so much for you to learn and you don't always know better, but we do not curse, and we never use the name of God in vain." She smoothed my hair back into place.

I didn't really know what she was talking about but I knew what I had said was wrong. I asked her if I could just stay in the house. She was surprised that I didn't want to go swimming with my "new friends," as she called them. I didn't want to go swimming or be with the other children. She didn't seem to understand that I was frightened by all the commotion and insisted that I go to the river.

I climbed over a rock wall along the river where ooze and slime came out of the moist, dark foundation from the high water table. Fungus grew on the cement walls of a huge old swinging bridge, as they referred to it. It was constructed of old faded splintering, boards held up by four cables, each bigger than my arm. Far away, I heard laughter and water splashing. I was so excited, my heart beat like a tiny lizard I had caught once. When I had held him to my chest, I could feel his heart beat against my own chest. The nearby picnic table was covered with checkered oilcloth. Gifts, stacked high, were wrapped in "baby" gift-wrapping paper. A huge banner stretched between volleyball poles was painted with the words, "It's a girl." A cake with pink frosting repeated, "It's a girl." A freezer of ice cream, paper plates, and matching napkins were on the table with a big, pink plastic stork carrying a baby bundle.

I'd always wanted to taste a birthday cake. I had always yearned for a birthday party. I'd never had one before and remembered one time asking my mother, "What's a birthday, Mama?" She just stared off into the distance and never answered.

I had no idea what this was all about, but my heart pounded at the sight of the cake. I couldn't wait to get my hands into it.

"It's all for you," Jeri said.

My very own cake. All for me. I'd waited and wanted a cake of my very own for so long. Suddenly my mind put on the brakes. Why is this cake for me? Must be some kind of a trick. I gotta' be real careful, these people are gonna' trick me. All of a sudden I thought I had the answer. These people thought that Jeri was bringing home one of my baby sisters and she'd gotten me instead. The group of girls anxiously waited for me to open my gifts, but I just knew that they weren't for me—they were for one of my baby sisters.

Dumbfounded, I refused to open the gifts.

"Come on Peggy, dear. Why won't you open your presents? They're for you, dear."

"I'm afraid they'll take'em back."

Everybody burst out in laughter. Even their laughter frightened me. I knew they were not happy for me. They were just happy for the Crosbys.

"Come on, Peggy, open your presents," the girls begged.

"Those ain't my damn presents," I screamed back at them. I saw their awful looks and ran to the other side of the house, but didn't go in because it wasn't my house.

Jeri followed and stood looking down on me. Her look was icy enough to freeze water, but I didn't care. I knew I'd said something bad.

"We don't speak that way here. Now aren't you ashamed of yourself? These are going to be your new friends. Just look at how you've behaved!"

"Them ain't my friends!" I screamed back. "They," Jeri said.

"What...huh?"

"They. They aren't. We don't say 'them' and 'ain't,'" she said.

"You don't speak that way, but I sure as hell do," I yelled back. "I don't want those damn kids for my friends. They won't like me, you just wait and see. I didn't choose them for my friends, you did."

"Now, little lady, you're going to get your first lesson. I'm so ashamed of you. Look at what I've done for you. I've taken you into my home and given you a home when no one else wanted you. The three other foster homes you've been in didn't keep you. Not even your own mother wanted you." She shook one manicured finger at me.

"I didn't want this damn party. Besides, it's not my birthday. My birthday is in March. This is the dumbest party I've ever seen, and all these people are dumb. Besides, I didn't ask you to come and get me." I could feel my fists balling up. "Whoever told you my mother didn't want me, and what in the hell do you know about it, anyway?" I took off running up the graveled driveway.

In the background, I could hear Jeri's voice screams, "Hunter, Hunter, she's running away! Hunter, come help me."

CHAPTER TWENTY-FIVE

When Hunter caught up with me, he gently persuaded me to come back.

That night, we went out to dinner. Jeri wanted me to meet all the Three Rivers folks.

The parking lot was packed. Everyone in town seemed to be there. Hordes of people ran to greet us the minute we stepped into the restaurant. There were all kinds of people bent on grabbing and hugging me. Many had more gifts. Women were kissing me and carrying on something awful. Some commented on how much I looked like Jeri—enough to be her very own daughter.

Their preacher, Reverend Pooly, was there. It seemed the word had gotten out to come to the restaurant to look over the Crosbys' new daughter.

"You're on display," Jeri said. "Everyone knew yesterday that we were getting you. They are all here to meet you."

"Are you sending me back if they don't like me?" I asked.

Jeri laughed. Even Hunter cracked a smile. He hadn't said much.

"No, no," Jeri said. "You're going to be the perfect daughter for us. Things will be all right, just wait and see."

Jeri ordered a steak, for me. I wanted a milkshake and hamburger, but she said that tonight was a celebration. So we had steak. There would be plenty of time for hamburgers and milkshakes.

Jeri told Hunter that my bad manners weren't going to be washed away in a few days. Hunter nodded. He still didn't say a word.

This was my first meal in a restaurant, and I didn't know what to do. I shifted my position watching the people eat. I was fascinated with everything. The butter was molded into small squares and had a flower pattern on each square. There was a single, fresh flower in a tall, thin, bud vase. The water glasses clinked with clear ice. Everything was so pretty.

"This was all done just for you." Jeri waved one hand expansively over the table.

I blushed with embarrassment.

The server put a big old sizzling steak down in front of me. I knew it was hot, but that didn't bother me any. Picking it up with both hands I bit into it. A big chunk of meat hung from my mouth.

Jeri didn't seem very surprised. Hunter choked on his coffee and had a coughing spell. Someone hit him on his back.

Jeri pulled her chair over to me and spoke, in her calm, sweet, baby-like voice. "It's all right. We all do silly things, even me." She cleaned my hands with a napkin, then picked up the knife and fork. She showed me how to hold the steak down on the plate with the fork while cutting with the knife. "If you're in question about how to eat, just watch someone else to see how they do it." She called the knife and fork "utensils," just like Mrs. Marshall.

With my mouth full, I spoke around a big chunk of dangling meat, "All these rules! Just like at Mrs. Marshall. Rules and more rules."

"I know, dear," she patted my hand. "It must sound terrible to a darling little girl, but you're going to learn and I'll never have to say another word, you'll just know. You're going to be a quick study, I just know you are."

I took the knife and fork and tried to do what she showed me. It was hard. I was clumsy, but I managed to cut off a few bites. Finally, in frustration I slammed down my knife and fork. "This is stupid!" I announced, picking up the pieces of meat with my fingers and stuffing them into my mouth all at one time.

Patting my hand again Jeri said, "Just go slower. It will get easier."

I proceeded to cut up all of the steak. I had all these tiny pieces on my plate, just like Jeri wanted. It did seem like I was catching on.

"No, no, no!" she scolded. "Just cut one bite at a time. Eat that bite, then cut another."

Dropping my knife and fork into my plate I said, "Do this, do that. No! Not that way. See, like this. How do you expect me to remember all this?" Looking around the room I saw people watching me. Many smiled, and some turned their heads away in embarrassment. When I looked their way again, some of the kids snickered. That stupid old Fanchon tried peeking when I wasn't looking.

I knew they were making fun at me, just like the people in Springville.

After I'd eaten, I started gagging. I put one hand over my mouth, and my cheeks bulged. I tried despartately to stop it.

Jeri thought I was choking.

Then it came. I barfed—all over me, the table, the floor. Huge chunks of steak. Little kernels of corn and french fries. To make things even worse, Hunter went running off, out the front door with his hands over his mouth.

Jeri dragged me out the front door and around the back of the restaurant to the rest room. It took her forever, but she scrubbed my clothes and cleaned me off.

I heard Hunter in the room next door. He was barfing, too. At least I'm not the only one who gets sick the minute I eat, I thought.

That first night, Jeri undressed me and put on my nightie. "I always sleep in my clothes," I said.

"We don't sleep in our clothes here," Jeri said. "We sleep in nightclothes. It's not healthy to sleep in your clothes. Besides, it's not comfortable."

Getting into bed, I pulled the covers up and Jeri kissed me right on the mouth. That was the first time I'd ever been kissed. Along with her hugs and kisses, her soft lips felt good. I'd never felt anything like that before.

I had something Jeri called linens, and they were just like those that I'd had in the TB institution—smooth, clean, and fresh.

Long after Jeri had gone to bed, I got out of bed and slipped out of the nighty, pulling on my pedal pushers, and shirt. I crept back in bed and pulled the covers under my chin. I knew Jeri would be in to check on me during the night, because she'd said so. I lay back and listened with my eyes closed, and felt myself slipping away. I knew at the end of darkness I would awaken to the sight of a friendly face, and the sound of kindness, but I just didn't know how long it would last.

During the first week, I itched to go into Jeri's bedroom. That was the one room I wasn't allowed in, because of her doll collection. From the open door, I could see the window seat with row-after-row of dolls. She had hundreds of them. She said she'd had them since she was a small child. All of them were porcelain—some just porcelain faces, some tiny, porcelain miniatures like real-life baby dolls. Some had rag bodies, and some were jointed at the elbows and knees. One was fair-haired.

Jeri said their hair was made from real human hair. One doll had tiny glass buttons that ran down the front of a silvery dress. That doll had high-heeled shoes that could be removed, and real earrings made of pearls. One was a real mommy doll, and Jeri said she was more fragile and precious than all the others. They were even prettier than dumb old Shelly's dolls. She even had one teenager with three whole changes of clothes, right down to shoes and bonnets and everything.

Later, Jeri taught me how to polish all her precious china, but she wouldn't even let me inside the room with her cherished dolls. Jeri said I was too old for a doll. I guess I was, but I'd never had my very own doll. When she said that a sudden thought presented itself. Well, Jeri, look how old you are, and you have hundreds of dolls.

When we cleaned the upstairs, Jeri would fuss with her dolls. It was like she knew exactly how every little leg crossed, where every crease in the dress should be, where every curl fell over which shoulder of each doll, even right down to how the bows on the bonnets were tied.

During my first few days at Jeri's, she took me on a tour of the house and told me all the "do's" and "do not's." There was so much for my brain to remember. Not Mickey and me, but Mickey and I, and my brothers and I. All that proper grammar I had to learn. It was baffling. Don't say "don't." Don't say "ain't." Singular is "was;" plural, more than one, is "were." How confusing. Left-handed people have problems. Mental problems. That makes sense, as I have problems. Don't do this, but do that. I wondered if I'd ever remember it all.

One day we entered Jeri's bedroom and walked over to her dolls. I fairly drooled at the beautiful sight. I couldn't pull my eyes away. Excitedly, I picked one up.

Jeri snatched the doll out of my hand. It flew through the air and landed on the floor. She looked at me sternly. "See what you made me do?"

That's what Shelly did.

I thought it was strange that all the dolls, even the one dressed in a Mexican costume, had blue eyes like Jeri's and that dumb old Shelly's. My eyes were brown. Mama and Daddy had brown eyes.

I wondered, is it something to do with the eyes. Is something wrong with people who have brown eyes? I wondered…if that had anything to do with that word "normal?"

I loved those dolls. I'd stand at the door of Jeri's room and gaze at them whenever she wasn't around. I didn't dare go in. From downstairs, Jeri could hear if I walked into her bedroom. The perfume she wore lingered in the room, a sweet floral scent. "Roses," she said.

I hovered outside her room for a while, yearning for a touch of her golden-haired dolls. They were unattainable, beyond my reach, everything delicate and soft. And I wanted it to...what? I wanted them to be mine.

Jeri told me almost from that very first day that when I grew up, they would all be mine. "Wouldn't you like that?" she asked.

On the other side of the room was a large "dressing table," she called it. The stool matched the dressing table. There were big flowers, hand carved from pecan wood, Jeri said. The dressing table had three mirrors. The two on the sides were on hinges, and she pulled them this way and that. Jeri sat on the little stool in front of the dressing table to show me how it worked. She pulled out a drawer.

I saw my reflection in the mirror. My eyes were bigger than an owl's. Sparkling back at me were row after row of shining stones-rings in special little slits, all in a line. Some rings were clear, with sparkles of pink, blue, and gold-green stones, ruby red, yellow. Jeri said that each ring had a story behind it.

I seemed to be surrounded by her voice floating around me. She went on talking in the half-teasing, half-angry tone she always used with me as she told me how precious those jewels were.

"This one," she picked up a ring, "was my very first baby ring." She put it on the end of her little finger. It didn't even come close to fitting. She picked up a big pendant and held it to her neck. "Doesn't this look good on me?" She lifted out a tray and slipped the pendant into a hidden compartment under the tray. She picked up another piece, then quickly put it away. "Oh, I don't care for this one, but I have to wear it. If I don't, Grandmother is always asking why." Carefully she put it aside.

On and on, Jeri rambled, picking up each ring, bracelet, and necklace, telling me where it came from, who gave it to her, and why. She also said that all those jewels would be mine someday.

My heart thumped with excitement. I wanted desperately to please her. I was frantic to fit myself into her mold. She must have had millions of friends and Aunties who truly loved her to give her all these things.

I wanted to try on a ring. My grubby hands, looked nothing like Jeri's. The nails were chewed to the quick. I didn't care though, I wanted one.

"Your finger wouldn't look proper with a ring," Jeri said. "It would call too much attention to your chewed nails."

Well, I still wanted one.

"All these things are precious to me...and so are you," Jeri said.

I thought, well, if I'm precious to her, why can't I touch her precious dolls or wear one of her cherished rings? Yet, I can polish her precious and valuable sterling silver and crystal. She seemed to have a way of teasing me with all her beautiful, things.

I trembled, wanting badly to touch them—just to feel the treasures in my hands. But I was no fool; I knew not to touch them.

Jeri said she came from "royalty." I didn't know what royalty meant.

Though everything of Jeri's was off-limits, the rule didn't apply to her closet. Jeri's closet was in the spare bedroom. I'd creep into her room-size closet and, with eyes closed, swirl around in the cloud of costumes and dresses and inhale her essence. She told me that what I smelled was called "Shalimar." I'd stand in the middle of the racks of clothing and wrap myself with all her long dancing dresses. The soft folds of some of her skirts were chiffon, and I could see through them. Rack-after-rack of ruffled petticoats hung in a row. I felt as if I were floating on an imaginary cloud in her closet.

For a moment, I belonged to her. Jeri was really my Mommy, my honest to goodness Mommy.

I wished, those girls in Springville could see me now.

They'd all be so envious.

Jeri's closet was something from a picture book. I swooned over her clothes. They were clothes just like I'd seen in the Sears Catalog. Everything was perfect. A lovely white lace parasol hung from the ceiling. Hat boxes were stacked high, in all shapes and sizes. Some boxes were tattered because they were old. One was red satin, some were lace, and some had big red roses. One that I will always remember was white with hand-painted cherubs swinging from the clouds, waving and winking at me. Coats hung, protected in bags. Matching shoes and bags hung in a row inside their very own tiny compartments.

Jeri said she was an artist, and she took me into a room that she called her "studio." I recognized the smell of turpentine.

"Oh, I recognize that smell. In the TB institution I had a spoonful of sugar every night with turpentine poured over it for a cough medicine."

"Now, you must be mistaken. Turpentine would kill you." "Nope. I know what I had. The nurses said it cut the phlem, whatever that is."

She gave me a strange look, "Well I don't believe that!" "Well, I don't care what you believe. I know more about that stupid TB more than you do," I answered back smartly. There were tubes of paint everywhere, with smelly paint rags and tubes of paint twisted every which way.

There were also a lot of canvases. Stacks-upon-stacks of all sizes stretched on frames. There were sketches, pencils, and charcoal drawings by the hundreds that Jeri did of her friends' children. They were grand, with their big eyes.

In the corner of Jeri's studio was a drawing board, an easel, and a long table with a cloth over it that reached clear to the floor. Behind the cloth, she stored all her supplies. There were big clumps of clay, along with funny-looking knives that she used for her carving.

It wasn't long before, I could hold a fork properly and cut a piece of meat to Jeri's satisfaction without drawing attention to myself. Jeri had taught me so well. I could set a table for eight with her lovely china and her silver. To Jeri's satisfaction I knew what to do with the salad fork, where to place the butter knife, the fish knife, and understood the difference between a red wine glass and one for white wine. Even though the Crosbys didn't drink, she had the glassware and I had to know where to place them at the table. Jeri didn't teach me to cook as she herself didn't know how, but she allowed me to learn myself. I learned well.

Every morning, Jeri sat at her dressing table and painted on her face with paint brushes. To me, they looked just like the brushes she used for her oil paintings, only these weren't full of paint. She used long, pointed ones for her lipstick, and a flat one with blunted ends for brushing powder on her eyelids. A short, stubby one was used for her eyebrows. It took her hours. She said, "Brush up and out, never down." She brushed white cream at the upper and lower corners of her eyes. She looked like a raccoon at first, but she would brush and blend, first this way and then that, always up and out. She said it opened her eyes wide. Right under the arch of her brow, she put a tiny red dot. "It lifts the eye," she said. "When you get older, everything sags, you know. Just watch me, and when you're old enough to wear makeup, you'll know how to apply it."

I often posed for Jeri. She started me out right away posing, and frequently painted me. Even when I hadn't posed, everyone commented that everything she did looked like me. I posed nude down at the river, sitting on a rock with the water up to my belly. In a couple of years, Jeri had me posing nude for a small group of other artists. I was comfortable with it. The older I got, the more I did it.

It wasn't long before I was posing nude for classes in the colleges, and other large art classes. It was the late 1940's, and there weren't many nude models. It served as a form of acting out for me.

I loved the crisp feel of the linens. I changed them every day...at least, until Jeri found out. After that, I could only change them once a week. She said it was too expensive to send them all to the laundry.

At night I lay in bed. I could see everything by the light of the moon. Jeri said this was my very own room. It had a maple dresser, low bookshelves under the window, and a bed. Jeri called it a three-quarter-size bed. The closet door was open.

The closet was as big as my bedroom. I crept out of the bed, being careful not to make any noise, and I looked into the closet. Far at the back, Jeri had long dresses in plastic containers. I didn't touch them. I just looked.

A huge box in the corner was filled to the brim with bedding. It smelled strong and strange with what Jeri called "moth balls."

It was September 17, 1948. I was eleven years old and two weeks before Jeri told me we would have to go to court. I didn't really understand what why.

With the sound of clanking chains, the courtroom came alive. It was cool inside the big building. The voices carried and echoed off the high ceilings, and people spoke in whispers, even when they didn't have to.

I watched a man in uniform lead a line of men all chained together. Their footsteps echoed, and the door creaked shut behind them. He led them to a group of oak, barrel-shaped chairs, almost right in front of me. One-by-one, he pulled the chain out that locked them to each other.

I had to appear in court. I was a witness to testify against Mama. I didn't want to be a witness. But Jeri told me I had to do this. In another way I was excited, as I wondered if I was going back with mama. From time to time, my thoughts meandered away in fear.

The courtroom was quiet when Jeri and I first entered. She held my hand. I was on the edge of my seat and really excited about getting to see Mama that morning. "Will my brothers be here too?" I whispered. She gave me that awful look I'd learn to recognize when I'd really done the worst imaginable thing which was whenever I asked about any of my brothers and sisters. I knew she didn't like for me to say one word about any of them.

A man entered first and said in a big, booming voice, "Will you all rise."

I was frightened when the judge entered, dressed in his long, black robe. The United States and the California flags stood on poles behind him. Within just minutes, the judge appeared to be asleep. The court was wild and crazy and noisy.

In the hallway outside the open door of the courtroom, I saw another line of men being led past the door. They were dressed in faded jeans and white T-shirts. They were chained together at the waist and at the ankles, and they looked dirty and dangerous.

My mind spun backward to Mama's threats I'd be put in jail. Maybe it was just a trick to get me to court. Maybe they'd chain me up with the men and put me in prison! Just like Mama said.

To the left was a large boxed-in place with chairs in a line. I wondered what all those chairs were for. Several men moved about the room. The seats squeaked as people moved in and out of them. A police officer in uniform took a deep breath and looked down at me. I looked for a way to escape but just then the door opened again, and Mama came in with a fat man dressed in a dark blue suit. He was bald. I wondered who he was. They walked past the rail and sat at a table way up front. Mama didn't even look at me. Mama doesn't recognize me. My heart sobbed. I don't look like the same little girl she left behind so long ago. I know she had to have seen me as she walked up to that table. Why did it have to be this way. I knew by her posture, her gestures that it was my Mama. I knew her stride, the way she swung her arms. Oh how I wanted to grab and hug her. But I didn't dare.

Jeri picked up my hand and held it tightly.

Why was she doing that? I didn't want Mama to see Jeri holding my hand. I knew Mama wouldn't like it. I sure hoped Mama wouldn't turn around and look at me now.

I wanted to run to her. I wanted to place my hands on her and run my fingers through her fine hair—feel whatever life might be in her after loosing her children and being beaten so badly by Daddy.

Mama never did turn around to look for me. It had been months since I'd seen my Mama. I just knew she'd be beside herself. But she wasn't. I just knew when she looked at me, she'd call out my name with emotion...but she didn't.

My heart pounded. I wondered how long my body could take the pounding.

A small, older woman occupied the little oak desk below the judge. She was white-skinned and frail. She looked angry. After shuffling through a pile of papers, the judge asked all others to clear the courtroom, "except those concerned with the case of said minor, Peggy Bearden." Looking at me he said, "Peggy Bearden, will you come forward please?"

With a sound of clanking chains, people hurried out. The courtroom hushed. I waited. I was really shaking now. I know it was noticeable because Jeri tried to hold me to keep me from shaking so much. Tears streamed down my cheeks. I'd never, ever cried like this before. I was trembling violently, snot running to the floor. Everyone searched for hankies. Jeri patted my knee, telling me it was "okay." I wanted to run, but I was afraid that I'd be taken to prison.

My mind cautioned, the officer's watching me. He knows that I want to run. That's why he's stationed here to make sure that I don't run away.

The judge leaned over a counter from high above and looked down at me. "Peggy, did your mother abandon you?" he asked me.

"What does that mean?"

"Well...did she go off and leave you alone?" "No."

Looking at me strangely, he spoke again. "Peggy, did I hear you that your mother didn't leave you alone?"

Again, I said, "No, she didn't."

Looking over his glasses, he said, "Mrs. Cunningham, will you explain this to me, please?"

The two of them whispered for a few moments. Both looked at me and shuffled through papers.

The judge asked me again, "Peggy, are you telling me you were not alone when your mother left?"

I shook my head.

"Peggy, for the court, will you answer 'yes' or 'no' so that you can be heard."

I was crying hysterically. Nobody could understand a word I said.

"Would someone please control that child," the judge demanded.

"Yes...I was not alone." "Who was with you, Peggy?"

Mumbling through tears, "My brothers and sisters." "Oh," he said. "Was there anyone else, like a neighbor or an adult?" "No."

"Did your mother leave you very often?" "Sometimes."

"I see you're now in the fourth foster home in just a short time. Are you happy with the Crosbys?"

Between every breath, I sobbed, and my hands trembled. I twisted my fingers to hold them still, but they still shook. I heard only murmurs from the judge and the man Mama was with. Why, oh, why, wouldn't Mama look at me? I was screaming inside, Mama, please look at me, Mama.

When Mama turned, for the first time in my life she was beautiful. I'd never seen her without a black eye, or busted lip, or bald spots where her hair had been yanked out. Mama went right by me without even looking. She and the man left the courtroom before anyone else. Mama never looked in my direction. Jumping up I ran out after her. Running down the hundreds of steps, I went way out into the street and watched her as she got into the car. She never turned around. I stood there jumping up and down, waving my arms, screaming "mama." Sobbing. I truly believed that she was there that day to take me home with her. I couldn't stop crying, my whole body shook. I was a burden to her. That day I pasted her face deep into my mind. I never wanted to forget how she looked, so beautiful.

Jeri caught up with me and gave me that look. She held me back while she and Mrs. Cunningham talked. I watched my Mama swing around the corner and out of sight. Before I got into the car, I stretched my neck, hoping for one tiny glimpse of her. Was that asking too much?

After court, that afternoon, Jeri took me to see BAMBI. It was my first movie. I loved Flower, the skunk. He was my favorite. I fantasized that Flower was the same skunk that Mickey and I found. Much later, when Jeri and I talked about the movie, she found that I really couldn't see it very well, and I thought it was a silent movie. That was when she found out that I couldn't see or hear.

The next movie I saw was CINDERELLA. I didn't have to fantasize. I really was just like Cinderella, only she was blonde and I was dark.

When we went to get glasses, I had to take ugly, pink frames because Jeri said so. I hated them. I couldn't pick out the frames because Jeri said those were the only ones the welfare would pay for.

"Well, why don't you pay for them yourself?" "They are too expensive for me."

"Well, my tonsils were more expensive than these stupid glasses, and you paid for that."

"Pegi, you are the most disagreeable, argumentative person that I've ever seen. Why do you always have to get your word in? Can't you be grateful for the things I do for you? Just once, show some gratitude. After all, I don't know where you would be today if I hadn't taken you in. Why can't you be normal?"

That word! What is normal? My thoughts rebelled. Why can't I be normal. Well—if somebody would just tell me what it meant, maybe I could be. How can I be normal when I don't know what it?

The next day, I went to another doctor for my hearing problem. He said my eardrums had been broken many times and that I had over an eighty percent hearing loss. I'd learned to compensate for it. There wasn't anything that could be done.

People kept asking me why my eardrums had been broken many times. I thought my hearing was fine. I didn't know what it was like to hear better, but I carried the dark secret of the beatings in an envelope of embarassment, and just shrugged off their questions.

For the first couple of years, and maybe longer, Hunter never said much to me. He seemed a bit of a wimp and henpecked. When he went swimming, he never asked me if I wanted to go. If he went to the store, he never took me. I never heard him raise his voice or curse. Hunter was a small man, slim but muscular.

As I grew older, it became obvious to me that Hunter would do anything for Jeri. He worshiped her. In fact, it seemed that everybody worshiped her, and talked baby-talk to her. Jeri talked syrupy talk to everybody else. The whole town liked her. She had more friends than anyone I'd ever known.

From the beginning, I knew Hunter cherished Jeri, and it was such a shocking reversal of how Daddy treated Mama that I studied their relationship in amazement. I'd never seen a man act the way he did with a woman. He carried Jeri's bag and opened the car door for her. He helped her at the table, even when we were at home. He'd pull his chair up beside hers after dinner and gaze into her eyes while he held her hand and the two of them just talked.

I cleared the table and did all the dishes.

Jeri was a good Christian woman. That first Sunday, I couldn't wait to go to Sunday School. Jeri told me all week about Sunday School, and I was excited. There were only about seven of us in my class, and Mr. Gray was the teacher. He was a big man with a long mustache. He was a great teaser. Right away, Mr. Gray had us praying.

I was excited, my stomach was really jumping. I'd waited so long for this. I remembered the church I'd longed to attend in Springville...the steps I'd run up searching for the man Jesus to help us…the same door I'd snuck in and they threw me out. Now maybe I could be one of them.

After church on Sundays, we went to Trembley's Drive Inn for lunch. That was the only time I could have a hamburger. The first Sunday after church, they took me to Trembleys.

"How much money did you take when they passed the money around?" I asked.

Jeri looked at me oddly.

Holding out my hand with the dollar bills scrunched in my fist, I said, "I took this much out when they passed the basket. How much did you take?"

Jeri and Hunter, looked at one another, and howled with laughter.

"Yes, Peggy, you are sure smart," Jeri said. "I think we have a smart one, Hunter." Everyone in Trembley's turned to look.

"Peggy took money out of the church offering," Jeri told them.

Everyone laughed.

Mr. Gray was there. I really liked him. He reminded me of Jake. He was funny, always laughing. He made a special point of teasing me. He came over and put his hands on my shoulder.

"That's about the smartest thing I ever heard of," he told me. "Yes, Jeri, you have one smart girl here."

That night after I went to bed, I hopped back out and knelt beside it. I vowed, I'm going to pray for my brothers and sisters, just like I learned in Sunday school. This will work. Now I know that if I pray, I'll get them back soon.

"Dear God, please keep all my brothers and sisters safe. Oh God, please bring my Mama back to me, and my brothers and sisters so we can all be together again. God, please, please bring us back together again. I promise I'll take good care of them. Amen. And God, forget my Daddy. I don't want him. Amen."

Every night for many years, I prayed that I'd be back with my brothers and sisters.

Jeri never cooked, and she didn't want to. Hunter did all the cooking. She continued to have cleaning ladies come in while I learned to clean.

There were far too many things for me to do, too many things to clean—gobs of windows that Jeri insisted I wash weekly.

Jeri made me use my right hand. She said left-handed people had mental problems and that I already had enough problems. No matter how hard I tried, Jeri always caught me using my left hand.

I tried valiantly to please her in every way. Just when I about had the grammar-thing right, now using my left hand was wrong.

The first few months I lived with them, she kept my left hand tied behind me, and only untied my hand when we were together. It was hard, and very, very confusing for me. Finally, I simply made it easier on myself by making sure I never used my left hand at all.

Another thing that Jeri changed was the spelling of my name. She changed the spelling from Peggy to "Pegi." Her name was "Jeri," so she thought it would be nice if my name matched hers. Then she changed my last name from Bearden to Crosby.

I sometimes celebrated two birthdays. It depended on how Jeri felt. If I had been good and she felt generous, I celebrated two birthdays: one birthday in March for my real birthday, the other in July for the day she got me. Most of the time, I celebrated my birthday in July. I'd never celebrated my birthday before anyway, and had even asked Mama what that word meant. So whether my birthday was in March or July didn't matter to me. I felt lucky to just have a birthday and eat cakes and ice cream.

If Jeri was mad at me, I didn't get to have either birthday. But it really didn't matter. But someone always sent me a birthday card. One of Jeri's friends always remembered.

By this time, I was quite confused. It seemed I really didn't know who I was. I certainly wasn't the same person I had started out being in Springville. The more I thought about all the changes, the more confused I became.

It made me angry when I thought about it all, and got me into a lot of trouble if I questioned Jeri. She told me that I had an "active imagination," whatever that was. I also listened when she told her friends that I was a very disturbed girl, and I'd had an unsettled childhood. I didn't understand that either.

I felt as though I were two people: Peggy Bearden and Pegi Crosby. Each one had a different set of standards. I tried hard to please Jeri, but it was all very perplexing. Many times I listened as she told her friends that I was 'A Bad Seed'. I didn't know what that was but I never forgot it. Peggy Bearden was the mean child, and Pegi Crosby was the good child. That was how I figured it in my own mind. At night, I'd fantasize about being the real me. I'd daydream about being with my brothers and sisters. My heart ached for them. I didn't miss Mama since she had made it clear in court that she didn't want me, and I certainly didn't miss Daddy, but I missed my brothers and sisters terribly. I couldn't get them out of my mind.

I had nightmares every night about the beatings from my Daddy. I had nightmares about all those babies. Babies bombed me. Nightmares of Mama's helpless screams awakened me during the night.

Jeri and Hunter were awakened from a deep sleep almost nightly by my crying out. When I didn't have nightmares, I was sleepwalking and falling down the stairs.

Everywhere I went, I stole food. If I had a pocket, I'd stuff it with food. When I was old enough and Jeri let me carry a purse, I'd stuff the purse with food. When she found out, she took the purse away. I'd stuff food into a paper napkin, paper cups...whatever I could find. I'd hide it under the seat of Hunter's car until I got home. Everywhere you looked, there would be food I'd hidden. Outside, when Hunter was gardening, he'd even find food stashed in the flower beds.

When I came in each day, they'd have all the food lined up on the table that they had found. Jeri searched my room daily, looking for food. I always had to find new hiding places. but Jeri always found them. I thought, What's wrong with me stealing food? I'm not hurting no one. I can't figure this out, I'm not hurting anyone. Why don't they want me to eat? Peggy Bearden was the one getting all the food, not Pegi Crosby.

Jeri said that I couldn't distinguish fact from fantasy. She said that I derived pleasure from telling things that were untrue, that it was an attention-getting mechanism. She called it my self-destructive imagination.

When I got into trouble, it was usually to get attention. At least, it was better than the silent treatment. I'd do anything to get into trouble. Becoming a thief got me into trouble. About the same time, I began to tell lies—or at least stretched the truth. I wasn't very good at that, either. I'd tell a lie, when the truth would have been easier. I couldn't understand the lying part. Lying protected my family and me. I had to know that I was important to Jeri, if only in a negative sense. I couldn't please her, no matter how hard I tried.

I listened while Jeri told someone that I was a kleptomaniac.

That evening, Jeri was talking with a friend who was telling her to bring me along, if I'd like to come. The lady smiled and looked at me, and said she'd enjoy having me.

I piped up and said, "I have kleptomania, you know."

Jeri laughed and said, "Oh, Pegi doesn't know what she's saying."

Later, Jeri asked me where I had heard such a thing. "I heard you tell people I had kleptomania," I told her.

She never mentioned it again. Not to where I could hear, anyway.

I did steal. I started doing it at times when Jeri wouldn't speak to me. At least the stealing seemed to get her attention. She'd scream at me. I liked that better than the silent treatment that could go on for days. It also made me feel better.

I felt like I was getting back at someone. It didn't matter who. Someone was being paid back for all my pain. It was something much, much deeper than just my Mama and Jeri. It was revenge on all society.

One dark, early morning, a dream seized me in my sleep. I was wandering in the big house when someone called my name. The sound was muffled. I was barely able to hear… or was it my poor hearing?

Sitting up in bed, I listened, hoping the voice would lead me to a safer place. The voice grew stronger, and it was coming from my closet. I stood at the door and the voice drew me nearer. It was clear now, the voice was coming from a big box in my closet. Listening intently, it's Mickey, he's calling me. "You can't go in there," Jeri said. There was hardness in her blue eyes that frightened me.

"But I have to," I pleaded. "Mickey, my brother…he's calling me. Listen, can't you hear him?" I could see my own face, and the faces of my brothers. My baby sisters beckoned me on.

"I said, you can't go in there," Jeri held me back with a firm hand.

Mickey's voice called again, and I struggled with Jeri, trying to twist out of her grip. Her hands tightened and she tried to drag me from the closet.

Mickey's voice still rang in my ears. I awakened. I was standing at the closet door in my bedroom, drenched in perspiration and gasping for breath, as if I'd really been struggling.

Back in my bed in the silence of my room, with the darkness of the night around me, I realized it was only a dream.

The dream always left me rattled and irrational.

I got up from my bed and went to the window, peering out at the rushing river below. The full moon hung in the sky, the bright stars twinkling.

I waited, expecting to see some strange form appear. I wondered, Mama saw the car drive into our driveway, and heard the car doors slam, and heard the voices and the car drive back out our driveway. Is that what's happening to me? Am I seeing images just like my Mama?

I watched and waited for several long minutes. Finally slipping between the covers I huddled there.

But when I closed my eyes, the memory of the dream came back to me. Again, Mickey is in the closet and wouldn't come out. He's in that big box under some blankets. He's older now, maybe fifteen. He's calling us. Abruptly turning, I hear their voices coming from outside my room, they're running up the stairway, taking two steps at a time… running and screaming toward me. "Sissy! Sissy!" Mickey says, 'we're dead.'"

I woke up suddenly. My body's flooded with panic. I stared at my clock. It was 3:05. I didn't sleep again that night. I was too frightened by the images of my dream. I held a towel in my mouth as I bawled, hoping Jeri would not hear me.

What did I do? How is this happening to me? I sat up in bed shivering, staring into darkness. The next night, the dream came again.

…It came out of a swirling fog. Mama holding a baby in her arms walked toward me through the brush and under the big trees. The shadows made my imagination stampede. The wind whistled through the trees, and the cries…of my babies who turned into ghosts that bombed me, diving down on me. As always their faces were hidden in a hazy blur.

Mama stopped in front of me. Reaching out I tried to touch her and caress the baby, but I couldn't. They were out of reach, turning into monsters, trying to grab me.

"What happened to the babies wasn't your fault...wasn't your fault...wasn't your fault..." the voice faded and faded, until it was gone.

Reaching out for them, I cried, "don't go. Oh Mama, please don't go."

I woke again, crying hysterically.

Hunter and Jeri ran to my room and comforted me.

Back in bed, I was never alone. Mickey would always come, and sometimes my baby sisters too. Sometimes I saw him standing in the corner of my room. Other times he sat at the foot of my bed playing with the two babies. I could see through him. He would vanish as quietly as he appeared. And then I would miss him—and when I longed for him he would return.

The images came every night. They were always the same, vivid and real, complete with sound effects. All the events were real. They had happened. The dreams were mirrors of my life. I tried to stop the dreams. Sometimes I did. Sometimes I failed.

"Don't argue with me! Don't argue, I say!"

Jeri gave me a stinging slap across the face. My head snapped back, and my hand flew to the side of my cheek. It stunned me for a minute, but the surprise was worse than the pain. That was the first time she'd hit me.

"I'm sorry...I'm really sorry," she moaned, drawing me closer. "I'm just upset, trying to take care of you. It's so hard to teach you in such a short time."

My mind accused me. It's my fault. It always is. I wish I could please her. I don't know what more I can do. I don't know how. Something is missing inside me. I can feel it, yet I don't know what to do about it. I should be more appreciative of all she's done, but I can't seem to control this burning anger inside me.

"Let's continue with our chores," she said as she gently put her arm on my shoulder. Sometimes it seemed that all I ever did was chores. She spent hour-upon-hour, days-on-end, teaching me how to do chores. Scrub, scrub, scrub, clean, clean, clean. The whole big house was nothing but windows. I washed windows 'til my fingers were cracked and bleeding. I dusted for days on end. Every day, I cleaned her glassware and polished her stupid old silver until I'd worn holes in all the cleaning socks.

The house was full of huge, monogrammed pieces of sterling silver. Jeri said that Bill Coty had given them to Hunter's grandmother when she was young.

"I don't suppose you know who Bill Coty is, since you are so dumb. But you'll learn from the history books when you go to school."

I sat for hours with silver polish and worn-out socks, polishing her silver daily, even if it didn't need it. I washed and dried her lead crystal, over and over. And if I'd been bad, I'd have to do it all over again.

She said I needed something to pass the time, and that I needed the training. "After all, some day these lovely things will be yours, and you must learn how to keep them sparkling."

Jeri said she had to teach me all by herself. She told me this repeatedly. I always felt so sorry that she had to do it all alone, with no help.

One of Jeri's favorite remarks to me was, "Yuk! No wonder your mother didn't want you. No wonder she left you." Or: "You'll be just like your mother."

That would light a match to my anger. I'd turn on her in an instant, screaming, "What do you know about my Mama? You weren't there! Nobody knows what happened, not even those stupid social workers!"

As I got older, she quit making those remarks, but I always could tell by her looks that she didn't like for me to talk about any of my family.

I'd decided I was just going to quit. All I ever did from the time I got up till the time I went to bed was clean, clean, clean. So I put all the cleaning solutions, furniture polish and oily cloths in a bag, the way Jeri liked to keep things. And I sat down defiantly on the little green velvet sofa.

Jeri came in with her hands on her hips. "What are you doing?"

"I quit!"

"Oh, no! We don't quit around this house. You should be ashamed of yourself, after all I've done for you. You owe me so much. Now, aren't you ashamed?"

"No, I'm not ashamed. Are you?"

Her mouth fell open. "Oh, my God! Why do you always defy me? We all have errands and chores to do. If we'd all quit, we'd have to live in a pig pen."

I was afraid to displease her. I looked into her outstretched arms and listened to her soothing words.

Jeri sat on the sofa and wrapped both arms around me and said, "I love you so much, Pegi. If I'd had my own daughter, she could never be the daughter you are. You are the perfect daughter for us. We all have things to do, and it's important that you learn these things. I know it seems like so much for you now, but that's because you have to learn it all at once."

Jeri kept me wrapped in her arms, stroking and rocking me as she continued to talk softly to me.

"It's so important to learn these things. Margie, Fanchon, and Mary, your new friends all do these chores.

We're going to see this whole thing through together, you wait and see." She rested her chin on the top of my head and stroked me. On and on, her voice rambled. "You should be grateful to have such loving foster parents. You know, few foster children can have a home like this one."

When she got through, I felt bad for her because she was not able to have her own child. I felt so sorry for Jeri because she had to have me. I felt sorry that she had no one to help her teach me these wonderful things that I had to learn. I wanted so badly to please her, just once.

Later, while on the telephone, I overheard her tell about the episode. It sounded different, though. It sounded like she'd done something wonderful in her way of teaching me. But why didn't I feel wonderful when it happened? The only time I felt wonderful was when she loved me. The rest made me feel bad.

Jeri's friends would comment on what a wonderful job she was doing, and how they admired her for her strength and love for me.

There was a side of me that adored Jeri, and the other side hated her. Peggy Bearden hated her, and Pegi Crosby loved her. Who was I supposed to be?

Nobody wants me the way I am. I told myself, why didn't she get someone who is perfect? I'd do anything to please her. I don't understand why she wants me when she says such terrible things to me and about me.

I was saddled with doing the light chores and the harder jobs of a scullery maid—cooking meals, doing the wash, and ironing Hunter's fancy shirts. One-by-one, a little at a time, I learned to do it all. Jeri didn't even like the way I ironed, but I got the job done and the shirts looked as good as those she'd done. She made me open the pillow slips and slip them over the end of the ironing board instead of laying them flat. She frequently reminded me that I should be grateful for being in such a fine home and having an opportunity to learn such fine manners and behavior. I truly tried to work myself to death. I felt I owed her so much for taking me in and teaching me such fine things—proper manners and good grammar.

Tears came easily for me. I'd cry if someone told me something good. I'd cry if they screamed at me. I'd cry if someone looked at me. I didn't feel that I was worthy of being a friend, or deserved to be liked. If one of my schoolmates moved away, I'd cry for days, even if it was someone who had teased me and called me names. I couldn't bear to have someone leave me. I'd cry looking at photos of happy faces of people I didn't even know.

Jeri told me—and everyone who'd listen—that I cried to get my own way.

Often after a confrontation, I would have an asthma attack. When she took me to the doctor, she always told him I had the attacks when I couldn't get my own way. She said that I was psychosomatic.

The harder I tried not to have an attack, the more I seemed to attract one. Jeri would turn on the oven and stuff my head in it. Someone told her to do that; it was supposed to make my breathing easier. It was worse, but Jeri wouldn't believe me. The propane fumes burned my eyes, and I'd cry. I'd cry and choke. Then, for just one minute, I could breathe.

"See, it did help," she'd say.

Instantly, I'd go back into the asthma attack again, only to have her push my head back into the oven. I knew what Hansel and Gretel must have felt like.

My Daddy used to tell me that I had asthma attacks on purpose, too. Now two people have said it, it must be true. My mind accused. What can I do to keep from having the stupid attacks? If I have them on purpose, why can't I stop'em?

After I began to worry so much about my asthma, I started to giggle. Some said it was the giggling stage that I was going through, but it wasn't. I sometimes giggled uncontrollably. Instead of crying, I laughed. It covered my pain.

Jeri took me to my first funeral, and I laughed aloud hysterically, nonstop. I was in the front row. Standing behind the casket and facing me was an old man with big nostrils. He was a heavy breather. Every time he exhaled, his nose made a whistling sound like a mule. After about ten whistles, I started to laugh. Finally, I was laughing so hard I started to shake.

When I looked up again, I stared right into the eyes of a boy younger than me dressed in a robe. He carried some type of burner with big chains and bells hanging down. He was trying not to laugh. When our eyes met, he broke loose. His chains and bells started to jingle and chime. The more he shook, the more the chains rattled. Jeri never took me to another funeral.

I laughed when the pain got to be too much. I laughed when life got too...overwhelming.

Jeri took me to the doctor again, and he said that I had grave emotional problems. Jeri said that I must learn to control myself.

I heard Dr. Feldmeyer tell her that I had a "dissociative personality."

Trying to be cooperative, I admitted to hearing voices. But I didn't tell them that the voices I heard were of crying babies.

The swimmers came daily at four o'clock. If my chores were done, I could swim too. At first, I could swim with the rest of the swimmers, but gradually that all changed. In no time, I was being punished every day for one reason or another. There were two sides to Jeri. When people were around, she was loving to me. She told everyone that I was the daughter she could never have. She'd hug and kiss me and tell me how much she loved me. When she and I were alone, she'd attack me about whatever popped into her brain. I never knew if I should reach out to her or cringe away.

I'd go away and bawl uncontrollably, because I didn't think I was worthy of her attention, thinking I owe Jeri so much. How can I ever repay her? After all, she took me in when my own mother didn't want me. For just a slim measure of love and attention, I'd work my knuckles to the bone. There was nothing I wouldn't do for her.

The minute no one was around, she'd give me the silent treatment that lasted for days. I'd try harder to show her how much I loved her by cleaning and doing things for her so she'd talk to me. Still, she wouldn't say a word until someone came around or she had something she wanted me to do.

I loved her in spite of it all. I worshiped her. I believed every word she said. I actually did feel that the whole problem lay with me. I felt that I was a burden to her.

She'd tell people such terrible things about me, about how hard it was for her to teach me right from wrong. Maybe it was, but she contributed to my confusion. I simply was unable to figure out if she liked me and wanted me, or if she didn't like me and didn't really want me.

I still threw up every time I ate. It was found that I had a form of bulimia, not self-induced. My stomach was unable to handle large amounts of food. It had shrunk from the lack of food in my early childhood. Through diet and eating smaller amounts of food, it was finally controlled. I wasn't cured of it entirely until I was in my thirties.

Jeri took me to see Dr. Feldmeyer, I was frightened out of my wits—and even more frightened of the hypodermic needle. I'd scream and carry on. Once I even ran away.

Even though I was living in a nice house and had nice clothes now, I still felt that there was something "different" about me. Nobody cared, nobody cared how I felt. Nobody cared if I got good grades or did my homework from school. The only thing Jeri cared about was that I did all my chores at home for her. Nobody cared if I saw my brothers and sisters and she always got angry when I mentioned it. Always daydreaming about my brothers and sisters, I was quiet, sullen, and withdrawn. Something separated me from all the other kids. I tried to play like them and join in the games they played, but the school kids seemed to sense that I was different.

From the beginning of my school days at Three Rivers School, I was called "Cootie." I thought it was strange that these kids called me the same name the Springville kids had called me. The kids chimed together and sneered, "Cootie." The way they said it, it sounded very bad.

I shied away from them. I dreaded the moments I'd stand in line waiting, choosing sides for a spelling bee. I wasn't even the last to be picked. I simply wasn't picked at all. At the end, I'd mosey over to which ever team I wanted to be on. The teachers and the students all shunned me. I was miserable.

Kids teased me about my Mama running off and leaving me. They said my Mama didn't want me because something was wrong with me, and that's why she had left. There was little hope that I could manage the school work or find friends in this new school.

If I told Jeri the least little thing about my abandonment, the next day at school, the other children knew everything. I'd be teased all day long. Every time my Mama got Rita and Kathy back, I always heard it from the other kids at school. They'd sneer, "Your Mama got your two sisters back, but she doesn't want you! You know why? 'Cause you're a Cootie!"

When I went home that night, I never asked Jeri if my Mama had gotten my sisters. I quit telling her anything, because I knew she'd tell her women friends, who in turn told their families.

If the Crosbys were with me, the kids would be nice and wouldn't tease me. If I was alone, the kids told me that they weren't allowed to talk to me. But they still made fun of me. "I can't play with you," Mary told me. "Mama says she's afraid of what you'll teach me."

Kids at school, said the Crosbys only got me to do Jeri's work. Sandy said her parents had known the Crosbys in Houston, and Jeri never wanted a child because she was so spoiled.

I'd heard the adults whisper things of that nature, too, especially at 4-H. Although I had many problems, I did my part and everyone else's in helping clean up after our meetings. I heard parents comment, "Jeri taught her well." What the public saw was just a shadow of what Jeri really was. Some of them seemed to know a hint of the truth. It was just like Springville; the people were aware a child could be in jeopardy, yet nothing was done, and while I no longer had to root through trash dumps for food, mental garbage from the past, plus Jeri's subtle cruelty, would take an even greater toll in the future.

CHAPTER TWENTY-SIX

Jeri had one brother who was more than twenty years older. Uncle Denny's wife was Florence. I had to call them "Auntie Flo" and "Uncle Denny."

Auntie Flo was very large. In fact, she was the biggest person I'd ever seen. She had huge, pendulous boobies that rested at her waist, wore high heels and gorgeous dresses, and was very fussy. She spent hours sitting at her vanity doing her hair and makeup, which I considered was certainly warranted as she was very beautiful. I loved her dearly.

Uncle Denny and Auntie Flo had one son, Bobby, who was a pilot in the Air Force, but they lived in Exeter. The first time we went to see them, I found out they lived on the same street as Mickey and Brian, in fact, just two houses away with an orange grove between. Coincidentally, they were neighbors of Mrs. Hogsbreath, the first foster home we had been taken to when we were spirited away from our home.

As we went by Mrs. Hogsbreath's house, I said, "That's where my brothers live."

"Pegi," Jeri said, "Why do you tell such lies? You know your brothers don't live there. They live in Strathmore."

"Oh no, they don't. That's the house."

Every time we went down to Exeter, in my mind, all I ever saw was Mickey chasing me down the road, still wearing that demeaning dress.

At Auntie Flo's, I always wanted to go outside to play, hoping I'd see my brothers. I had it all planned. If I could get outside, I'd disappear into the orange grove and go the back way to their house. I knew I could do it in just a few minutes, but I wasn't allowed out of the house as Jeri watched me like an old mother goose.

Once I overheard Auntie Flo ask her, "Well, have you ever asked if her brothers live on this street?"

"No, I don't have to. I know they live in Strathmore. That's what I was told. It's just another of her lies. Florence, you know how she lies! I don't know why she does it. She tells the biggest lies, when the truth would be easier."

"What do you think it would hurt if she saw her brothers? You know, Geraldine, it might just help."

"Well, it's not my idea, it's the welfare agency. They think she'll be better off without seeing any of them."

"I'm sorry, but I have to disagree. You're an educated woman, Jeri. You're bound to know how important her brothers are to her."

"I'm just telling you what her social worker says."

"I'm sorry, but I can't believe she's right. She should know how important Pegi's real family is to her." Auntie Flo crossed her arms resting them on the shelf of her bosom.

"She'll forget them some day. Hunter and I are her real family now."

"Oh! You're impossible, Geraldine! This attitude stems from your own attempt at control...your own jealousy!"

One day Jeri and I met Auntie Flo in Visalia to shop. Jeri and Auntie Flo were good friends, shopping together weekly, then we'd have lunch in a hotel.

The first time we went into the big hotel, there were cloth tablecloths and napkins, small round pats of butter with a tiny stamped picture on them, and a clear, shallow dish full of water with a tiny sliver of lemon in it.

By this time, I had acquired the genteel manners that Jeri had taken such great pains to teach me. I very daintily squeezed my lemon into the water, then picked up the fingerbowl and drank the water.

Jeri let out a big gasp. Her hands flew to her chest. "Oh, my God, Pegi! How crude! You never cease to amaze me." "She's trying to please you, Jeri," Auntie Flo said. "I'm not meddling, but I think you are too strict. You're expecting too much from her."

That same day, while in town, Auntie Flo wanted to buy me some dresses. I was very excited. I had never had anyone besides Jeri fuss over me.

I liked watching the people on the streets as they entered one shop after the other. I stared at everyone and everything—people hurrying along, teenage girls giggling, children eating ice cream. I always watched and looked for my Mama or my baby sisters. Will I know them if I see them? I wondered constantly.

We went into a five and dime store which Auntie Flo called "J.J. Newberry". We also went into Montgomery "Monkey" Wards, which had wooden, noisy steps going downstairs. I had never in my life seen anything like it. I wanted everything in that store. I rubbed the material of the dresses between my fingers. I loved the softness of everything.

Then we went into the toy store. If she caught me, Jeri wouldn't let me touch one thing. "Don't touch this, don't touch that. Look, but do not touch." Just around the corner were the dolls...shelves upon shelves, clear to the ceiling with dolls. Each stood high in its box.

I had never had a doll. I stared at the dolls of every size and description. One was a big baby doll that reminded me of my sisters. Oh, how I wanted to pick her up and hold her. "Please, Jeri, may I touch her?" I begged. "Just once, please?"

"No." Her voice was firm.

Auntie Flo said, "Do you like that doll, Pegi?" "Oh yes. Yes I do."

"Well, I'll buy it for you."

Tears came to my eyes. I was so happy, I laughed and cried at the same time. I jumped up and down. I danced around and around with joy.

"No, Florence, not this time," said Jeri. "When Pegi learns not to beg, she may have a doll. She must learn that she can't always have her own way."

My heart fell. I ached inside. I didn't know what to do. Why did I even tell her that I wanted that stupid old doll. All I wanted was to hold her and touch her. I didn't beg, I rationalized.

Auntie Flo and Jeri argued. I couldn't understand what they said, but I could tell that Auntie Flo was extremely angry.

Sometimes Jeri acted like she loved me and wanted me, but other times she acted like she couldn't stand me. My mind bounced back and forth like a ping pong ball, but having the baby doll offered, then cruelly snatched from me like my own baby sisters left an additional scar.

Grandma and Grandpa Denison lived next door. I stayed with them a good bit, and Grandma even cooked for me—although she really taught me how to cook well. I liked her teaching me, and loved working beside her while she showed me how to can, and I'd help with the jars. She treated me with much love and patience.

They had both been born in New York. I loved to listen to the stories they told about "Geraldine," as they called her. Grandma said the school kids gave Geraldine the nickname of "Jeri." I could tell by the way they talked that Jeri was spoiled. She had wealthy aunts and uncles who gave her many fine presents, mostly dolls and rings.

Grandpa had two sisters who were old maids, and both had been in mental institutions for many years. Grandma and Grandpa talked of the old wealthy aunts every night while the radio played softly in the background. Usually it was ONE MAN'S FAMILY or AMOS 'N' ANDY.

I always listened to their stories. The aunts were rich. One had been in real estate, and the other was a stockbroker, one's husband was a veterinarian in New York. That aunt always carried a large paper bag full of money. My grandparents laughed about the time she had gone off and left a large sum of money in a paper bag on a bus.

Grandpa said they were both insane, twisted and sick. I never knew what he meant, but the insanity in her family bothered Jeri. She seemed preoccupied with it and was always wondering if it would affect her.

One summer, Jeri went to New York to visit one of her old aunts. Somebody had called and asked her to visit. When Jeri returned to Three Rivers, she had expensive jewelry—diamonds, emeralds, and fresh-water pearls.

Within a few days, the Tulare County Sheriff was at our door asking questions. The aunt that Jeri had visited claimed that Jeri had stolen her jewelry. The sheriff took it from Jeri, but she got an attorney and later got the jewelry back. I never knew the real truth about whether it had been actually stolen or not.

On Sundays, Auntie Flo and Uncle Denny came up to take Grandma and Grandpa out to the Buckaroo for dinner. We went also. Every time we went to the Buckaroo, all the cowboys from the bar would come into the dining room to talk with Grandpa and always bought him drinks. For some reason, he never touched the drinks, but then, he was close to ninety years old. There would be dozens of untouched drinks lined up in the middle of the table, yet he never so much as took a sip. I thought it was stupid that they bought him drinks and he wouldn't drink them, so I asked if I could have one. "Please Jeri, may I just have a sip?"

"No, Pegi, it's against the law."

"But I tasted it when I lived in Springville," I shouted back at her. "It wasn't against the law then!"

"Pegi, listen to me. Yes, it was against the law. You must not argue with me. Just do as I say."

There was one part of me that wanted a drink, but another part wanted nothing to do with it. If a person went by me and I got a whiff of alcohol breath and sweat, I'd back away, frightened by a reminder of the past.

During dinner, Uncle Denny went outside to the bathroom. When he returned, he was carrying a large, long box wrapped in paper. He handed it to Auntie Flo. Auntie Flo set the big box on its end beside her chair.

I wondered what was in the box, perhaps a present? My mind raced—maybe for Grandma or Grandpa? Material for Grandma to make a new dress—that had to be what it was, I decided. Everybody gave Grandma material for a new dress. I loved presents, even if they weren't for me. It felt like warm sunshine when someone else was surprised. My heart seemed to jump up in my throat. I had the feeling that something exciting was about to happen, and I couldn't stand to see a present just sitting unopened. I kept squirming and looking under the table at the big box.

After we'd finished eating, Auntie Flo picked the big box off the floor and announced. "I believe this is the proper time. With our family together, I'd like to give Pegi her first doll." I felt like a firecracker had gone off in my chest. I bounced up and down in the seat, and tore at the paper, ripping it off into shreds.

"Careful, Pegi! Careful. Go slow, now..." I heard Jeri's voice in the background.

"She's beautiful," I screamed.

She was beautiful in the big box. Her eyes were glass. They were closed, but when I picked her up, they opened and she looked right at me. She looked right into my eyes. I was thrilled. She had brown eyes, just like mine. Running around the table, I kissed Auntie Flo's cheek, "Thank you so much. Thank you, thank you." I hugged her.

When I sat back in my chair, I looked at Jeri, and I could see that she wasn't very happy. My mind tried to assess her mood. Why isn't she pleased?

"Don't you like her?" I asked.

"Oh, yes, she's lovely," but she frowned as she said it. "You know, Pegi, that is a very expensive doll." Her icy words were like a curse.

She let me keep it, but her strange attitude suggested she should be the only one in the household to own a doll.

Many months later, I got a package in the mail. I knew by the handwriting it was from Mama. Mama had never sent me a box before, in fact, she had never bought me anything. I was thrilled. To my mind this really proved Mama loved me, because she had sent me a present. It was a small Kewpie doll. That doll meant a lot to me. She had never had the money to buy me a doll, so this was an extra special present.

"Oh yes, your mother never comes to see you, yet she sends you expensive presents," Jeri said. "If she only knew what you were like, I bet she wouldn't even think about sending you a present." The words were like a harsh slap.

A few days later, I got up from my bed and went to take my Kewpie doll from the shelf. She fell to the floor already in pieces. I knew Jeri had broken my doll. I just knew she had. Why? She had a long row of beautiful dolls.

Months later, I received another package in the mail from Mama. This time it was a wristwatch. I was thrilled. Though I really didn't care if I had a watch or not, it was from my very own Mama. That was what mattered.

Later I heard Jeri tell people that my mother never came to see me, never called, yet she'd send me expensive presents. She told her friends that it was easier for her to send presents to salve her guilt than it was to come to see me.

The Crosbys traveled and taught dancing. On the weekends, I went with them, but during the week I had babysitters or I'd stay with Grandma and Grandpa. I had babysitters until I was sixteen years old.

After school, the Crosbys taught dancing to students of all ages. They performed in television shows with the young dancers. Although I learned to dance, I was never allowed to participate.

"The parents of the students paid for their children to take dance lessons," Jeri said. "You understand, don't you, Pegi?"

"Yes," I said because it was the answer she expected; however, deep inside, I really didn't understand at all.

I rationalized that Marjorie's mother taught piano, and Marjorie was the best piano player around. I wondered why I couldn't dance with the others?

Two summers later, Jeri and I went to Visalia to shop. We were in J.J. Newberrys, standing at the counter looking at bobby socks, and panties. I gasped as I looked across the counter, and there was Mama with my two little sisters, Rita and Kathy. Kathy was walking so she must have been about three years old. My heart stopped. Yet I knew they wouldn't remember me. I wanted to run to them all and just squeeze the life out of them.

This was the first time I'd seen any of my brothers or sisters since that horrible day at the Marshalls when I was taken away. I studied them closely, my mind racing, Mama wouldn't have someone else's kids. While I wanted to run to hug Mama and my sisters, I knew Jeri would get furious if I did.

I was in a daze and didn't know what to do. I stood there, not hearing or seeing anything but the three of them feeling like I was suspended in a tunnel. From somewhere in the background, Jeri called to me.

"Pegi! Pegi!" Her voice got louder and louder, and finally she grabbed me by the arm. She shook me, "Didn't you hear me? Come on." She pulled on my arm, and I pulled back. We were in a tug-a-war. "What's wrong with you?" she said to me. Across the counter, Mama reacted. She had heard Jeri calling me. I raised my eyes and looked straight into Mama's face. Mama raised her hand to her mouth and squinted. A surprised look spread across her face. "Oh!" escaped her lips. Jeri still had me by the hand, trying to pull. "Come on, Pegi. I'm not telling you again. Come on. What in the world is the matter with you?"

"No!" Pulling myself from Jeri, I yelled, "That's my Mama and sisters. I have to see them."

Jeri grabbed me. "You don't know what you're talking about. That can't be your mother and sisters. Your mother doesn't even have your sisters. Be real, Pegi. You still live in that fantasy world of yours. Why can't you accept that you'll never see them again?"

"How do you know this isn't my Mama and sisters? You've never seen them!" I screamed, pulled myself from her grip and ran around the counter to Mama, who by this time was running toward me.

I flew into Mama's arms. After a moment, out of the corner of my eye I saw Jeri shrug her shoulders in disgusted acceptance.

Jeri bought lunch for all of us that day. Mama told us that she'd just gotten the three younger children back, but Scotty was in school. She said she hoped by the end of the year that she would have all her children with her. I felt warm hope flooding through me.

I knew Mama loved me and that she had wanted me back all along. She'd just said so and I tingled with anticipation at the thought. Jeri scowled. I knew she didn't like what my Mama had just said.

I tried so hard to talk to my two little sisters. They were terribly shy, and seemed to not remember me. I loved them so much, and had been waiting so long for this moment. I told them I was their big "Sissy", hoping to spark some recognition.

"No, Shelly's my big sister," Kathy said. "And Roger's my brother, too."

I sensed Jeri would be mad at me if I acted like I cared about them more than I did her. I just let my eyes drink in how they looked.

For the next several days, I told all my friends about seeing my Mama and sisters. Every time I'd run up to tell somebody, Jeri got that awful look on her face. She fumed. Once she took my hand, pulling me away from a friend.

"Oh, you know how Pegi is, always exaggerating and lying," she said, waving my statements away like smoke from a cigarette.

I jerked my hand away and stood tall, "I'm not lying. I did too see my Mama and sisters."

That summer, I kept begging Jeri to let me spend a day with my own family. Finally she agreed by telling me that the social worker would permit it. I was so excited I could hardly wait. We were to meet Mama in a coffee shop. Jeri left, telling me what time she would pick me up. I was surprised to see Jake with Mama, but I was happy as I liked Jake very much.

Mama still didn't have a car, but Jake did. I jumped into the back seat of his car with both my sisters. The girls were shy, but they seemed to like me being with them. I couldn't help it—tears kept coming to my eyes I was so happy.

We drove out to Elderwood to see my brothers, Mickey and Brian. This was the first time we'd been together since the family had separated, almost four years before, and it was like the happy ending in a fairy tale.

I didn't know until this day that my brothers had moved. My brothers saw the car pull in, as they were expecting us. They almost knocked the door off the hinges running out to greet me. We just stood staring at each other, not having anything to say. Finally we ran off from the adults. They showed me the bunk house, as they called it, which was where they slept. There were almost twenty iron beds lined up in a row, with all the bedspreads alike. The bunk house was clean and neat, with scrubbed and shiny wooden floors. When it came time to leave I was felt like I was being torn into small pieces. I didn't want to leave and when I started crying, so did Mickey. He was just like me, and cried easily.

We returned to Mama's house in Visalia in the early afternoon. We weren't there long before Mama and Jake left in his car. She said they wouldn't be gone long. There wasn't any food in the house for my sisters and brother and by this time we were all hungry. Jake hadn't fed us while we were in Elderwood.

"Don't worry, Pegi," Scotty said. "I'll get us some food." He was probably eight or nine years old. He left the house, and came back a little while later with a box of cornflakes. Out the door he went again, and this time came back with milk. He made still a third trip and came back with sugar.

He crawled up on the counter and got bowls down from the cabinet, then sat on the counter and poured the cereal into the four bowls. During that day, we ate the whole box of cereal.

Scotty had become the care giver for his two little sisters. He was learning to take care of them, just as I had done. It was a sad thing for me to see. They weren't any better off than before. Mama really hadn't changed. I didn't want to live with my Mama, but I didn't want to leave my brother and sisters.

Then it was time for Mama to return me to where Jeri would pick me up. On the way, she told me, "I want you to throw the biggest fit you can tonight. Scream nonstop until they can't no longer stand it. Maybe they'll bring you back to me. Cry and scream. Beg to live with me. Threaten to commit suicide. I know if you do that, they'll let you come back to me."

When I got back home to Three Rivers, I just couldn't do what she had wanted. A part of me loved Hunter and Jeri and a part of me loved Mama, but I loved my brothers and sisters more than any parents—I was so confused. I wanted to be with my brothers and sisters, but I had become wise enough to know how it would be. I didn't want to live that way ever again.

With the Crosbys I had security; I knew I wouldn't have that with Mama. If I could see my brothers and sisters, I'd be happy. But I knew I couldn't do that either and I still didn't understand why. Adding it all up, I couldn't put on the act that Mama asked for me to do.

Internal tug of war was costly. I felt like my whole family had somehow slipped through my fingers along with my beloved Patches.

Jeri said that social services thought I needed to be an only child, and pampered because of being the "little mother" for so long. Another time she told me it was the other foster parents who didn't want my sisters to have any contact with me.

I think it was the foster parents who didn't want us to see each other. Mama could go visit my brothers anytime, and sometimes she spent the night with them. My brothers told me so that time when Mama and Jake took me to see them. So it had to be the Crosbys and the Marshalls who didn't want us to see our brothers and sisters. They were jealous of any affection we might have for one another.

Mother left my sisters and Scotty alone in a car behind a bar in Visalia. She got them back again later and did the same thing again. My two sisters were abandoned three times that I know of.

Jeri always let me know when my mother abandoned my siblings. She would make a special point of telling me. And then finally one day she told me Mama had committed her ultimate infraction and would never be permitted to have her children again. Jeri's eyes flashed in triumph as she announced Mama had moved to Los Angeles. A strong resolve rose up in me. I would not give her the satisfaction of seeing me cry, but that night my tears drenched my bunched up pillow. I cried not for myself, but for what Mama must be feeling.

Now every other Sunday, Jeri and Hunter drove to Fresno to teach dancing. We passed the house my brothers lived in, the same house where Jake and Mama had taken me when I had visited them. I begged Jeri to stop so I could visit with them. I stretched my neck as we passed, to see if they were in the yard. I never understood why they were always moved right into my path, and yet I wasn't allowed to see them.

"I simply do not know how you come up with all this, Pegi," Jeri said in an exasperated tone. "First your brothers lived on Avenue 344, and now they live way out here. Why don't you make up your mind?"

The Crosbys never stopped to let me visit my brothers. The minute we left in the morning for Fresno, I'd start begging to stop there. I didn't know why I couldn't be dropped off to spend the day with them. It seemed so simple.

They'd look at one another and drive right on by. "Jeri," I asked one day, "Why do you drive to Fresno this way?" It was a much longer trip to go through Elderwood.

"Oh, we like the drive. It's a very pleasant drive, don't you think?"

Actually, it was farther out of their way. It was always pure hell for me. They told me they couldn't stop at my brothers' without the welfare agency's permission, yet they never tried to get permission.

Jeri always would let me know when my sisters were moved from home to home. I'd always beg for them to take one of my sisters. For several years, they were moved back and forth to other homes. Every time Mama lost Kathy, she was taken to a home in Dinuba before going back to Farmersville with the Marshalls. I always begged to have her live with us.

One day when I came in from school, I was surprised to see an ugly blonde girl sitting on the sofa. She had a big nose and no upper lip, and squinty blue eyes.

"This is Dora," Jeri smiled. "You always wanted a sister, so we got one for you."

Immediately I wondered why she hadn't gotten one of my sisters, or Scotty. "I don't want this stupid sister," I declared, insensitive to how my words must have hurt the girl.

Jeri smiled again in an obvious attempt to assure Dora. "Well, why didn't I get to pick out my sister? I certainly wouldn't have picked her. I don't like blonde hair and blue eyes. Why didn't you go get one of my brothers or sisters?"

Jeri stared at me. "You are never satisfied! Why are you so disagreeable? I did this for you." She flung her arms wide in obvious dismay. "You're the one who wanted a sister, not me. This is extra work for me to have the two of you. Well, this is the way it's going to be. This is just the way it is. You're never happy!" She shook her head. "It wouldn't matter what I did for you."

Dora didn't stay very long. I don't think she liked Jeri. Dora had lived in a home in Exeter for many years, and she wasn't used to all the work that she had to do for Jeri. One day, she simply told Jeri that she wanted to live somewhere else. The same day, the social worker came and took her away.

Surprisingly, I hated to see her go, and thought she'd left because she didn't like me. She still went to Woodlake High, and I saw her everyday. I hated her because she'd left me. I didn't have the nerve to leave the Crosbys, even though I wanted to, and yet Dora had had the guts to do it. It was just easier to hate Dora than to admit that I couldn't leave Jeri.

Mama came to Three Rivers to see me once a year. She had to visit me once a year, or I'd be put up for adoption. It wasn't the Crosbys' responsibility to take me to see my mother, Jeri had said.

I'd receive a letter first, telling me that Mama would be there on a Saturday. Friday night, I'd go to bed and not be able to sleep because I was so excited. I'd think about seeing Mama the next day, and thoughts of what I wanted to tell her would stack up in piles. I knew she loved me, because she was coming all that way to see me.

I'd get up early Saturday morning, so happy. Taking great pains at getting dressed, I would wear my favorite dress. I wanted to look just right for Mama; I wanted her to be proud of me.

One Saturday I waited and waited, pacing. I walked the length of the driveway, I hoped to meet her on her way down. Soon it was lunch time, and I took time out for lunch. Up and down, back and forth, I went back into the house to check out how I looked and to recheck the time.

Eventually Jeri made me lie down for my daily nap. I protested loudly, but it was no use.

Hopping up from my nap, not worrying about putting myself back together, I started out again. Waiting for Mama, I walked the drive. Up and down, back and forth, over-and-over, back into the house to check out how I looked and to check the time.

Long after dark, Jeri came out and made me come inside. I still strongly believed my Mama was coming. She must've had some car trouble or something. I got out her letter and read it over and over to make sure I hadn't made a mistake. Maybe she had told me the wrong date, or I might have mis-read something. I cried myself to sleep that night. I dreamed of a tiny voice of a baby screaming. It was a teeny infant, one that nobody cared about, only me. I cradled it in my arms while the baby cried, clamping my hand over its mouth, silencing the faint cries. After all, I didn't want Jeri to know I had a baby in my room. I woke up suddenly, my heart racing, my breath in gasps. I was weak. I knew it was only a dream, but I couldn't go back to sleep.

I hated it when I dreamed about the babies. I never knew if it was my two sisters, or the other babies.

Early Sunday morning, I got up. Again, I read Mama's letter, still thinking maybe I had the wrong dates. I checked and double-checked the calendar, hoping Mama hadn't lied to me.

I re-read those letters so many times the folded crease began to tear and split and over time, I was unable to read Mama's words written in the creases. I rewrote the words along the edges so that I'd never forget them.

After church, I went through the very same thing. I walked the driveway all day, waiting for Mama. Sunday night, I pounded my fist into the pillow. I pulled another on top of me and burrowed like a mole under the covers, hiding so my sobbing couldn't be heard. Hour-after-hour I prayed for Mama to come down the long driveway to see me. Many times, long after Hunter and Jeri were sleep, I'd creep out of bed and run to the front bedroom to watch the driveway. I just knew that Mama was still coming. Finally I would go back to my bed and cry myself to sleep.

I went through this for months on end, year after year. I didn't ever want Jeri to hear me cry. I didn't want to give her the satisfaction. She always made such nasty remarks about me crying and my mother not showing up. Like, "What do you expect, Pegi? She ran off and left you. Do you think she's going to come and visit you? Who would ever want to come visit you? You know very well she won't come, Pegi. She never does."

And she never did.

Mickey on left. Brian on right. I took these pictures the day I went with Mama and Jake to visit them in Elderwood. I think it was 1948 as I was just learning to use my left hand to write. Mickey on right when he was 17 years old.

Baby sister Kathi at eight years old.

Left to right: Jeri Crosby, Grandpa Denison, Grandma Denison, Uncle Duane, hunter Crosby, Aunt Florance, Cousin Bobby, and myself at 12.

Hunter and Jeri Crosby

Mother on left with her two sisters

My mother's parents, the Burlesons. I never knew them.

CHAPTER TWENTY-SEVEN

One hot summer day, Jeri's eyes were red and swollen from allergies. She fumbled for a Kleenex. I sat on her bed, fingering the soft bedspread while she gave me directions for preparing our evening meal.

"You can do that, can't you, honey?" Jeri coaxed. "Yes, Jeri. I'll fix dinner."

"Oh, you're such a good girl. I couldn't have a better daughter if I'd had you myself."

With her kind words of love echoing in my mind, I prepared the best meal possible. Right down to baking her favorite blue berry pie. I wanted desperately to please her. I worked until way past my bedtime, cleaning and scouring. Before I went to bed, I went into Jeri's bathroom.

Both medicine cabinets, the counters, the top of the sink, the back of the toilet, every space was crowded with her medications—Valium, Miltown, Promazine, Reserpine, Seconal, Librium, Quaaludes, and Dalmane.

At night, when it was time for her to go to work, she always managed a miraculous recovery. She would get out of bed, and walking slowly with head down and hair hanging in her face, she would go to the bathroom, pick up one of her bottles of medication, shake several pills into her hand, and take them. Within a few minutes, she would be fine. Sometimes she would come out of the bathroom dancing, and other times she'd be a raving shrew.

Jeri made weekly trips to Exeter for prescriptions. She took pills for everything: pills to sleep; pills to wake up; pills to give her pep, and pills to calm down. The bathroom looked like a drugstore. Everywhere she went, she had her purse stashed full of pills. If anybody mentioned having the least ache or pain, Jeri would pull a bottle of pills out and offer, "Here, have one of these."

Jeri had more cats than the Pied Piper had rats. The cats had kittens, and the kittens had kittens. She had inside cats, outside cats, shed cats, and river cats. At one time, she had thirty-two cats. "Tabby Tom," as he was called, always waited for Hunter at the end of the driveway. He would hop onto the hood of the station wagon and ride down the hill every day. "Sissy" was fixed and never left the house. She sat on the back of a chair most of the day. Sissy was a Manx with Siamese markings. We had several cats like her.

In the spring, when all the females had kittens, Jeri would hunt around to find where the kitten's were hidden. When I came home from school, I had to fetch the latest litter, and then put the tiny kittens in a pillow case, along with a rock. Jeri expected me to tie a knot down close to the kittens and lower them into a pail of ice-cold water. The first time that Jeri made me the chief kitten executioner is still seared in my mind. The litter floated to the top, rising and falling, meowing and clawing inside the pillow case. I saw all those tiny creatures fighting for their lives, their mews grew louder and louder. Suddenly I screamed. My consciousness fragmented into small pieces:

The babies—I hadn't thought of them in a long time. I hadn't let them crawl into my mind for a long, long time.

The kittens' meowing and crying abruptly turned into the desperate cries of a baby. Running up over the hill and down the other side, the crying baby followed me. I ran through a pasture. The crying seemed to hover over my head. I heard footsteps chasing me. The branches that brushed against me were the hands of babies trying to grab me. The pale, crying face of a baby loomed in front of me. It dove down at me haunting me. I thought, I'm crazy just like Mama.

Babies crying, twisted my heart in agony. One-mouth open screamed and sobbed, arms stretching toward me in imploringly. The faces surrounded me, all of them screaming, crying.

A stabbing pain shot through me as my knees buckled, and I sank to the damp ground. But still the faces—the crying babies' faces came closer, closing in on me. Their cries echoed throughout the hillside, ringing in my ears, louder and louder.

I ran to my room and hid under the covers, but I still heard the baby cries.

Hours later, I had to go back and get the little, dead kittens. I had to take them out of the pillow case and bury them.

Two nights in a row, I had nightmares. It was always the same dream. I was back home in the wooded mountains in Springville—looking for Mickey, knowing he was there, but I had lost him. Frightened, afraid that he'd fallen down a steep slope, I scrambled through the clinging brush, calling frantically for my brother. The trees, reaching out for me, became distorted monsters. Babies cried from another direction.

No matter how attentively I listened, or how fast I made my way through the mountain, I kept losing them... losing them... In my dream I would get right on top of the cries, scrambling, looking behind ever shrub and bush. In seconds, they'd be in a different direction. I would then run after them again.

When I awoke, I tried to calm myself by closing my eyes and breathing deeply, telling myself that it wasn't really happening to me. I sagged into the bed, coughing to clear my throat. My breath rasped as I struggled to keep my lungs filled with air. I didn't want to have an asthma attack. The next spring, when I saw the cats mating, I'd try to chase them away from each other. Of course, my efforts were in vain. It almost drove me crazy watching the male cat rape the females. There were always more kittens born, and more to dispose of. And during those nights, I would always have nightmares of babies crying.

I tied the tiny kittens in a potato sack and tossed them into the river. That way, I didn't have to listen to their cries, and I didn't have to bury them.

I felt hostile anger after these incidents, but I didn't let it out. If I did, Jeri would get angry, too. She'd shout, "Who do you think you are to get angry for helping me, after all I have done for you? I've given you a home, when nobody else wanted you. I even gave you a name. I gave you my own name."

I tried not to hear her words, but they echoed in my brain like the imaginary babies' cries. And I continued to have nightmares. Jeri wouldn't let me stay over at anybody's house because of them. My dreams scared others, and I also sleep-walked. Almost nightly, I got up, put on my glasses, walked to the stairs, and fell down them.

One side of me hated Jeri's guts for making me drown and bury those little kittens. Out of retaliation, I sometimes spied on her and listened to conversations. I heard her tell one of her woman friends that I was two people.

I remember climbing the stairs to my room, looking at myself in the mirror, I thought, that makes sense. I'm two people because I love and hate Jeri at the same time. What does she mean by her remark? I know that one of me is Peggy Bearden, the other is Pegi Crosby. That makes me two people. Simple? But I had this eerie feeling that I really had nothing in common with her and that there was something very wrong with the way I was treated. I was lonely for my brothers and sisters, for my own sense of belonging. I knew that I really didn't belong there. They had chosen me. I hadn't chosen them. I was not the person they were trying to make me into. I was like a chunk of Jeri's modeling clay, and she was trying to mold me into something I was not. I felt like I was truly two people—one for Jeri and one for myself.

She told her friends that I was a "very disturbed girl, who seems to live in a world all of her own."

I walked a tight rope of caution being careful to please Jeri. No one seemed to notice I didn't have feelings or thoughts of my own, as my foster mother's wishes pasted themselves over my own. She monitored everything I did, everything I said, everybody that I talked with, and what I had on, down to my fingers and toes. She worried about me wearing anything that might belong to her, especially her fine jewelry.

Ester Peck, one of Jeri's friends had a retarded daughter, so Ester was always with the kids at all times. She gave Jeri reports on everything I did, every place I went. I would be in trouble if I made a slip of the tongue.

Lena Hayward, the telephone operator, knew everyone who called me or other kids I called. I think the operator recorded what I said. Jeri always knew word-for-word exactly what I had said.

There were many people on the same telephone line, and therefore when the telephone rang at our house, it rang at all the others too. Our ring was two longs and one short.

I never liked to talk on the telephone. I wasn't one to linger on the phone like some of my friends did. Actually, I wasn't allowed to. Most of the time when I called someone, I stated what I had to say, then hung up without saying "goodbye." I just hung up. Most people called me back and asked me why I'd hung up the phone on them.

I was a straight "F" student throughout school. Everyone teased me about it, even some of the teachers. Some called me "dumb."

Miss Kozel, my fifth-grade teacher, said, "You're mean as shit and twice as dumb. No wonder your Mama left you." Miss Kozel was a big old woman with loose jowls that hung down like an old, sad dog. When she spoke or shook her head, her jowls wiggled like Jell-o. She told Jeri that I constantly day dreamed and gazed out the window. "Well," I said when she called me dumb, "you may be right. But I'm only planning." "What are you planning, Pegi?"

"I'm planning for the day when I get back with my brothers and sisters, and how I'm going to find them."

The whole class erupted in laughter. The boys stomped their feet and shook their heads; the girls covered giggles with their hands.

Miss Kozel demanded, "Class! Class! Come to order now. Pegi can't distinguish the real world from the world in her mind."

"I can too!" I shouted.

"Come to order now, class! Class! Class, come to order!" One day after she had made a particularly demeaning remark about me, I picked up a pair of snub-tipped scissors and chased her around the room. There was never any mention of this. For some strange reason, no one ever told. When I started Woodlake High School for the first time, I had one teacher who realized I had many problems. Mickey also went to Woodlake High, and he was into sports. Mr. Bacconni knew Mickey first, and I think Mickey talked to him about our pasts. I had a few classes with Mr. Bacconni, and he was wonderful to me. For the first time, I was a teacher's pet. He nominated me as a pompom girl and gave me a lead part in the junior class play. After the play, he took the cast to Visalia for pizza, but Jeri wouldn't let me go.

Hunter and Jeri never helped me with my school work. They never even asked if I had homework to do. Hunter had nine years of college. He had degrees in engineering and chemistry before attending medical school, where he studied to be a dentist. I had a horrible time with mathematics, and every time I asked him for help, he'd get very impatient with me.

I didn't have any idea how to study, and I really didn't have time for homework. I came home and prepared dinner for Hunter and Jeri. By the time I finished all my chores, there was no time left for homework. I asked Jeri once if she would get a tutor for me. She told me it would cost too much money.

"Well, why can't the welfare office pay for a tutor for me?" She told me that I had mental problems that kept me from learning. She also said that she thought it was caused from my abandonment.

"We call it a learner's block," she said. I didn't think she'd lie to me. It made sense.

One year in my high school album, a straight-A student left me his "brains," noting that I'd need them to graduate. After buying the year-book, I went home and burned all my class annuals. I always wondered why the staff allowed the seniors to put something as degrading as that in the yearbooks.

In the summer months, I worked for the Pusiteris. Juanita Pusiteri had polio and spent all of her time in an iron lung. Juanita's husband was a professor at the College of the Sequoias. They had two small girls. The Pusiteris had a housekeeper who took the summer off, so they hired me. Working for the Pusiteris was Jeri's arrangement, not mine. She said I needed the experience. She also said I needed to learn how to be gracious to others. Jeri said that she and others had done so much for me that I needed to learn how to return the favors. Jeri also told me that I needed to give back to the community what I had taken. I never understood what she meant by "what I had taken."

I had to save all my money and buy my own school clothes when school started. At the end of that summer, I had less than sixty dollars, and I spent every nickel on Jeri. After I did that, Jeri would brag about me. She'd tell everyone what I'd done. She made a big show demonstrating her love and hug me, telling everyone that if she'd had her very own daughter, she couldn't be nearly the daughter I was. Of course, after such a demonstration, I couldn't do enough for her. I couldn't buy enough for her. Instead of eating, I saved my lunch money, and when I had enough to spend, I'd buy a bottle of cologne. In my mind she was the only thing that mattered to me. She was more important than I was.

If I saved my lunch money to pay on a skirt in layaway for myself, it was a different story. She'd call the store and tell them not to let me put clothes in layaway.

One day when I got off the school bus, the social worker's car was in the driveway. There was no mistaking that County car. A sick feeling always crept over me, at her monthly visits.

I opened the front door, but didn't close it, and I stood there listening to Jeri telling her all the terrible things I'd done. For some reason, as I stood there in the doorway eavesdropping, all the stuff sounded so much worse than it had actually been.

I overheard Jeri ask the social worker if she had seen a movie called THE BAD SEED.

The social worker said, "No."

"Well, you must go see it," Jeri said. "Pegi is just like that little girl in the movie. I'm also worried that she may cause Hunter and me to have a bad reputation in the community.

We have always had such a good reputation. We've worked hard to maintain our good standards in this community." She continued, telling the social worker that I was dangerous. "But I do feel that there is hope."

I closed the door quietly, then opened it again, pretending I had just come in. This time, they heard me.

"Pegi, Pegi darling," Jeri called out. "Pegi, is that you? Your social worker is here, and she wants to talk with you. Say 'hello' to Mrs. Cunningham."

After I exchanged greetings with her, an awful silence settled in the room. I wish she'd tell me something about my sisters, my mind prompted.

Jeri wrapped both arms around me and sat me down beside her on the sofa. Stroking my shoulders, she mopped the hair out of my face. "All in all, she's a pretty good kid. We only beat her on Fridays, whether she needs it or not. Don't we, Pegi? Run along now. Do your homework while you have time."

Closing my bedroom door, I leaned with my back against it. I couldn't make sense of her actions. My world and Jeri's was one of topsy-turvy contradictions. Jeri said that I was two people, but with a sudden flash of adult discernment, I knew she was too.

I had heard her telling the social worker such horrible stories about me, but when I was in the room, she'd made a big show of affection and said wonderful things about me. Other times she'd sit me on her lap, brushing the hair out of my eyes, and proclaim, "We are getting along just fine. Sometimes things are a little rough, though, aren't they, Pegi? We had to start from scratch, you know. We're working through the problems. It's just taking us a while. A bit longer than it takes most people. Pegi knows she can just talk about anything she wants with me," Jeri would ramble in direct contradiction to the statements of intense problems she had just related.

How could she possibly do this, when I had just stood at the door and heard her say those awful things about me? I wondered.

In reality, I couldn't say how I felt. This attention was too precious to do anything disagreeable to Jeri in front of the social worker. She only showed me love when someone else was around, and hardly noticed as I fiddled with her rings or stroked the fabric of her blouse.

Jeri caught me smoking and had me put in Juvenile Hall often, but she always came and took me back in a few days. She did it for punishment, so I would learn that I couldn't get away with anything. Jeri said it was good for me to go to Juvenile Hall, explaining it would make me grateful to be back with them. She said it would make me realize life wasn't all that bad at the Crosby's.

I was forever being grounded. It didn't matter what I did or didn't do. I'd sit in my room, surrounded by only the things represented by my life with the Crosbys. There was nothing to remind me of Mama, my brothers and sisters... Patches. It was as though God had taken a large pair of scissors and cut my past off from the present. I kept trying to drag my real family out of that black hole and at least keep them on the window sill of my mind, but it became harder to hold onto them—more difficult to understand just what was expected of me. I simply couldn't find myself, and actually began to believe I was a "wretched creature", a bad seed doomed for prison or a worse fate.

Every time Jeri locked me away, I felt shunned. Yet I hung on and clung to her more tightly than ever. I was her misplaced baggage, lost and found and lost again.

She also took me to child psychiatrists. The Crosbys had a friend who was a psychiatrist, a Dr. Dillon in Kingsburg. He arranged with another doctor to see me. Jeri literally had to drag me into his office, where two chairs faced the doctor's desk.

"Mrs. Crosby, will you explain Pegi's problems?" the doctor asked, looking at me over the top of his glasses.

Jeri's voice became a hum in the background as she related her version of what I did, I said, I felt. Most of what she said, I didn't want to hear. She told the doctor how much she distrusted me and how she was unable to believe a word I said. She talked of my lying, my fantasies, and my thievery. Jeri also told the doctor, "Pegi is a thousand different people. Is that possible?"

"Oh, yes," the doctor said. "There are people with many different personalities. Is that what you think is going on here?"

"Yes, Doctor. Pegi is definitely two or more people." I tried not to listen. It was all so tainted and unfair.

"Why does Mrs. Crosby have so much distrust of you, Pegi?" the doctor asked.

Shrugging my shoulders, I answered, "I don't know."

"What kind of fantasies do you have?" he asked.

"Just planning when I'll get back with my brothers and sisters, is all," I said. "I don't see anything wrong with me wanting to see them. This isn't fair."

"What sort of things are you planning with them, Pegi?" he asked.

Before I could answer him, Jeri jumped in. "Pegi, how often have I told you, it's not me who won't let you see your brothers and sisters. It's their foster parents who won't let you see them."

"Oh, yeah. The last time you said it was the welfare office. Now it's the foster parents."

"See, Doctor!" Jeri said, turning to him. "See how she is! She has an answer for everything that I say!"

"Shh...let Pegi talk, Mrs. Crosby. Go ahead, Pegi, tell me what you're planning."

"Well, my brain is constantly busy remembering the last time I was with my brothers and sisters. And I'm always planning on how it's going to be when I'm with them again. And besides, when I grow up, I'm going to sue!"

"Whom are you going to sue, Pegi?" the doctor asked.

"Oh, I don't know. That stupid old welfare office, maybe."

"What are you going to sue the welfare office for, Pegi?"

"I'm going to sue them because they wouldn't let me see my brothers and sisters."

"Well, Pegi, many things are not fair in life. When you grow up, you'll understand. I think it would be far better for you if you just realized that you can't be with them."

"Well, I won't do that!"

"It looks to me as if you deliberately make things hard on yourself," the doctor said. "Mrs. Crosby is concerned for you. If she wasn't concerned, she wouldn't be here with you. I understand that the Crosby's furnish you with a lovely home on the river in the mountains. Is that so?"

"What does that have to do with seeing my brothers and sisters?"

The appointment ended in what appeared to be a stalemate in the contest between me and my foster mother. Of course, they always assumed her point of view was correct. She was the adult in the situation.

Another time, I was taken to a different doctor. Jeri didn't come in with me this time, for some reason. When the doctor came into the waiting room for me, Jeri jumped up and said, "Pegi regurgitates dreams, Doctor." The doctor's eyes darted to me, then back to Jeri.

The doctor held the door open. "Come on in, Pegi." After he spoke with me, he spoke with Jeri. That night, on the way home, she said, "Pegi, I want you to understand that when I punish you, it's not because I'm mad at you. It's because that is the only way I can teach you a lesson. The doctor told me that you said you're always being punished. Well, I just want you to know why."

Jeri and I went through several sessions of this nature. The doctors, all of them, mainly listened to what she had to say. There was never a doctor that I could talk with. They always told her everything I said. Eventually during the sessions, I would reach the point where I wouldn't even say one word. I'd sit the whole hour with my mouth shut, looking down at the floor. The doctor never took his eyes off me. He stared a hole in me.

"Tell me your name," he said.

Why, you stupid old coot! You know my name.

I wouldn't even answer that, because I knew that he knew what my name was. I would never even talk to them. Finally, they said that I was unmanageable.

I wouldn't talk, but my mind raced, is it my fault that I was abandoned? Was it because of all those babies? Was I born into a bad family, or am I in a bad family now? Did I cause all this? I don't know. I'm confused.

Why didn't anybody else understand? All I wanted was to see my brothers and sisters, and I couldn't understand why it wasn't allowed. I always believed that it was all of them: Jeri; the Marshalls; and the welfare office in league with each other against me. I dreamed constantly of suing when I grew up.

Always the night after I'd seen a physiatrist, I'd cover my head with my pillow to muffle the sound, then sob myself to sleep.

One year the Crosbys took a dancing tour of the United States. Jeri had one of her lady friends come stay with me while they were gone. This was the friend who always tattled about everything I did.

When they returned, a long list waited for Jeri about everything I had done. One item was the theft of six dollars. I had become a terrible thief.

I certainly did steal anything I could get my hands on. It didn't matter what it was. Most generally, it was something I didn't want. I just took it because stealing made me feel better. It was recompense for all that had been taken from me. It really did make me feel better.

I'd steal things to give to Jeri. If I had money, I'd spend it all on Jeri. If I was in town without money, I'd shoplift expensive gifts for her. Jeri never questioned that, but if they were used gifts and she knew they were used, she'd punish me. If she knew where I had been, she'd call and ask if they were missing a slip, rhinestone earrings, or whatever. One time after one of these incidents involving a used gift, she planned a diabolical punishment.

A week or so after I'd had my monthly, Jeri confronted me with a tall brown paper bag in which she had apparently stored all my used Kotex. She told me to come down stairs with her. Dumping the bag out into the wash tub, she smiled as smelly used Kotex tumbled out. Turning on the water, she told me I had to wash and reuse them. Another wicked smile crossed her face as she turned and left the laundry room.

I stared down at the bloody mass of paper, cotton and gauze. The sweet sickening smell filled the room as terrifying memories of bloody discharge from newborn babies filled my mind until it swam in helplessness. Vomiting, I ran from the room, up the stairs, through the dining room, living room, leaving yellow trails of vomit along the way. Jeri ran after me screaming, "What are you doing? Look at the mess you're leaving! Clean it up!"

"I'm not cleaning up that mess or the mess in the laundry room, and there is no way you can make me do it!" I yelled back at her from the shower. I scrubbed and scrubbed and couldn't seem to wash off the bloody sweet smell. The more I washed the stronger the bloody smell became.

Immediately I heard her on the telephone telling the social worker that she wanted me out of her house, "Now! Right now!"

It was only a couple of hours until the social worker arrived. On the way to Juvenile Hall her voice droned on about trying to place a "trouble making" child like me in another home.

Where was she taking me? Was I going to another stupid foster home? Was I as expendable as the baby kittens Jeri had made me drown?

CHAPTER TWENTY-EIGHT

I was bounced back to Juvenile Hall again—the dull gray existence of bullying girls and echoing halls. I'd been there before when Jeri wanted to punish me, but this time it was different, and I found myself enveloped in a paralyzing fear with this realization. The two people inside me fought a tug-of-war with my will: Pegi wanted to go back with Jeri; Peggy whispered, "Who needs her? Find Mama! Find your real family, girl!"

The two people warring inside me bordered on madness, leaving me limp with confusion. I sat on the hard bed longing for my pretty room at the Crosby's, and lonesome for Jeri. Yet my longing was laced with anger.

I hadn't thought of Patches for years, but wished I could bury my face in his shaggy fur, wrap my arms around his neck, let him lick away the salt of my tears. Where was God? Didn't anybody care about me?

Peggy whispered, "I don't need anybody!" Pegi would reply, "I need the Crosbys, I really do...I want to go back." "Never!" Peggy would silently scream.

There were times I could picture twins fighting in the same womb, and I had never felt so bereft and alone.

During my stay in Juvenile Hall, I never mentioned that I was a foster child. Instead, I told others that the Crosbys were my parents. Although I didn't want to go back with them, I didn't want to give up that identity. By now, it was the only one I knew.

In the '50's and '60's, "The Crosbys" were very well known throughout the surrounding counties and states because of their dancing and their dancing exhibits with children. There were frequent photographs and long articles in all the local newspapers about them. Jeri had always said that they put Tulare County on the map.

The first thing I wanted to do was shower. The matron told me I could only shower at certain times. I told her I still had vomit on me, so then she let me shower. When I got in the shower I didn't want to use their soap. I wanted my own.

The matron laughed and said that I had to use the same soap the others did. Standing in the shower, I washed and washed the soap before rubbing it on my body. Later, some of the girls wanted to use my lipstick, and I wouldn't let them. Finally after much teasing from them, when they called me selfish, I gave the lipstick away. I suddenly didn't want it anymore.

As the days dragged on, I finally came to the stark realization that my first instincts were right. This time at Juvenile Hall was different. The Crosbys were not coming to my rescue this time—not coming to take me home when I'd endured enough punishment.

I was flooded with a drowning terror. They had abandoned me...just like Mama.

Pegi told me I'd gotten what I deserved whereas Peggy declared, "Good riddance to bad rubbish."

And as time passed, it seemed as though I had fallen into a deep, dark pit of loneliness...falling...falling in slow motion, the fingers of my mind not even bothering to reach out to try to save myself.

In this dark free-fall, I found myself shuttled from one foster home to another in Tulare County. It didn't seem to matter that no one wanted me for any length of time. I was numb with the frostbite of loneliness and fear.

Finally, the court decided that I would go back to my mother because there really was no other place for me.

Somehow Jeri must have gotten word of the court's intention to award custody back to my mother. After all this time, she suddenly appeared to visit me in Juvenile Hall. By now I was humbly grateful to see her—anxious to share my good news about Mama. Her response was like a slap.

"Pegi, you know your mother is ill." She almost spat the words in my direction. "She's really not able to handle you with all your problems, and she never has been. She won't be able to take you now." I took a step backward from the force of her words.

"You know, Pegi, your mother could have had you anytime she wanted to these past years, and she didn't want you. The welfare office would have given her hundreds of dollars, to keep her children and she'd never have had to work."

I stood staring at Jeri. The cruelty of her words seemed to choke the breath from me.

"They've already told me that I'm going to live with my Mama," I stammered. "Why did they tell me that, if I'm not going to live with her?"

"Well, I don't know." Jeri's long, sleek red nails tapped an impatient staccato beat on the table between us. "But I'm telling you, your mother is too sick, that's all I have to say. I just want you to be aware of that. I only want the best for you, dear." The ingratiating tone returned. "You've always known that, haven't you?" Jeri pulled me to her and stroked my hair.

I could feel every muscle in my body tense in revulsion at the phoniness of her gesture. Yes, Jeri was two people too: Jeri, the gushing, over-loving actress, always dancing on the stage of life; and Jeri, the self-centered, manipulative woman who spat cruel words, demanding obedience and attention akin to worship. I saw the Jeri who harshly drew blood, then abruptly covered my wounds with the salve of phoniness.

It was as though I truly saw through her facade for the first time, and a cold shiver ran through me. Would that I had possessed the same ability at that time to be able to discern the demons she had imparted to me. But I was just seventeen and would only recognize them in the future.

CHAPTER TWENTY-NINE

I was beside myself. Mama wanted me! She was coming from Los Angeles to get me, and it was such a long way to travel, so it was obvious how much she loved me.

Before I could be turned over to Mama, I had to go to court which is where we saw each other for the first time in years. As the judge talked to Mama and me, I kept stealing sideways glances at her. It had been so long since I'd seen her, I'd forgotten what she looked like.

This woman didn't even resemble my Mama. Or had my memory framed a different portrait of her? My Mama was gorgeous, with long, thick hair. This woman's hair was stringy, and I could see light between every strand. My Mama had big teeth like mine. This lady had little bitty teeth that made her mouth look funny.

And who was the man with her? When Mama had written to me she never mentioned anything about a man. I didn't know what to do. I just stood there, staring at him. He didn't say anything to me either, just looked at me. He wasn't nearly as old as Mama, and really wasn't much older than I was.

All these years, I'd dreamed that my Mama would run toward me, grab me, kiss me. But she didn't. I was face-to-face with her, and awkwardly didn't know what to do, and neither did she. She was a total stranger. I felt sick. What had I done? I really didn't want to go live with this woman. But now I had no choice. I wasn't prepared for the jolt of the image I had carried for years like a precious souvenir now being so abruptly smashed before my eyes. Had my imagination sculpted Mama into the perfect beauty on a pedestal? I wanted her to be and tried to mentally put a gloss over the miserable little creature I had now consented to live with? What had I done?

From the beginning, I had a hard time calling her "Mama." I knew she was my mother, yet she'd never really been a mother to me. I couldn't call her Winnie, and I stammered on the word "Mother."

Mama said the man was her husband. Why hadn't anyone told me she'd remarried? Had Jeri known and not told me? He was younger than Mama by more than ten years. He didn't talk to me, so I never spoke to him.

As we walked down those long steps of the court house that hot day the two Pegi's were battling again. Pegi, wanted to stay in Tulare County. Peggy said, "Oh come on, it's going to be alright."

Earl opened the door of that new baby blue Buick, lowered the front seat as I stepped into the back seat and lowered myself down on the white leather seats.

"Whew," said Peggy. "See, I told you that it's going to be just dandy. Look at this car. It's better than that pink Thunderbird that Jeri drives."

"I don't care anything about this car or Jeri's old pink Thunderbird, I don't want to go," Pegi answered on the verge of tears.

After Mama and Earl were in the car he pulled out from the curb and maneuvered the car out to Highway 99.

Mama opened her purse and took out a pack of Lucky Strikes. She lit one and handed it to Earl. Turning around in her seat, she shook a cigarette out, "Would you like one? Do you smoke, Pegi?"

"Whow," said Peggy. "Now you can smoke."

Pegi was terrified for an adult, to see her smoking. She really wasn't a smoker, "Thank you," she said as she took the cigarette out of the package. The two Pegis' were finally happy as they breezed down Highway 99 on their way to Los Angeles.

I was horrified when we pulled into that dingy, dirty, old motel in Los Angeles. It had a kitchenette and crawled with big black bugs like I'd never seen before. There was a small cookstove in one corner with only two burners.

I opened the tiny closet to hang my clothes and my nose was filled with the same sweet ugly smell from the past. Looking down, I gazed into a tall brown paper bag filled with bloody rags. Paralyzed in the same position, I heaved and heaved into the offensive bag. Running to the bathroom, I jumped into the shower, washing and washing the bar of soap before I rubbed it on my body.

In the year of 1954, Mama was still using those bloody rags for Kotex and washing them every month. And every day I could smell those rags when I entered that tiny apartment. As much as I tried, I couldn't wash the smell from my body, or cleanse it from my mind.

Mama bought me a sleeping bag, and I slept on the floor. Her husband worked nights and slept in the daytime. Always, if I stayed inside, I had to be quiet not to waken Earl. Most of the time I waited outside, walked downtown, or sat in the park. Unhappiness was my only companion.

Earl drank all the time when he wasn't sleeping. He told me that he and Mama weren't really married. I really didn't understand what he was talking about. By the way he admitted it, I could tell it was bad. I'd never known of anyone living together. I thought people had to be married in order to live together. Because he was the one who told me, I felt that somehow it was my fault.

One afternoon, one of Mama's friends asked, "What was the name of the private school you went to, Pegi?"

"What?" I asked. "Private school?"

Mama jumped in and rattled something off before I got a chance to answer. With my hearing problem, I attributed it to misunderstanding.

Looking back, I know now that my Mother told her friends I had been in a private school all those years. I thought it was funny they believed her when she lived in such a dump. Mama never could accept the truth.

Earl drank continually, and was always sloppy drunk. I hated being around him. Mama would scream at him, "You promised me you wouldn't drink when Pegi came to live with us."

Other times, they hung out in the bars and dragged me along. I liked that. The bars were full of young men in uniforms. I liked the atmosphere inside the bar, but I didn't drink because I was underage. I was game for anything and everything. I was continually searching for...I didn't know what. Perhaps love...love in any form.

From the beginning I realized that Mama carried a huge baggage for what she'd done to her children. I learned how to work on this guilt to get my own way. I knew it wasn't right, but I did it anyway. I knew she was trying to make up for what she'd done to me, and I leveraged it to my advantage whenever I could. Jeri's sly spirit of manipulation must have smiled encouragingly at my guilt trips placed on Mama.

Late one afternoon, before Mama got home from work, a shiny car pulled up in front of the motel. I recognized the county car. I stood at the window and watched two women walk to our motel door. I had the door open and was standing in the doorway by the time they reached it.

One said, "We're looking for Winifred Bearden."

"Her name isn't Winifred Bearden anymore, it's Winifred Wells," I corrected. "She's at work and won't be home until six o'clock. I don't have social workers anymore. Why are you here?"

The other woman said, "We want to talk to your mother about signing adoption papers for Rita and Kathy."

I invited the two women in, to wait for my mother.

My mind began prompting, I promised my little sisters when they were born that I'd take care of them. I haven't been able to live up to that vow. Now I can, by making sure Mama signs those adoption papers. Mama is going to sign! I'm going to make sure she does. I know I can make her sign! My sisters aren't going to have to live the way I did. They'll never have to live through the hell I have. I'm going to give them a Mommy and Daddy. This is the only way I can live up to the promise I made to them so many years ago. Yes,

Mama will have to sign those papers. I knew it would be a showdown, but I had Rita and Kathy's lives in my hands at that moment. I had saved Rita's life by fighting Mama at the birth...and by God, I'd save her again now so she could live a normal life, not like one of Mama's discarded bloody rags in the closet.

Standing at the window daydreaming, I watched Mama walk through the alley as she came home from work. I kept my eye on her as she walked up the steps and opened the door. When she stepped into the tiny living room she was surprised to see the two women sitting on the sofa.

"Mama, these women are from the County, and they want you to sign adoption papers for Rita and Kathy," I began.

Mama started screaming, "No! No! Those are my babies! No one will ever take them from me. I'll never sign!" Her face distorted with anger. "I may never have them with me again, but I'm not giving them up!" Pointing to the door, she screamed, "Now get out! Get out of my house!"

Pulling Mama around to face me, I screamed louder. "Yes, you will sign those papers! You aren't going to put those two kids through what you put me through. You don't want them. You'll never take care of them. You sign right now!" Turning to the social workers, I said, "Give me those papers. She'll sign them right now."

Mama looked at me, obviously horrified at my resolute assault on her which must have seemed like a mutinous attack on her motherhood.

Grabbing the papers from one of the ladies, I nervously spread the papers on the table. "Where does she sign? Show me where."

One of the women wedged herself between Mama and me and pointed to the line. "Here," she said. "Right here."

"Okay, Mama—sign, now!"

With tears running down her cheeks, Mama signed, and ran from the room, sobbing loudly.

Both the social workers hugged me before they left our tiny motel. "We could have never done this without you," one of them said.

For the first time in all those years, I knew my mother would never get her children back. She didn't want them and couldn't care for them. The reality of it all finally hit me. I may have been the sacrificial lamb for the rest of them, but at that moment I knew they would never have to endure the cruel instability, loneliness and lack of love I had had to endure. A warmth spread through me like spring sunshine—I knew I had done the right thing.

What I had no way of knowing was that this mental crossroad was the final domino stacked on all the others of the past. It was a crushing weight which would cause enough imbalance to topple my life.

The lamb was about to be sheared...

CHAPTER THIRTY

Mama shuffled around in sorrow, with a rag in her hand, sniffling and mumbling to herself. Directly she said, "Not one word of this to Earl when he comes in." "Why would I say anything to Earl? I never talk to him?" "Just in case. Just making sure you don't, that's all, she said.

Me and Mama continued packing for our move and Mama continued sniveling.

It wasn't long I felt that old familiar weight on my chest, and started to cough. Within minutes I was in a full bloom asthma attack.

"Oh my God, do you still have those attacks?" Mama asked. "Yes Mama, I still have asthma." I never attributed my asthma attacks with anything traumatic in my life, as everyone said I did it purposely. After a horrible night, by morning I was alright and able to help move. We had no furniture as most of these small places were furnished.

Our new home way a 4–plex along main street of South Gate. A one bedroom with me sleeping on the sofa in the living room again. The backyard was long, and narrow, the length of the 4-plex with clothes lines stretched the whole length. Across one side a 4-foot high block fences separated the duplex from the house next door. I looked into mama and Earls bedroom at the sagging mattress. "Are you going to sleep on that ugly nasty mattress?" I asked.

Mama glared at me, "Well yes, she answered.

"Well for sure I know the Crosby's would never sleep on a mattress that looks like that or expect anyone else to either." "Pegi, how many times do I have to tell you? You are not at the Crosby's anymore."

We hadn't been in our new home long. One Saturday morning I was sitting at the kitchen table still dressed in PJ's. I could hear mama and Earl giggling in their bedroom. Before long they opened the door and came out playing and dancing. Earl had a towel, flipping mama on the backside. They continued to play and laugh.

I pulled my pajama top over my head, peeking out the gaps between the buttons. I continued to watch mama and Earl play around. Earl came over to me, ruffled my hair, and said, "Pegi, Pegi, we're having a baby. A brother or sister for you. Which do you want? 'My face must have been one of horror as Earl and mama at the same time, screamed, "What is wrong with you?"

Mama said, "Oh she is the most disagreeable kid I have ever seen.

Earl flopped down on the sofa on top of my blankets. He pulled mama down onto his lap and kissed her for a long time. "Here Pegi," he said, picking up change from the table. "Go to the corner and get us a newspaper, will you?" He handed me the change.

I wanted to get out of there. Grabbing the change I hurried out the door. Walking to the corner that morning still dressed in my PJ's, my mind a thousand miles away, remembering those babies from so many years before. I was just overwhelmed. I lost my way—I lost my memory—not knowing where I was. I began to run.

Crying babies bombarded me drowning kittens flew through the air. In a state of panic I ran on, not knowing where I was or where I was going. Laying on the ground, lights flashing, police cars fire trucks, all around, I had no idea where I was.

A tidal wave of blackness broke over me. My entire world seemed to be obliterated out of my grasp. Time ran in circles, flowed backward, skipped ahead from now to then. I made an attempt to come into the present as I heard all the men in uniform asking me question-after-question. Memory flowed back slowly and I knew the answers, yet I wasn't able to answer. There seemed to be a steel wall between my mind and my mouth...a wall of disconnect.

"What's your name?" one asked. "Do you know who you are?"

"Where do you live?" the voice was gruff.

The bleak realization spread through me like a bolt of vicious lightening—I had gone crazy...blacked out. I had been teetering on insanity for seventeen years, fighting the two Pegi's which shared each other, death-locked inside of me. The last thing I remembered were the cries of babies which had driven me out of the motel room, fleeing the chubby fingers which clutched the air trying to reach me. I was taken by ambulance to the emergency room in South Gate Hospital. Soon I was transferred to Norwalk State Hospital.

I'd driven by the state hospital many times, yet had never really seen it. Tonight it seemed like a huge sinister castle and was by far the most intimidating thing I'd ever encountered as I stood at the gate with the officer. He rang the night bell. After the gate was unlocked, he led me up a row of steps where the intern waited with the door open. At the top, the policeman gave me a rough shove. Stumbling on the edge, I caught myself.

I was examined by a doctor, who asked me one question after another.

"How was your childhood?" "What childhood?"

"Do you hear voices?" "No, I hear babies crying."

"She hears voices, all right," the doctor pronounced more to himself than me as he scribbled rapidly in a notebook. "Lock her in F5," he spoke into an intercom. But first, I had to fill out heavy paperwork.

I was then medicated and shown to a cramped room filled with other patients, where I was to be "locked down" the first few days for observation.

The moment I stepped into that ward I was overwhelmed by the sickening menstral smell. It seemed intensified more than ever before. I spent my days running to the bathroom to vomit and wretch. If a nurse came near me who was having her period, I'd run off puking.

I was fed three cups of pills a day, and spent time in a fog wondering why these people were mad at me. I wouldn't talk to anyone, and when I did, they just said, "Don't pay any attention to Pegi. She's crazy." I'd never taken pills before, but these weren't bad. At least they helped me to not think about everything…my baby sisters, Mama, the Crosbys.

I really didn't think these doctors and nurses knew what they were talking about. I'd never taken pills before, but I heard them say I had. I'd never even had a drink like they said...well, not since I was little and lived in Springville.

Word spread among the hospital staff that I was a mad woman and crazy. I was terrified of the other patients and the staff, who claimed they had a wild woman on their hands.

I wouldn't talk with Dr. Green's office because I refused to even think about my problems. Instead, I counted the books behind him that were on the shelves. When I finished, I'd start over. The next time, I'd count the squares of the tiles in the floor. Then the squares in the windows. Then I'd go back to the books. I never spoke to this particular doctor, and he never spoke to me, just stared.

After the hour of silence, Dr. Green said, "It's time to stop for today."

At this point, I went into the black hole of my early memories. That's what I call it. I had no tools for living. I didn't have a clue, not one. Someone else had told me who I was, what to do, when and how. I'd been thrown away. Absolutely thrown away, and I had no idea why.

They say I have no feelings. How can they say that? I'm scared to death of everybody and everything.

My primary feeling as a kid was being afraid of everyone. Whatever I told the doctors was used against me. It was always that way. If I shared an experience with anyone, they turned it around and used it against me.

I was locked down in a little room with no doorknob. A psychiatrist came in every day. He'd knock once before entering, introduce himself, and ask a few questions. While he spoke, I looked him over carefully.

"How are you feeling?" he asked. "I'm here to help you, you know."

Nodding, I said, "I'm okay."

"Are you comfortable?" he continued. He didn't sound terribly concerned. I wasn't sure what I saw.

"Yes."

Why do they ask me how I feel? How do I know? Besides, I hear them telling the other nurses and doctors that I have no feelings. That's what Jeri said. I wonder if they found Jeri? Did I tell them anything about her? I can't remember. Jeri knows everything. Everyone, even Jeri, said I had no feelings. I'm not sure if I even know what feelings are.

"I'm fine," I told the doctor. "I'd like to go." "Do you have a place to go to, Pegi?"

"Yes. I'm going to my parents in Three Rivers." "Why don't you tell me about them?"

"No. I don't want them to know where I am."

Once when he spoke to me, I told him my name was Pegi Crosby and I was an only child. The next time he came, I told him my name was Peggy Bearden and I was the eldest of six children.

"We'll talk more tomorrow." He patted my knee and left the room.

Every day, the doctor visited. Every day, he said the same things.

I don't belong here. I don't belong at home, I don't belong with the Crosbys. Just where do I belong? I'm not prepared for this! I'm not prepared for life! I haven't the slightest idea what to do. I don't know what's wrong, or how to go about fixing it! Somebody else has always fixed me.

I remained in the locked ward for twenty-nine of the ninety days I was in the hospital. Just outside my door, they gave shock treatments. This was the only time my door was unlocked. After the patients received shock treatment, they were wheeled into my room where I watched while they came out of their stupor. I saw it all: the mental patients' listless bodies, twisting and convulsing on the cold metal table. It was obvious they were confused.

Every one of them came to me with questions. Many cried and called me "Mommy." Half the time, I didn't know what the hell they were talking about. Just watching the procedure was a frightening experience for me. I kept quiet about it, though, because I'd seen too many patients led down the hall and given a shot because they acted out. I didn't want that to happen to me.

One time, when I was out of the locked ward, I became even more frightened at what I saw. Hundreds of women paraded the halls, all wearing muumuus, all alike.

This was by far the scariest place I had ever been. Padded cells were full of very disturbed people.

An old woman rolled in her dung. Like an animal in the zoo, another threw dung at the door whenever someone looked in. Mildred sat in a corner and masturbated. At times, her whole hand was inside her vagina.

One sat in the same chair day after day, rocking back and forth, hitting the back of the chair hard enough to knock herself silly. She was led to her dormitory every night by the nurses, and brought back out in the morning where she sat in the same chair all day.

Gertrude sat with her fingers twisted so hard her knuckles were white, her hands red and swollen from the blood being cut off. The nurses on the ward said she had to restrain herself from choking another human being. None of the other patients ever went close to her. I never knew if she was a murderer or not. That's one example of rumors the staff started.

Harriet rapidly paced the hallways, both arms swinging. Her mouth was always open, and she moved her tongue from side to side.

Ramona dug through the trash bins for used Kotex to put between her legs. At her feet lay all the bloody Kotexs. She'd look for the bloodiest. She'd wear them until they dropped out. She left used napkins dotting the hallways and all over the ward. Every time I saw those bloody used Kotex, I'd puke. The women smoked in the bathroom. The smell of smoke and the sickening bloody smell combined together, I puked and puked. Standing in the corner of the bathroom, the nurses talked among themselves about me washing and washing. "I'm washing the soap before I use it," I told them. To me, they acted like I didn't realize what I was doing.

Lucille was nearly bald. She sat in a corner and pulled out her hair, one strand at a time.

The minute a doctor came on the ward, Maxine ran to him, pulling off her clothes along the way. She screamed, "You want to play with my titty? Look, Doctor, look! Why don't you fuck me now, Doctor? Come on! No! No! You don't want to do it here, do you? Everyone will know what kind of doctor you are, huh, Doctor?" The remainder of the day, she ran through the halls naked.

The nurses were always calling other wards for a male technician to help restrain a patient.

Later the women were given make-up. Some didn't like theirs, and wanted mine. I wouldn't let any- body use mine. Some called me selfish. Finally I gave the make-up to the women.

In the classified ad section of The Los Angeles Times, I was lucky enough to spot an ad: "Pregnant? Let me help." I memorized the phone number, and planned my escape.

Within a few days, I went over the fence and ran to the first pay phone I could find, maybe twenty blocks away. I didn't know if the staff would look for me, but I wanted to be far enough away so I wouldn't be noticed in my muumuu. Only the patients from the state hospital wore muumuus, and I didn't want people on the street to know that I'd escaped.

I didn't have a dime. I got the operator and asked her to ring the phone number collect. When the person accepted my call, I told her I was seventeen years old, not pregnant, but I needed a safe place to go.

After finding out where I was, she told me to stay there and someone would come for me.

They took me to a home with working parents and an older grandma, along with their three children. I was a mother's helper. I worked there and saved my money.

It was there that I met and married my first husband, who was a Marine. It was a way out for me.

CHAPTER THIRTY-ONE

I was a mass of nerves up to the moment I gave the final painful push, and my daughter came out into the world.

The doctor put the loud, protesting, dark-haired baby on my breast. Finally! My very own baby! She's beautiful, and she's all mine! The thoughts did somersaults in my mind. This is what I've always wanted for so many years. My own baby. Now you, my little one, will replace all those I lost so many years ago. No one, absolutely nobody will ever take you from me. I'll see to it. I'll never do to you what was done to me. I promise!

With that vow a feeling of peacefulness came over me, unlike anything I'd ever felt before. It clung to me as I held the tiny infant wrapped snugly in a soft blanket. Tears stung my eyes as I held her in my arms and gazed down on her.

James Newman and I were married and had two beautiful children, three years apart. My husband was in the Marines, and later was transferred to North Carolina. Jeri paid for the air-fare for Shaunda and me to fly to be with him. I had been living with my mother, and Jeri knew I was very unhappy, therefore she graciously suggested that she'd buy the ticket. A couple of years later James was shipped to

Korea and I went home again to my mother. Really I had no other place to go.

I loved my children. For once, I felt normal and lived a normal life. I vowed to be a good parent and the strong basis of that pledge was that I would never drink like my mother and father had.

James was from a large family in Texas. They had a closeness I'd never experienced. I liked this big group of people very much and treasured being a part of it; however, I didn't like my mother-in-law, Zola. She was an alcoholic. My husband's parents were divorced and both were alcoholic. James father was a wine-o.

I don't really remember how it happened, but the family didn't like the name I'd given our daughter, and they called her "Sandi". I didn't like the name Sandi. I loved her name, yet I didn't have the self-esteem to insist that her name wasn't Sandi.

Most of the time, we lived with James' mother. A couple of times I talked James into moving out on our own, although we never could survive financially. But at least we weren't packed into one bedroom, like when we were living with Zola. Zola picked James up from work, on his payday. The two of them would drink all night. She'd bring me a bag of beans and a sack of potatoes to feed my family for the rest of the week.

James said I was jealous. I was, but it stemmed from much more and was deeper than that. I tried to go out with them, although I didn't drink. James and Zola seemed to know everyone. There were many women around. James wouldn't dance with me, yet he danced with those other women. He told me he wasn't able to say "no" to them.

"But you can tell me no!" I screamed at him.

We argued continually over it. Many nights, I'd disappear from the bar and walk home through the middle of Houston in the dark. James never asked where I'd gone or how I had gotten home. He simply didn't question it. He never hesitated to take me with him, because he knew I'd get angry, walk home and then he could do what he wanted to do anyway.

During the walks home late at night, I was always stopped by the Texas Rangers. The first time I was stopped, the Ranger asked, "Hey, are you Captain White's daughter?"

"Yes, I am, and I'm just walking a short way," I lied.

Every time the Rangers stopped me, I'd tell them I was Captain White's daughter, and they'd leave me alone. During these late-night walks, I got to know one Texas Ranger. I had an affair with him that lasted during the years I lived in Houston.

The first time I got onto a bus in Houston, I thought it funny that so many people were standing and hanging onto the metal bar overhead. The people swayed, lurching forward and almost falling into the aisle as the bus rounded corners.

I was holding my baby, Sandi, and staggered back taking a seat with an African American woman. She took Sandi from my arms and bounced her on her knees. Sandi reached out her tiny hand and began to rub the old lady's black face. Sandi looked at me, then back at the black woman.

People stared at us. They turned in their seats, whispering to others around them. Others poked the person in front of them and pointed at me.

I couldn't figure out what was wrong. Again, people were snickering and sneering at me. When I hopped off the bus with Sandi in my arms, all the people stared at me until I was out of sight. I tried to see behind me, thinking maybe I'd started menstruating and blood had covered my backside.

Another time, I was with James and Zola in a bar when a black man in uniform came in and sat at the bar next to James's mom. The bartender came over and told him, "Hey, buddy, you'll have to go to the back door. I'll bring a beer to you. We don't serve blacks in here."

I tapped Zola's shoulder and asked, "Did you hear what the bartender said to that black man?"

"Yes. Leave them alone. You stay out of it," she snapped. The bartender already had an open bottle of beer in his hand. When the young black man went to the back door, he was going to follow and give it to him.

I couldn't stand it. I said, "Bartender! Bartender, this young man has been in Korea. He's been fighting for your ass, and you aren't going to serve him?" Turning to James, I said, "You've been in the service. Are you going to allow this?" "Shh, Pegi, Pegi! Will you be quiet? You're going to get us in trouble."

The black man didn't want to cause any trouble. He went to the back door, where he got his beer and left.

It infuriated me to see anybody mistreat another human being like that. However, Zola made fun of me for what I had done. She told me blacks weren't treated like whites, and because I was from California, I didn't understand. She gave me a long list of things I shouldn't do.

Zola was white trash—far worse than any African American I'd ever known. I couldn't handle how she treated the blacks, even though she treated me just as badly. I simply couldn't fathom why, just because a human being came in different colored wrappers, they were looked down upon.

The Newman's were terribly prejudiced. My mother-in-law would shout, "When in Texas, do as the Texans do!" Frankly, I thought they were ignorant. Was it that calibre of thinking which had allowed the town of Springville to let my brothers and me starve? Was this another form of what had happened to us long, long ago?

I just didn't understand, and wanted no part of how these people lived. Afterward, I went to great extremes to treat blacks with the utmost respect. Every one of them would ask, "You're not from around here, are you?"

When I rode the buses, I always went to the back of the bus and sat with a black person. I was working in a restaurant in downtown Houston when the "sit-ins" started, and I proudly served the blacks.

I loved being a part of the big family, yet I was jealous of them. James' mother reminded me of my father, although she was not abusive. But on the other hand, introducing me as her daughter-in-law from California who "loved niggers" was certainly verbally abusive.

"I will not live this way!" I told her constantly.

During the few years I lived in Texas, I had an opportunity to meet some of Mama's sisters, and see my Aunt Anne again. I asked her to tell me what had happened the day when she had come to visit us.

She whispered in an angry voice, "Don't you ever mention that your Daddy almost killed me. I had to stay longer was so that I'd heal before going home. Don still doesn't know your daddy beat me up!" She continued, "and I don't want him to know now. Do you understand?".

I asked her, "when you came back to Texas why didn't you tell all the sisters how hard and abused we were?"

Again, "Peggy, I don't want to hear any of it. Drop it!"

I imagine everybody was frightened of my Daddy.

I finally talked James into moving back to California. We moved in with Mama. The four of us crowded into one bedroom again.

It was close to Christmas time when we moved back, but we spent Christmas with Jeri and Hunter. I'd always been in touch with them through letters.

By now, Mama had lived alone for a long time, and she had a better class of friends than before. She dated businessmen with nice homes and jobs. Her closet was full of long fur coats, capes, and fur-collared sweaters of every color. Mama always looked nice. She'd joined social clubs, and always wore a dress and heels. Her apartment was lovely, and expensively furnished.

While I lived with Mama, I'd steal her fancy furs and give them to Jeri for birthdays and Christmas. Mama never asked me any questions. I never knew if she missed them or not, because she had so many, or if she knew I'd given her expensive clothing to Jeri.

A mental analogy began taking place: my long-suppressed childhood rage came tumbling forth when Mama was around my children. My dark pit of early memories began to plunge me into anger and rage. The old demons returned whispering there was nobody I could trust, nobody to protect me.

When Mama was home, I'd curl up under a blanket and stare at her. Full of panic, I found myself afraid to move. There were no more corners left in my mind where I could hide.

The more I watched her around my children, the more I remembered the festering childhood resentments. She wanted to be "Nana" to my children. Deep inside, I didn't want her to be their Nana. She was critical of their manners, their grammar. When you got right down to it, she didn't even act like a grandma. Although I rationalized that she probably really wanted to be a grandparent, she just didn't know how.

One evening, Mama was getting dressed for a date. Before he arrived, she gave me a long lecture on how she wanted my children to act.

"For Pete's sake, Mama, they're only babies. Besides, how can you be so concerned about these babies? You really don't know how to handle kids. You didn't even raise your own!"

"What do you mean, I don't know how?"

"You know very well that you didn't raise your own kids. How can you raise mine? What do you know about grammar? I know more about manners and grammar than you'll ever know."

I couldn't bear for her to tell one of my children what to do. The love she showed me was fake. How could she show my children love and attention? I resented her. She told my two children she loved them, and I knew she meant it to the best of her abilities, however, she had never told me she loved me.

James worked nights, so my mother and I were alone in the evenings. I tried to talk to her, but I was young and really didn't know how. Just for starters, I asked her about the time Daddy had beaten her so badly and she was in the hospital.

Mama told me that when she had wakened in the woods, she was lying in a gully surrounded by a pool of blood. When she touched her head, she found it full of dried blood, and new blood was still oozing from her head.

She said her pain was unbearable. She was weaker than she'd ever been—so weak she could hardly move. Her eyes left my face and looked back into the past. "I felt I would be better off dead than to be alive and face one more beating. I saw no reason to get up; it would be easier to just let myself die." Her eyes misted at the remembrance.

Mama said it was the thought of her kids that forced her to get up. "I had to live. I had to find somebody to help me. Help my kids, if nothing else."

Mama said when she tried to stand, she couldn't support herself, so she fell down the hillside. It took several hours to get out of the gully. She made it to the top, only to tumble back to the bottom. She stayed there, hidden, knowing she would die.

She forced herself to crawl up to the top again. After resting for what seemed like hours, she dragged herself down the dirt-covered hills. From crawling on the ground, she tore her dress to shreds until she was finally dragging herself along completely naked. She kept herself moving, listening for cars or trucks and looking for lights from ranches.

Mama told me she never tried to stand during that awful night. The more she moved, the more blood spurted from her head. She dragged herself naked on her belly, with her head down, crawling across the mountains and fields. She would crawl for a while, then rest, exhausted from the effort.

Finally, she made it across the last hillside and saw a barn and house. There was a barbed-wire fence separating the hills from the pasture. It must have been more than a quarter mile away.

It took her longer to drag herself under the fence than it did to crawl to the house. When she got closer to the house, she screamed. Dogs ran toward her, barking loudly, then ran back to the farmhouse.

People came to the door more than once, but were unable to see her because she was on her belly, hidden in the tall grass. She was still too weak to stand. She finally crawled to the door of the house. A young girl pulled a curtain aside and stood staring out at Mama, but she was so frightened by all the blood, she closed the curtain fast. She didn't tell her parents that there was an injured lady in their front yard.

"The only reason I knew I had to survive was for you kids—it was the thing that urged me on as I crawled out of that gully for miles to find help. It would have been easier to lie there in my own blood and die, but I knew I couldn't leave you at the mercy of your father. And you accuse me of not knowing how to raise my own kids!"

With that she lapsed into the shadows of her own hell for a period of time. Mama sat for hours in a daze. Was she having one of those dreams she had had before, about seeing and hearing cars? I felt deep twinges of guilt at having initiated her trip into the darkness of the past.

Teasingly, one day she said to one of my children, after I had told them to do something, "Come to Nana. You don't have to do what Mommy says."

I boiled inside. How dare she tell my kids something like that? I wanted to scream, I hate you! I hate you! I'm horrified of becoming just like you. I truly hate you for what you did to me—my brothers and sisters! I cried inside and something snapped.

Running to the kitchen, I came back with a butcher knife, and chased her out of the house pursuing her down the block. I was like a crazed animal, and couldn't seem to find the reins of self-control. I do believe I would have killed her, had I caught her.

My emotional strength from my childhood days, had not yet formed scars.

Mama never came back home. She did sneak back to get her car sometime later. When I came home a few days later, she'd moved out and taken only her personal belongings. She left all her furniture. Within weeks, she'd quit her job and moved back to Texas to be near her sisters. I must have put the fear of God in her. I had no idea that I could chase her out of the state. I just wanted her out of the house and my life. I guess I got it.

Somewhere around this time I had my second breakdown. My two children were young. I caught my little daughter pulling out a bureau drawer to reach a bottle within those few seconds it took me to reach outand hit my daughter of perfume. I whacker her with all my might and knocked her to the floor. The blow was hard enough to break her little neck. Within those few seconds it took me to reach out and hit my daughter, my life of being beaten by my father flashed before my eyes.

In a wave of stark terror, I looked down at Sandi. She was unconscious, both arms stretched out on the floor. I lifted her tiny head and put in in my lap, rocking her back and forth.

It was as though I drifted into the past. Daddy was high over me holding that Christmas tree limb hanging limp at his side. The sharp crease of his trousers stroked my face. The scene drifted. Mama ironing his trousers and daddy screaming in the background, his face moving closer then away, shouting! Yanking his trousers off the table, he threw them on the foor, "Bitch! Can't you do nothing right!"

grabbing Daddy's trousers, Mama had ran to the sink to wash them one more time.

Still in a daze of trying to comfort Sandi, my minds eye watched Mama wrestling with Daddy on the bed. He was straddled over her holding a knife in his hand and was carving a big X on her belly. She was covered with blood. "I'm cutting this bastard kid out of ya", it ain;t mine, Winnie, and you know it, don't you?.

The toe of Daddy's shiny shoe, was level with my cheek. Coming to my senses with Sandi's head in my lap, I realized that I'd done what I vowed I'd never do to my children. For the first time in my life, I saw my Daddy in myself. At that moment I knew my daddy would be abused by me, in a flash of revelation, I knew I needed help and I didn't have the slightest idea of where or how to get it.

I went back and lived with the Crosbys and attended beauty college. I had almost a thousand dollars a month income from Social Security for myself and my two children. I gave the checks to Jeri for our expenses. She paid for my school, which was less than four hundred dollars. I had the money to pay for my school, but she insisted that she wanted to do something for me. For the next year, all I heard about was how much she helped me. She told me she had to go without in order to do for me.

I didn't really know. I'd never lived alone or had to manage one thing. I believed that the monthly income I gave her wasn't enough to support my two children and myself and believed she was going in the hole.

I got the children off to school in the mornings before I left for school. Jeri kept them for a few hours after school; they arrived home before I did. She trained them well to be her little top sergeants.

She also took them for all their doctor appointments. I couldn't bear it if one of them had to have a shot. I'd run from the room screaming. Just a small thing like taking my kids to a doctor was too much for me. I still had a fear of doctors from my days in the TB sanitorium. I'd be almost hysterical before I got one of the children into the doctor's office.

At the sight of blood, I'd run for my room, jump in bed, and cover my head. I had the same aversion with my children's teachers. I couldn't attend a student, teacher, parent conference. Just the thought of it was too much for me. My precious little kids would be crushed because I didn't attend like all the other students' parents did.

Memories of my school days flashed through my mind: old Miss Tarr pushing me into the tall, dark cloakroom; stealing lunches and puking. I couldn't deal with any of it. I hadn't the slightest idea where to begin. Therefore, Jeri took the children to their doctor appointments and went to their teachers' conferences for the next few years.

Everyone waited for me to get home to prepare dinner. I was back into the same groove, which was all right with me. It was far easier for me to have her take care of us. Every day, I asked Jeri for lunch money. I didn't keep one dime for myself. It was just better that way. In reality, I needed a caretaker.

When Hunter bought me a new car, Jeri was furious. "I've been married thirty years, and I've never had my own car," Jeri said one morning.

I drove by the Old Youth Hostile, which was on the route I drove by many times a day. Sometimes I'd pull over to the edge of the road and look down at the window where I lay hidden so many years ago, wishing that someone would rescue me. I never had the nerve to drive down the long driveway. I wanted to, yet every time I thought of doing it, I just couldn't bring myself to do it.

I kept a spotless house, and did everything else, including shopping and laundry. One day I asked Jeri for a dollar to buy a jar of mayonnaise to finish making potato salad for a picnic. She flew into a screaming fit.

"I don't have a dollar to give to you for your friends. It's all I can do right now to take care of you and your two children. Not that I'm complaining. You just don't understand how much it costs, Pegi."

I started dating, Jeri found something wrong with everyone I dated. Finally, I started dating Hunter's best friend, and soon married him. Luke and I were perfect strangers, and he was over thirty years older.

I wanted to get out of the house and away from Jeri and felt that this was the only solution for me. I only stayed with him three months before booting him out. Luke bought my children beautiful gifts, which he'd leave at Hunter's and Jeri's. They thought he was wonderful and loved my children because he left such great gifts. They felt so sorry for Luke because of the way I'd treated him.

I bought a small beauty shop and a home. Now I lived alone with my two children, and I really didn't want a man around. All I wanted was to live and take care of my two children. I was almost thirty years old, and I'd never lived alone. I'd never managed my own life. I'd never written a check or paid a bill.

And at that point in time the unthinkable happened. Since childhood I had regarded drinking as despicable.

It had been the cause of my father's drunken rages, my mother's promiscuity and child neglect. But I found myself sliding down into the quicksand of genetic patterns. Though I didn't realize it at the time, the strangle-hold of my love/hate relationship with Mama became the victor over my own actions. I had promised myself to never be like her, yet by some wicked transformation I was becoming her!

I started drinking.

CHAPTER THIRTY-TWO

Drinking became the magical release and cure for me. It made me feel normal, gave me the secure feeling I'd been searching for, allowing my low self-esteem to climb to new heights on a fictitious ladder whose rungs had been dipped in alcohol.

I crossed the line. I wasn't the only one like this. The drinking people I met were like me and had the same feelings I had. My new friends turned me on to the "magic stuff." It made me feel great, so I drank every day for the next eleven or twelve years. No matter what, I drank! It became the most important thing in my new world.

I rationalized, this is wonderful. This is my tool for living and coping. When I was little and watched all those people drink and wanted a drink so badly, this is what I was looking for. This feeling! This wonderful feeling. This is what I've been searching for all these years! I feel normal at last!

I was a workaholic as well as an alcoholic. I drank at home in the beginning, because I was told that "ladies" didn't drink in bars. I met a whole fraternity of drinking friends, and for many years went from house to house with my bottle and my kids. Every day I ran home from work, fixed dinner, put my children to bed, then drank all night.

Later, I left the kids with babysitters while I went out. I wouldn't arrive back home until it was time for them to get up for school.

I was like a tiger released from a cage. It was the first time I'd ever handled any money, the first time I'd paid my own rent, car payment, car insurance, or anything else. I was totally inept and therefore spent every cent I had. The word "save" wasn't even in my vocabulary.

These were the years I acted out. When I drank, I couldn't keep my clothes on. When I was drunk, I danced naked on the tables and skinny dipped in the river or swimming pools. At parties, I stripped off all my clothes. Quite often, someone would be pulling up my pants as I was pulling them down. One Sunday, I spent the whole day at the golf course drinking "Skip 'n go Nakeds." That night, I ran naked down the main street of Three Rivers.

When the era of streakers began, I considered the fad had been in my honor! I was the first streaker in Three Rivers. When it rained, I'd run naked down the main street of town. God! What fun! I thought.

The next day at school my children would suffer. Other kids would call them names and tell them what their mother had done the night before in the bars; however, nobody seemed to realize that whoever told them must have been in the bar also.

One day Shaunda came home from school crying, "Nikki said she couldn't play with me because I'm pregnant. I'm not pregnant am I, Mommie?" Her lower lip quivered.

"No sweetheart, you're not pregnant. Mommie is." I knew deep down that she didn't understand all that, and in reality I didn't either. I didn't do half the things that many of the married people did, yet I was the one they talked about.

I finally remarried. He was a drinker too, and he wouldn't work. Later, he brought in his twelve-year-old son, whom I couldn't support. This marriage lasted less than six months and produced an adorable red-headed boy, Danny.

When I drank, I went straight to oblivion—I was a blackout drinker. On the day after, I couldn't remember the night before.

The only thing that had changed for me was that I had my own home and business. Every day after work, I did the marketing for Jeri. I cooked their meals before I went home to prepare my children's. I cleaned all day Saturday, and maybe three times a week. In return, she kept Danny.

Jeri became more demanding. She was the centerpiece of my life. She'd call me at home to go back to the market or drugstore to get something I'd forgotten. She'd ask me to leave my home and my children, disregarding my inconvenience, even when she knew Hunter would pass right by there on his way home.

In the small community of Three Rivers, everyone drank and partied nightly. For me, it was one big party. When people told me I drank too much, I'd laugh and say, "Look who's talking."

What I didn't understand was that they didn't over-react to liquor the way I did. They might have too much to drink, but they had the sense to go home. They didn't end up in a blackout. They didn't leave their family.

I married again. While still married and living with my husband, he found a marriage license in the car. It stated I'd been married the night before in Nevada, to someone I didn't even know. I had no memory of the marriage or even being in Nevada. This marriage lasted only four months and the one marriage in Nevada I never took the time to have annulled. I simply forgot about it.

For the next ten years, I did nothing but drink.

Later I met a drunk who was the groundskeeper of the Three Rivers Golf Course. Giz was sixteen years older than I was. He had been born in Texas, still had his Texas accent, and a personality much like my father's. I'll never know why I was infatuated with him as he was really a drunken bum who treated my children and me terribly. I knew he didn't like Jeff, but he adored my baby Danny, so I thought things would get better. Giz said terrible things about Shaunda. But he said terrible things about his own daughter.

My low self-esteem wouldn't allow me to terminate this relationship. It got worse and worse. I lived in this sick relationship for six years, but put a band-aid on my wounds by satisfying my thirst for booze, sex and expensive possessions. The band-aid was soon to become the wound.

CHAPTER THIRTY-THREE

I came to and looked around the street. Nothing appeared to be familiar. I had no idea where I was or what day it was. I was parked in front of the Western Union office.

I glanced around inside my car. My mind was a raw blur. I couldn't get it together. What's wrong with me? I thought. I shuffled through my purse, fiddling with some papers inside. I don't know what's happened. Where am I? Where are my kids? What's happened to my money. God, why can't I remember anything?

I found a handful of change, then counted and recounted it. At least, I had a gasoline credit card. I'll fill up and start home. I tried to push myself toward some action.

I couldn't find the gas card. What had happened to it? I turned the key in the ignition. The car was on empty. I didn't even have enough fumes to move off the street. I panicked as I dug through my purse, searching for more money and my gas card. My numbed mind formed desperate questions. God, where am I? What day is this? Panic froze my mind. Gee, this car stinks! It's full of beer and vodka bottles. Who was with me? I don't ever drink like this.

My car was full of puke—the stench was putrid. It was hot and smelly. I opened the car door, and bottles clattered to the pavement.

I'm nearly naked. What's happened to me? Where are my clothes? I've never found myself like this before. And there is nobody I can ask.

A cop drove by and gave me a strange look. He passed me several times, then finally pulled up behind me and got out of his patrol car. He walked up to my side of the door. "May I see your driver's license, ma'am?"

"I can't find my wallet," I told him. "I guess I lost it." "You have California plates. Where in California are you from?"

"Three Rivers, California. Where am I, officer?" "You're in Sulphur Springs, Arkansas," he replied. "Arkansas! What in the world am I doing here?"

Arkansas? How'd I get here? God, where are my kids? I could feel the rapid beating of my heart which threatened to choke me. I must have driven to Arkansas. Questions swirled like snow flakes in a windstorm. Whom can I call? Jeri? Oh, God, not Jeri. Yeah, she'll know what to do. But I don't want to call her. Who else? Who else would know what I should do?

I didn't know what day it was, and I was afraid to ask.

But I sensed I'd been gone a long time.

The officer's booming voice startled my dreaming, "I don't know, ma'am. I was hoping you could tell me. Don't you know your name?"

"Yes. My name's Pegi Newman. I don't know what I'm doing here. I've always had money, but I don't have my wallet or my gas card. I've lost everything."

"Is there anyone you could call, ma'am?"

"Yes, I could call my mother, but I don't really want to. I'll have to give this some thought first."

"Well, ma'am, I'd like for you to move off the main street until Tuesday."

"I don't think I have enough gas to do that."

"Follow me. If you don't, I'll get enough gas to move you. For now, though, I want you off our main street until the holiday is over."

"Holiday? What holiday is it, officer?"

He looked at me strangely. "It's the Fourth of July." July fourth? It can't be. When did I leave California?

Why can't I remember. What was the last date I remember? Sometime in May is the last I can remember. Where are my kids? Does Jeri have them?

I followed the officer to an area behind a service station off the main street. He told me he lived just across the street and that he would keep an eye on me.

"We're just a small town here. Ya'll be safe."

Tuesday morning arrived and I was just down the street from the Western Union office. My heart hammered, and my palms were clammy. I knew if I called Jeri, I'd have to listen to a long lecture. I'd listened to her lectures long enough. I'd go to any length not to go through another one, especially about this predicament. I decided to send a telegram.

I stood in front of the Western Union office, waiting for it to open, counting my change. I was the only person around. Several hours later, the police officer returned to where I was parked. "Your mother, Mrs. Crosby, called me. She's wiring you fifty dollars. She said for you to come straight home." He invited me to his house to take a shower.

It took me three days to get back home. I never did find out what happened in that long, dark tunnel of time.

"Pegi, I don't know what happened, and don't care to know," Jeri told me. "But I've told no one about your nasty little adventure, and I don't want my neighbors to know."

I'd been gone about six weeks. That episode was the first step into a downward, spiraling free fall off the cliff of any hope of sobriety. It was as though I'd been deprived of so much as a youngster that now I was making up for it by drowning myself in drink and sex, never having enough.

Three other times over the next few years, I went through something similar to this experience. I always came out of the blackout in one of the southern states, looking for Texas. I was always almost naked, with no money. Once I took my crystal, china, and dog, but left the kids. I have no idea what I was looking for, except that Texas was where I had been born. Was I looking for long-lost relatives? I didn't know.

All those years with Jeri, one thing she'd taught me was that possessions were more important than anything. That was what I'd learned from her, and now I was teaching it to my children by going off and leaving them and only taking my precious, expensive things.

Jeri never wanted anyone to know about my trouble. "We don't want our neighbors to find out," she said. "Neighbors talk."

As my children got older, it was harder to keep secrets. They told everything. One time when I got back to Three Rivers, someone said, "Pegi, you did something I've always wanted to do. Just take off and leave the whole bunch."

The difference was, she only thought about doing it—I did it.

Once I came out of a blackout sitting on a plane on my way to Hawaii with Jeri's credit cards.

It was around 1965, and Jeri and Hunter were semi-retired. They joined some social clubs and began drinking heavily. Both of them went to different functions frequently, and it took much of the responsibility off me. I didn't have to prepare their meals every night.

Jeri still took heavy doses of prescribed medication along with her drinking. When I prepared their meals nightly, we had cocktail hour that lasted until nine o'clock, before dinner was served.

My children were home waiting for their's while I cooked their grandparents' dinner first. In later years, I managed to run home and put dinner in the oven for my children, so they could eat while I was at Grandma and Grandpa's.

Jeri often called me after 2:00 a.m. on many weekends, wanting me to come and help her with Hunter. Either she couldn't get him out of the car, or he'd passed out in the bathtub and she couldn't get him out.

At parties, after Jeri got drunk, she'd tell everybody that Hunter was impotent, useless, dead. She'd cry that he had a "hooked cock." The drunker Jeri got, the more she'd cry about Hunter and his sexual inabilities. I never did find out what a "hooked cock" was.

At parties, Hunter was always an ostrich. Down at the river, he'd try to literally bury his head in the sand. It's a wonder he never smothered.

In the late '60's, I had neighbors from Los Angeles. Both were artists, and much older than I was. Red and Ellie were retired. We became good friends, and I introduced them to Hunter and Jeri.

Three Rivers was a mountain town, and all the homes were built on large lots or many acres. Nobody had fenced yards, even if they had swimming pools. Actually, it was a small Peyton Place. There were parties every night, and always much drinking. If the sheriff stopped anyone for drunk driving, more than likely he'd take that person home never to jail.

Once, when I'd had a wreck and gone to the hospital, the sheriff went to my home and got my children so they wouldn't be left alone.

Late one night after the kids were in bed, I went down to join the party and found the Whitson's switching with Hunter and Jeri. I spied on them from the bushes. This went on for many years. Over the years, when I went to the Whitson's, I walked in on many local people switching partners with them.

It wasn't long before I was involved in the switching too. Not only did the drinking numb my senses, but because Hunter and Jeri thought it was okay, it seemed acceptable. By now I had been married four times, and I was living with a man who was sixteen years older than I was. Giz was like my father in many ways. He was a compulsive drunk, gambler, and a womanizer, but he had a fantastic sense of humor. Giz didn't support me—he lived off me. He'd give my baby Danny, who was one and a half, beer and a cigar.

Everyone laughed and thought it was funny.

I didn't laugh because it wasn't funny to me. But my low self-esteem, harnessed any action on my part. Giz told horrible things about me to his friends and to my face. He twisted things, and in the end, I didn't know what the truth was, or even what the topic of the conversation had been. It was a barbed form of mental abuse.

He was terribly judgmental. If a woman slept with a man outside of marriage, she was a bitch. But it was perfectly all right if a man did the same—except for his brother-in-law.

Giz bad-mouthed him plenty for sleeping around, but it was perfectly okay for Giz to sleep with whomever he wanted, including young babysitters his wife hired, while he was still living with her.

Giz liked to tell a bar full of men that I looked like a better piece of ass than I was. He told everyone about our sex life. His comments always found their way back to me. He craftily preyed on my low self-esteem in much the same way Jeri had.

Giz berated my thievery when he was just as big a thief, stealing equipment from the government yard for his woodcutting business. However, I was addicted to Giz's behavior like a black widow's mate. He had the same personality as my Daddy, and the same type of drinking cowboy friends. Giz wanted to be a gangster, but didn't have what it took.

Years later the secret to this habitual addiction was unlocked. One night I found Giz with another woman in a place where he lived off and on. When he wanted another woman, he took them there. In a drunken rage, I went home and got a deer rifle. With the gun loaded, I aimed at the woman's head and pulled the trigger. By the grace of God, the bullet lodged in the barrel.

I never wanted to shoot or kill anybody. My life was being controlled by the drinking and this sick relationship. It's hard for me to believe that I was ever attracted to such a humiliating relationship. I still have a wrenching, nauseous feeling when I think about it.

Much later, my daughter Shaunda told me that Giz molested her. She said she told me at the time, but I did nothing about it. Sadly, I have no memory of her telling me. I do remember that Jill, who also was a drunk, told the Crosbys that she'd heard Giz molested my daughter. Jeri told me. When I confronted Giz, he became so enraged that he went directly to the golf course and waited until Jill and her husband were in the bar. Even though the bar was full of local people, Giz publicly denounced Jill for passing along such rumors. He threatened to sue both of them for libel if they didn't quit. He also demanded that Jill retract her statement to everyone in the bar, as well as the entire community, and he made them drive to the Crosbys and tell them that she'd lied.

Giz came home telling me that Jill had gotten down on her knees begging him not to sue her husband. She begged everyone's forgiveness. Giz repeated the story to everyone who'd listen in Three Rivers. Because he seemed so indignant and angry about the accusations, I believed him. But today, more than twenty years later, I know he was lying.

I believe Shaunda now. Looking back, I know he was capable of molesting her. He was filthy, and he called his own daughter a "fucking cunt" for getting pregnant out of wedlock. Yet it was all right for him to molest a thirteen-year-old girl.

During one period of time, when Shaunda was a runaway, I got into therapy again. One Saturday while I was cleaning Jeri's house, I blurted out, "I'm going to therapy."

"Oh my God, please, not again," Jeri waved one hand dramatically. "Please, Pegi, don't tell anyone in town. It'll make us both look bad, you know."

Still searching, I married again, this time to a man who had been born in Portugal. We lived on a ranch south of Tulare and Shaunda came back home to live with us.

John's kids told me he'd beaten them with chains and shovels. He was one mean man! One of his sons was a brother in the Catholic order. When Brother Manual came home one summer, he told me about the last time he'd come home, when his mother was dying.

His mother had cancer, and had been moved to a convalescent hospital in Visalia. She was in a coma, and when he entered her room, he found his father on top of her with his pants off.

The description made me feel deathly ill. I went home and crawled onto the sofa. I was in emotional pain, though I didn't understand what was wrong. The temperature was above 100 degrees, but I was freezing. I got a blanket, crawled into a fetal position and cried myself to sleep. It was then that I had flashbacks of my Daddy on top of my Mama when she was in Tulare County Hospital in a coma. It took several days for the dream to surface and present itself to my conscious mind. When it did, I got drunker and drunker. I decided I was going to leave this marriage too. The alcohol had now devastated my decision-making abilities. I did the unthinkable—I went back to Three Rivers and continued to live with Giz.

In retrospect, I think I was looking for someone to "fix" me. I thought if I got married, everything would be all right. I was looking for a way out. I'd lost more than thirty-five years of myself. I believed Jeri's definition of me. She'd succeeded in making me a stranger to myself, and I thought someone else would eventually come along and take responsibility for me. I'd dreamed about growing up, getting married, and living happily ever after. But that wasn't what was happening to me.

When I was single, Jeri would say, "Why don't you just get married." If I was dating someone, she'd say, "Oh, marry him. Things will be all right."

When I'd get married, things weren't all right. They generally got worse. My life was totally unmanageable now and I was completely out of control.

The last time I went to Texas during a blackout, I went to see Mama. She had a four bedroom home and was taking care of old women. I watched her intentionally break an old lady's arm.

Jeri and Hunter sold their home in Three Rivers and moved to Seal Beach. Their main reason for leaving Three Rivers was because of my drinking, my kids, and my lifestyle. But we were still close; however, they were far enough away that they couldn't see everything, or be degraded by my actions.

A couple years later, at seventeen, Shaunda married and moved to Woodlake, a nearby town.

I finally left Giz and moved to Visalia. It was to be my fresh start, but I had no idea my free fall was accelerating to a body slam with the earth.

CHAPTER THIRTY-FOUR

The room was dark. On one wall was purple and black wallpaper with shiny, blinking stars. Weird sounds came from an entertainment center—music like I'd never heard before. I heard water running from the shower behind the wall, near my head. I was on a high waterbed and someone was lying beside me, his face turned from mine.

Who is this, and where am I? My mind scrambled to make sense of this strange place.

The bedroom door opened and a man's booming voice hollered, "Eric, get up. You're late for school."

A young boy's voice whispered, "Don't move. Be still. If my folks find out you're here, they'll kill me...and you, too."

"Folks?" Oh God, Pegi, what have you done now? His folks won't kill him, they'll kill me! He must be a kid. God, Pegi, you've really done it this time.

Eric hopped out of bed, grabbed a towel, and was out the door in a flash. I was still bombed and in a stupor. I couldn't open my eyes. I felt my face, and realized that my hair was glued to my face with semen.

Hurriedly, I put on my clothes and tiptoed from the house, carrying my shoes. I left the front door open and headed for home.

My boys were still asleep in bed when I arrived.

It was then I realized that I'd gone off and left my purse at Eric's house. I had three hundred dollars or more in it—all the money I had to my name. I wasn't sure I wanted to go back for it, and besides, I'd forgotten where he lived.

A few days later, I received my purse in the mail, containing all my money.

For the next few nights that followed, I found myself in jail. I'd either been picked up for drunk driving or being drunk in public. All those years I'd lived in Three Rivers, Deputy Carl Sisk and Dean Moore had protected me by taking me home, or finding someone who would. Now I wasn't in Three Rivers, and every time I left the house, I was picked up for being drunk. I accused the cops of following me. Most of the time, I was picked up early, and they only detained me a few hours. One morning, I didn't get out of jail until eight A.M. When I arrived home, Danny greeted me at the door. He was dressed perfectly for school and had his lunch packed.

"Where were you, Mommy?" He was only six years old.

"I had car trouble and couldn't get home."

"I waited and waited for you. I could have got on the bus, but I was scared. I didn't know where you were."

Even though he was late, I drove Danny to school. All I could think about that morning was how badly I wanted to be a good mother. I loved my children more than anything, yet I didn't know how to be a mom. I didn't want to be a drunk like my Dad, but that's exactly what I'd become.

I started crying and couldn't stop. The harder I cried, the more I thought about Jeri and how she'd scream at me for crying, and tell me that the crying just proved I was guilty. I cried even harder.

I didn't want my children to have to live this way, but I didn't know how to stop what I was doing. Where were the brakes?

When I came back home after taking Danny to school, I sat at the table drinking coffee and crying. Probing questions shook a finger at me. Is this what I'll be doing the rest of my life? Is this all there is? I want to change, but I honestly don't know how. I always thought alcohol was a magic potion—now I'm not so sure! What happened? It's all changed! Damn! I hate God. He's never done anything for me but put me through hell. I know there can't be a God to put a person through the hell I've lived in.

My hatred for God didn't stop me from praying however.

I prayed that this would never happen to me again.

The next day, I was back in jail for public intoxication. After five or six hours, I was released. As I walked up the ramp at the Tulare County Jail, I looked into the sky and begged God to help me. The image of a big man emerged into my view. He was grinning down at me. I blinked to clear Him from my vision, but His image remained right in front of me. If Jesus was God is that what He looked like, or was I hallucinating? Maybe I was starting into D.T.'s? But maybe this was the man Jesus I'd heard of when I was a child. When Daddy beat my Mama I had run up the stairs to His church, pounded on the door, but no one had answered.

Was this what He looked like?

When I got home, I got down on my knees and prayed for God to take away my desire for drinking.

Right there on my living room floor, I took those first three steps that the big book of Alcoholics Anonymous talks about. I didn't know anything about the first three steps then. What I did know was that I was powerless over alcohol, and my life was unmanageable. My life had never been manageable.

I already believed that only a greater power could restore me to sanity. I just didn't know if He would, because of all the bad things I'd done with my life. I got on my knees and asked God to please, just please help me. I didn't ask Him to help me not to drink, because I didn't know that drinking was my problem. I simply asked Him to please help me.

The image of the man resurfaced—fading in and out. Finally the image became that of a man I recognized as Homer Gentry. What was God trying to tell me? Were my heart and ears open to what He was saying? Homer was a man in Three Rivers I'd once known. People there talked about how he didn't have to drink anymore. Mr. Gentry was Shaunda's eighth-grade teacher. I knew he once had a drinking problem, but now his life was much better.

For years I'd hidden from my past, now I realized I had to face it. Despite my fears and shaking hands, I managed somehow to get to the phone and call him. His wife told me he was teaching, but she'd get a message to him. Within an hour, he called me back. He sent a woman over to see me right away.

I was terrified that day. Little did I know that the little ray of hope would grow into a raging flame. I never drank again. I was thirty-eight years old. I went to two Twelve-Step meetings every day for the next four years.

That night I went to my first AA meeting holding Danny by the hand. I took a sleeping bag and he fell asleep on the floor. For the first year of my sobriety; this was the pattern. Danny and I both were both so withdrawn, neither could carry on a conversation with anybody.

I busied myself, washing cups and dumping ashtrays.

Another member would ask, "How are you, Pegi?" Looking at the floor, I'd answer, "Fine."

Then she'd ask, "How are you, Danny?"

Sticking his thumb in his mouth, he'd bury his head between my legs, too withdrawn to answer. Neither of us had ever had anybody care before.

My craziness didn't end by not drinking. I still had a multitude of serious issues to deal with, many of which needed professional help. The shell I'd built around myself had grown so hard nobody could break through, no matter how valiantly they tried.

For my entire life, I'd been totally empty inside. I'd closed off my emotions early in my life. I didn't consider other people's feelings because I didn't know how. I didn't understand the pain I caused. All I knew was that there came a point when I knew there was something dreadfully wrong. I'd never learned any life skills, not even how to raise my own children. I simply didn't know how. I couldn't feel pain, physical or mental. The only release I could remember was crying. That was my only release. Being fearful of women, I wouldn't allow one to get close to me.

All the people I met in recovery were the "huggingest" people I'd ever seen. The minute one came for me with her arms outstretched, I'd put up my arms to protect myself and ward them off. Not knowing whom to trust, I trusted no one. I pulled away from their closeness. As far as I knew, every kiss, every hug, had a price. I was empty inside, but that was all right because empty was safe. I didn't have to deal with my feelings.

None of the adults who should have nurtured me as a child ever did. Those I'd trusted either inflicted harm or failed to protect me. By keeping silent, I thought I could make it all go away, but more importantly, I didn't believe I deserved another chance at happiness.

When I went to my first AA meeting, I had no idea what the people were talking about, when they spoke about their "feelings". There was a tidal wave of demonstrative love which threatened to drown me by the twenty-some men and women sitting around a big table drinking coffee and smoking. These were about the smoking-est, coffee drinking-est people I had ever seen. They talked about their feelings constantly. This big bunch of people radiated with love. They just wanted to hug each other all the time.

Well, I didn't like it. I didn't like being touched by people I didn't know. I'd put my hands up right away and not let them near me. The only love I knew came from zippers going up and down in the back seats of cars.

If I hear these people talking about feelings one more time, I'm going to puke! I told myself while arranging Danny in his sleeping bag at my feet. What is this thing called feelings? All my life, I've heard about feelings this... feelings that. At times, I thought I knew what they were, but now I know I really don't. Why don't I have them? Jeri always said I had no feelings. All those doctors and nurses said I had no feelings. Where do I get them? What are they? I'm empty—a vacuum, I know I am! Nothing in the world can fill this robot-like emptiness.

In AA, we tell our story and try to identify with another AA member. When a newcomer enters AA, they tell their story to the best of their ability. With each new day, week, month, and year more is revealed. We are told in AA that God never reveals to us more than we can handle.

Now, once again, I had to hear the word "God." What had He done for me? Nothing! Was it because I was just a piece of shit? Because that's really all I felt that I was—just a piece of shit. All God ever did was abandon me—just like my Daddy.

One of the things you do in AA is find another person you can identify with. That person is usually your sponsor. It has to be somebody you can trust, someone you can talk with. A sponsor is generally somebody with two or more years in sobriety, someone who can help you through difficult decisions and show you how to work the Twelve-Steps of the A.A. program.

I didn't have the nerve to pick a sponsor, so someone chose me. I didn't like that, but I didn't have the nerve to say anything, so I ended up with someone I didn't like. Every time I talked with her, she told me choice tidbits about the other AAer's, so I knew she was talking about me too. One of the last times I spoke with her, she said, "Oh, have you heard what they're saying about Sherlene?"

"Oh, you mean that she's so nice...that only a jerk would say something about her?"

"Humph," she said, giving me a freezing look.

Even though I still had an inner battle going within about females, I disapproved of bad-mouthing another woman.

During the first four years of my sobriety, the little girl, Peggy, appeared to me during a meeting of Alcoholics Anonymous. In the early stages of my sobriety I had awful flashbacks of the little girl, Peggy.

I knew it was my child-self. I could tell by looking at her, and she looked just as I had at five years old. She wore the same tattered, ragged dress with all the torn lace and missing sash. I tried looking away, but she'd dance right in front of me. If I moved my eyes, she'd change positions to be in the center of my focus. She'd dance off toward the men, trying to get their attention. Twirling in her dress, she'd show off her bare bottom. Nobody else was watching the little girl, therefore I surmised I was the only one who could see her. Once again I thought it was the results of "drying out".

The little girl Peggy only appeared a few more times early in my sobriety. I desperately tried to push her aside. One of the last times she appeared to dance on the table during the meeting, I dropped my head into my arms and didn't look up. I didn't want to watch her. When the meeting was over, she was gone. Sometimes she'd appear standing in the door, staring at me.

What was she trying to tell me, and why did she only appear during the meetings? My child-self never showed up at home. Was the twirling bare-bottomed little Peggy hinting at some necessary key to continue sobriety?

Could this be why she only appeared during the AA meetings? Peggy, of my inner self, seemed to be sending some mysterious signal to Pegi the grown woman.

CHAPTER THIRTY-FIVE

Inside, I was a child, younger in my thinking than my six-year-old son, Danny. To leave the past, I had to wipe the slate clean.

Many of the first meetings I attended were birthday meetings. That was where the members celebrate one or more years of sobriety. Whoever was having the birthday led the meeting, describing how it was before, and how it was now.

I was never able to celebrate a birthday. Even though I wanted to more than anything, I couldn't. The more I'd try to celebrate my AA birthday, the more frantic I'd become. I'd never had a belly-button birthday, so how could I celebrate a sobriety date.

My first sponsor told me I didn't have good sobriety if I didn't celebrate my sobriety date. It wasn't my intent to have "good sobriety." I only wanted to stop drinking.

Because I'd spent thirty seven years living in totally abnormal conditions and craziness, I realized it would take me far longer than most to get myself back on track. I figured it meant more than ten years of really hard work in a Twelve-Step program. If I'd known what to expect and how long the healing process would actually take, maybe the change wouldn't have been so scary.

Upon my entry to AA, I was Pegi Newman, maiden name Crosby. I'd been adopted by the Crosbys and had been raised as an only child.

The Crosbys didn't drink during my growing-up years, and I couldn't figure out why I had become a drunk. I'd never thought much about who I really was. The Crosbys and I had settled into the fantasy that I had always been their daughter. I'd had this perfect life as the only child in this wonderful family. It took me almost eight years (after sobriety) to wake up to the reality of who I really was. I had to come to terms that I wasn't Pegi Crosby, and never had been.

If I happened to run into somebody on the streets I'd gone to school with and who might ask about one of my brothers, only then did my past life surface.

In group, when we spoke about where a child is in her family role, I never knew where I fit into my family role. I almost went to my grave not knowing who I was.

I learned that your role makes up your part in the family drama: superachiever, caretaker, victim. I always stated that I was an only child, therefore I had no role in my family. My core material was a collection of selected perceptions, repressed feelings, and false beliefs. This became the filter through which I interpreted all new hopes and dreams in my life. That primitive child's adaptation allowed me to survive childhood, but it was a poor filter for adult survival. That was why I wound up in Norwalk State Hospital at the age of seventeen. Finding a strong faith in this group of people, I tried to hang onto them while moving into the future. I had a strong fear of abandonment and loss, even without knowing what that loss was. I just knew that somewhere along the way everybody would leave me. And if you didn't, then I'd do it to you first, thinking that I'd do it to you before you did it too me. I was constantly seared with the fire of anxiety. I just couldn't bare the feeling of abandonment. My insides would roll with the fear of being abandoned.

In a sense, the group became my family. They gave me support and nurturing. I got a new sense of myself. I couldn't have done it alone.

Simply not drinking wasn't enough for me. It had to be much more. My every thought and action had to change.

I began to think, "Wouldn't it be wonderful to have a sober husband?"

The first thing my ears were open to was, "Now you're sober. Things will be different. No more drinking, blackouts, fighting, and divorces."

It didn't take me long. In two weeks, I looked across the table and there he was. It was love at first sight. I felt good when he was around. Within a few weeks, we were living together.

Herman had two daughters—Sandy who was in her late twenties and lived outside the home, and Julie, seventeen, who lived with him. I knew that Julie smoked marijuana. Danny was only six, and I had no idea that her pot smoking would affect him. He had been told repeatedly that drugs were bad. Julie wasn't any different from any other girl. She lived with the dream that her mother and father would get back together. Julie's father wouldn't give her money, and she bought all her clothes at the Salvation Army store while he donated money to non-profit organizations and the

National Council on Alcoholism. A few months later, Julie graduated from high school and moved out on her own.

It was at this juncture that I lost sixteen year old Jeff in the horrible automobile accident. His death resurrected the crying of babies, the visions of babies, the mummy wrapped in newspaper. I fought to stay sober as the AA group wrapped their arms around me and my grief.

I'd been sober a year and a half when my brother Mickey called to tell me that Mama had died. It had been fourteen months since I'd lost Jeff and I was still trying to deal with the images from my past which had appeared at his death. Inch by inch things emerged from my subconscious, floating upward to present themselves to my conscious mind.

While on the telephone with Mickey, things began to surface, I finally knew why I'd had all those visions that began at the mortuary when Jeff was killed.

Flashes of old scenes of memories from my early childhood flooded my mind like a movie running backward: Mama standing at the sink holding a baby under the water; Mama screaming at me to hold a small squirming body under the water...

My heart pounded frantically, forcing my thoughts away from the pictures of what I knew was so frightening. But they were right there, trying to struggle out. Most of us have had the experience of being on the verge of saying something in a conversation, and suddenly forgetting what it was. The poison from my past festered in just that manner. The feeling would last for days while I rummaged through the closets of my subconscious trying desperately to remember what my mind had discarded so long ago.

During the days I'd stay busy so that I wouldn't have to think. I was overwrought with fear and tried to sweep the memories under the rug, but they kept oozing out.

But one common element kept trying to surface: visions of dead babies. I would awaken from a sound sleep hearing babies crying. I'd get up out of my bed and go into the empty bedroom, where I'd collapse into a corner to cry and sob. Finally, I'd get up and get in bed with Danny. For a long time, that was the only place where I could sleep.

Although the deaths were not my fault, and didn't happen by my hands, I was still frightened and didn't know where to turn. During my sleep, visions of Mama floated over me. I could still see her flashing eyes and hear that tone she used when she wanted to make sure I was listening. "Peggy, don't ever tell about those babies. You know you'll get in trouble. I'll get in trouble. You'll never see your brothers again. You must keep your lips buttoned!" The movie of my life began to run again, backward in jerky movements. Sometimes it would pause at the beatings I received from my Daddy, but that wasn't the real horror. It was those babies diving at me, bombing me again... being abandoned...Patches digging with dirt flying...a dead squirrel which turned into babies crying...Mama with dead babies...me with dead babies... something wrapped in paper, a tiny bundle... the bloody glob under Mama's bed...

and finally of Mama drowning her babies.

I saw myself moving in fast-forward, jerky movements. The reel stopped, rewound, and froze the action so I could study it more closely. And deep within my mental repository, I began to fully comprehend the common threads of all my visions and memories.

Finally, for the first time in many years, I felt relieved. Even though I was terribly frightened at what I'd just experienced in a fiery furnace of recall, at least now I knew why I'd had such a difficult time in my life. It was much, much more than simply just being abandoned and losing my brothers and sisters.

I was freed and no longer had to carry Mama's secret. I gave myself permission to forget all those dead babies. I had crossed that threshold of the door to all the painful memories as it now swung wide open over the next several years.

Losing Jeff had opened a wound I would fight for the rest of my life. I received Social Security for Jeff, before he died and myself. Herman needed the checks for his pet store and I gave them to him. After all, he was furnishing my children and me with our needs, I rationalized.

At the end of the year, Herman and I were married. I simply adored him, and so did Jeri and Hunter. He had the money, and that gave him the power. This was the type of man Jeri had always wanted me to marry. For once, she was happy. I had pleased her. This was something I continued to strive to do.

Herman was my seventh husband. I didn't have any business getting married again. I still didn't know who I was. I'd been sober only a few months, and my brain was still full of cobwebs. All I ever wanted was a better life, and now that I was sober, I was positive it would be better.

Everyone told me not to make any serious decisions during my first year of sobriety, and I knew that a lot of people thought it was a mistake to get married. But why shouldn't I? This was what I'd always hoped for. A sober man. Everything was perfect. He was sober, and I was sober.

I thought in sobriety, it wasn't possible to make unwise decisions. I had that perfect AA marriage, and now that I was sober, I was sure we would work things out. I honestly believed I couldn't have made it without this relationship.

Herman was truly my first love. I was happy. God had given me one more chance at being a good wife and mother. I'd messed up all the others, but this one was right. I worshiped him, and it was unthinkable to believe that our love would end some day.

It was an all day and all night job with Herman. I ran myself ragged doing for him and doing what he wanted. My day with Herman never ended until I went to bed. I had never worked so hard in my life, even at Jeri's bidding. Little did I realize that I had just traded my obsession for pleasing Jeri to one of pleasing my husband. When there were problems, I just thought that someday I'd get it right. Someday I'd be able to please him.

Like me, Herman had been in many failed marriages. We fantasized about our marriage. He was the first person with whom I thought I could spend the rest of my life.

I was thirty eight years old, and had my first orgasm with him. If I'd had them in the past, I was too drunk to remember, or maybe too young. I had yearned for the type of passion and love I'd read about and watched in movies. I had dreamed of being swept away by a man with consuming passion. That was what I had in this marriage.

In reality, I had dreadful sexual hangups. My mind was twisted about sex. I wanted to like sex. I'd heard from so many that it was grand. I'd thought I was frigid. If I was drinking, sex was easier. But if I was sober, I'd never have sex. That was one of the reasons I married so often. I really hadn't slept around much.

I entered every relationship hoping for the best. Most of the time, I got it, but I didn't know what the hell to do with it, how to deal with it, how not to be frightened by having managed to get exactly what I wanted. No one told me what I needed to know. So I kept on confronting one after another, convinced that a man would come and help me make sense of myself, help me become me...rescue me.

Jeri supported my theory. "If you don't find someone to marry now, you never will."

I still thought she was right, and I knew nothing. I willed myself to fall in love one more time. So I stepped in, laid myself down, and told myself that this was love. This time it would be different.

And what I fell into was the most obsessive, the most destructive, the most dangerous relationship of all.

CHAPTER THIRTY-SIX

Right from the beginning, I knew something was wrong with this marriage. With my self-hatred and low self-esteem, I blamed myself and continued to try harder at pleasing Herman. He provided me with a weekly allowance for the household expense, and in return, I had to give him an accounting of every penny I spent. Most weeks he handed me the checkbook with a twenty-dollar balance, telling me not to overdraw the account for our weekly groceries.

Herman manipulated every situation, and I let him do it. When it came to many people in AA, Herman was obsessed with them. He would run into the house in the evenings and proceed to call all his men friends about the forthcoming meetings. They'd decide over the telephone who was going to lead the meeting and who would call on whom.

The school was calling me every day with complaints about Danny and his behavior. I was never aware of any strange behavior with Danny. He was quiet and withdrawn, but I thought that was a fairly normal personality trait. I didn't think it strange behavior. Then the school called with questions concerning me, particularly targeting concerns about my pregnancy with him.

I was too new in AA to tell them the truth when they asked if I drank alcohol while pregnant. I was in denial, even though I wasn't drinking. I told them that I never had. The school called me at least once a week with questions about Danny, and continued to probe further into my pregnancy with him.

At the time, I didn't fully comprehend about the abuse of my children. Their lives were so much better than mine had been. They were clothed and fed. They had a nice home to live in. In 1976-77, not much was known about child abuse. Most of the abuse my children suffered came from me, but I buried the memories in blackouts. It took nearly twenty years for some of it to surface.

Herman kept two sets of books for his store. He falsified over ten thousand dollars on his taxes, and I had to sign. I was against it, yet I still had to sign. He even complained about my reluctance to Mr. Gentry, his AA sponsor, who laughed and belittled me. He was my good friend who had introduced me to AA.

When Herman got mad at me, he'd go into the bird room of the pet store. He'd pace from cage to cage, pulling the little birds' heads off. This should have been a malevolent signal about his violent nature; however, I didn't recognize it as that as I was in love and pleased with the fact that I was sober. I mistakenly thought because of those two factors, this marriage could be saved.

During the summers and weekends, the employees could bring their children to the store, yet my son Danny wasn't allowed to be there. Herman and I fought over it continually. Danny was a latchkey kid. At home, Herman would fly into a rage over the employees' kids being at the store, though he was the one who had given permission for them to be there.

Finally, after he had a heart attack, I told one employee to leave her children at home. She told Herman that I'd told her she couldn't bring her children to the store anymore.

Herman immediately reversed that decision by saying, "Oh, Linda, bring your children. They're no problem."

I was still very close to Jeri and Hunter, and viewed them as my true parents. I rarely spoke about my real family, except to the few who had gone to school with us. I was into my forties, and my past was long behind me. It seemed like a bad dream.

For once, I'd done the right thing, in Jeri's eyes, and as a result our relationship grew even closer so that one day I felt comfortable enough to ask her, "Why wouldn't the welfare office pay for a tutor for me? That was the main thing that made school so hard for me. All the other students teased me about being dumb. That made me an outsider."

"You know you had severe mental problems, Pegi," she told me. "We were told that you were retarded."

"Retarded!"

"Well... maybe not retarded. Maybe that isn't the right word. But you did have a mental block. And there was one time when we had you tested, and we were told you were retarded."

"If I was labeled as retarded, why didn't you find out if it was true?"

Enraged, Jeri jumped up from the table and threw her arms into the air. "I'd rather not discuss this any further! You're trying to blame me! It's all my fault. Everything is all my fault. It doesn't even matter what happened to you before we got you. It doesn't matter that your own mother didn't want you! Okay! Okay!" She lifted her arms to signify surrender. "You always blame me because you don't have your real mother to blame."

She took a deep breath and sighed. "She's the one who caused it all, you know! She's the one who didn't want you! I'm the one who did want you, and who helped you! Now you blame me!" Her eyes blazed with anger. "Okay! Okay, I'll take all the blame! You're still the same. You haven't changed a bit. Your mother could have collected hundreds of dollars from welfare had she kept you children. She didn't want you. When will you believe that! Don't ever bring up this matter again!"

Jeri was still taking vast amounts of prescribed medicine. It finally dawned on me that Jeri was addicted, though she would have never admitted it as it was all prescribed.

At the same time I was getting off alcohol, my seven-year-old Danny was learning how to smoke pot. Lord help me, I truly didn't know. Even when I was drinking, I never would have allowed him to use pot. Herman's daughter had introduced my son to it. I didn't find out until he was fourteen and seriously hooked into the dark addiction.

It blew me away. I had no idea. Those last five years, I had thought I was getting my life together. For once, I was the mother I'd always wanted to be. I'd had another chance to do right with this child—a chance I'd never gotten with my other two. Because I was sober, this one child had a decent mother. Now, I was faced with the fact that my accolades to myself was really a cruel joke.

In retrospect, I was too busy with my fellowship. I was going to two meetings a day, and I worked full time for my husband. I thought our life was picture perfect, but the picture was seriously flawed.

I was sober four years when this marriage ended. I hated and blamed myself for so many things. Herman was truly my first love, and this was the first time I'd realized that it took more than love alone for a relationship to survive.

Jeri continued to be a big factor in my life. I couldn't do anything without her. I had to have her approval for everything I did; however, she also remained close to my ex, Herman. Every time I said something to her regarding our breakup, she'd say, "Well, that's not what Herman said!" When I bought a new car, Herman called and told her before I even had the chance. He told her I'd embezzled from his business, which wasn't true. I did take money without asking but I didn't embezzle.

When she found out Danny was on drugs, she wouldn't believe it at first. She told me it was all my fault—which it was. I had enough guilt; I didn't need her to heap on more. Herman told Jeri that I had known Danny was on drugs when he was seven. But I didn't, and neither did he.

Jeri and I fought about it. When I called her, she'd tell me to never call again, and hang up the telephone on me. I finally quit calling, and she never called me again.

Danny truly missed his grandparents. I told him daily that he could call them anytime he wished, yet he never did. He was crushed. I blamed Herman for all of it. He also tried to sever my relationship with my daughter.

Hunter was also abusive. Hunter and I had never argued. The problem was between Jeri and me. Hunter was a lovable, wonderful man who was willing to have peace at any price. He crawled into his shell and stayed there. Hunter never called me. He allowed Jeri to do what she wanted. His permissive acquiescence made him just as guilty as she was in my opinion.

What the Crosbys did to me was insidious. It was not physical abuse in a legal sense, but it was certainly mental cruelty. It was as if she had drilled a hole in my head and poured in all her twisted mind-controlling, demanding thoughts. They kneaded and shaped me into the child they wanted me to be, and I tried to adhere to the measurement of their visions. They whistled, and I danced like the dancers they taught.

I now felt like a puppet whose strings had been cut. I fell in a heap with no place to go. While in therapy, a counselor had suggested that I go to a psychiatrist. Swallowing my fear, I went twice a week for almost two years.

One morning, I cried to the doctor about Jeri. "I just don't understand why I always do this to myself. Why do I listen to her, when she just makes everything worse for me?"

"Why do you?" Dr. House asked.

"I don't know. Self-inflicted punishment, I guess, but I love her so much."

"Do you really? Do you call this kind of treatment 'love'?" "Well, she doesn't want me calling her, so I'll stop. Beginning today."

He folded his arms over the massive barrel of his chest. "I think that would be a good idea, but I feel it's going to be very hard for you, since you're so dependent on them. However, in the long run, it will make you stronger...help you to think for yourself. Who knows...maybe you'll even find who you really are." His kindly eyes probed mine.

I felt good when I left Dr. House's office that day. This first step was a huge jump for me, because I truly loved them both. I still had to deal with commitments to my past while holding hands with the future. And I knew I had to face myself in a different way, in a way I'd never done before, and by leaving behind the person I'd been, I had to bury the little food-foraging Pegi on the garbage dump of her past.

I had to get away from those patterns. It wasn't possible to separate the good and bad from my own past. I could only think of destruction. To leave the past, I had to wipe the slate clean, even if it was with a handkerchief full of tears.

Dr. House told me I was bordering on having two personalities. Some psychiatrists had told me I did, but others said I didn't. That only added to my confusion, proving to me that the professionals didn't know what they were talking about. Now, in retrospect, I believe I was two: Peggy Bearden and Pegi Crosby.

It was hard, at first. I was terribly addicted to Jeri Crosby until my decision to turn my back on my past. I'd had to have her approval for everything I did. I called her daily, sometimes twice a day, for advice and guidance. She'd praise me and sympathize with me. Then she'd abruptly change all the rules. I actually permitted her to stomp me into the ground. I couldn't go back to her cruelty. I had to let Shaunda take Danny to raise as I couldn't deal with his drug use. No one knew of my inner turmoil.

My severance with Jeri cut off a portion of Herman's communication; he no longer had Jeri to deliver all his dirty little messages. So now he called Shaunda, my daughter every week-end asking questions, "Is your Mom dating? Who is she dating?" He also called many of my friends, and AA friends. One of his employees, who was also in AA, began calling me nightly to find out which meeting I was going to.

I now found that I hated the people, the town, the state, my past, and my future...I hated it all, and I hated all of them.

The circumstances became a noose which threatened to choke my sensibilities. Unwittingly, I allowed this noose to lead me down a path which would ultimately drag my neck into prison.

CHAPTER THIRTY-SEVEN

It all began with such a touch of innocence, a fervent desire to better my life—start afresh again. It was 1980, and I had enrolled in Fresno State, planning to better my education with some basic courses. And perhaps there was an underlying challenge to prove to myself that I was definitely interested in bettering myself.

One lunchtime in the student cafeteria, I overheard several girls talking.

"Well, when I was hired they let me know the escort service was just a front."

"A front? For what?" The attractive blonde to the girl's left took a bite of her tuna salad sandwich.

"Oh, come on, Julie, you can be so damn naive sometimes." The third student at the table shoved her tray aside, took a compact from a brown leather purse and began finger-combing her auburn bangs.

"Paid sex," the first girl told her. "Prostitution."

I thought the blonde might choke on her tuna sandwich. "You're hookers?" Her eyes grew wide.

"Yep, no more whining to Mommy and Daddy for money. No more student loans. You'd be amazed at the money we're making." The redhead drew a slash of magenta lipstick across her mouth, and blotted it with a paper napkin.

My table was just a few feet from theirs, but I scooted my chair a little closer. I didn't want to miss a word.

"Wined and dined in the most expensive restaurants first, and then a little fun." She snapped the silver compact closed. Her long auburn hair glistened in the sunlight from the cafeteria window. "You ought to think about going to work for the service too, Julie. Better than waiting on tables, that's for sure! Money, money, money," she giggled.

Well, I didn't know if Julie would think about it or not, but I couldn't get their conversation off my mind as I left the cafeteria. My thoughts circled this track like race cars for several days. I began to make plans—not to join the ranks of the other escort girls, but to actually open a house of prostitution.

Sometimes life presents us with choices between good and evil, then lavishly rearranges circumstances, in order to sit back and see just what we'll do with those opportunities—which path we'll take.

I had recently divorced and received a $40,000 settlement from my ex husband. At this particular moment I hated men and all they stood for. Their money, their power. My ex-husband could manipulate anything and have it his way.

Revenge.

Why not get even by taking advantage of their lustful, nasty natures? I'd get even by sabotaging them where it hurt the most—in their wallets. Not only would I savor some retribution for the past, but by setting up a house of prostitution I could further my own dreams of becoming wealthy.

Life, which had rearranged my circumstances to see which path I would choose, must have raised an unapproving eyebrow.

I began to make elaborate plans. I would find a house with five or six bedrooms, but it had to be in an excellent neighborhood. The women must be beautiful, refined, genteel, very stylish, good conversationalists also. "No cheap women", I wrote on my list. They must have no bad habits—drinking and drugs would absolutely not be tolerated. I had seen what both could do—turn a man into an absolute animal...

But where would I find the women? I decided it would be prudent to never use local women; therefore, I'd advertise for "models" in newspapers elsewhere. They could fly in and be met at the airport for their "appointments". This would be a first class operation, I vowed, but first I had to find just the right real estate.

It was a warm autumn day filled with sunshine which dappled the pampered and manicured lawns of the Fig Garden area of Fresno. A panorama of lovely homes swept by the windows of the real estate agent's car.

We pulled into the driveway of a large, obviously well-cared for white stucco home. The red tiled roof spoke of its roots in Mediterranean architecture. I made mental note of the fact that the front yard was large enough to erect a high privacy fence so that the house could not be seen from the main street which went by the front of the house. Instead, I'd put in the driveway off the side street, with a long gate. I knew this was exactly what I'd been looking for once I toured the interior. There was a large living room, and a huge formal dining room. Perfect! We would serve meals if gentlemen wanted them, and if the girls were there for a day or two, they would need to be served meals. There was a small two bedroom bungalow in the rear which could serve as an office or my home.

Immediately, before the agent and I even left the property, that thought amended itself. I would not live, or office on the premises. I needed to find an apartment nearby in order to protect my identity. The bungalow could serve as the housekeeper's quarters. I needed to find a couple—a broad minded couple—who could act in that capacity.

The sales transaction was quickly finalized as I walked through the empty rooms, my footsteps echoing on the hardwood floors, as I excitedly visualized the furniture I would purchase for it, and my antiques which could be used. I began dressing the house like an anxious mother adorns her daughter for a wedding.

In order to conserve money, I bought used furniture in good taste, painting, refinishing and upholstering it myself, while carpenters built the high privacy fence around the property. I even upholstered the headboards on the beds. I chuckled happily to myself as I worked thinking, I can take junk and mold it into a class act. I stood back and admired the elegant burgundy watermark satin headboard I'd just upholstered.

The carpenters built slender glass shelves in the windows to display my exquisite glass collection. Sunshine, filtering through cranberry glass, created clouds of roses which drifted happily across the thick carpeting. The house was ready. Now, all I needed were the people.

On a trip to Reno, I met Printus. He was a bartender, and when I told him I was going back home he asked where home was.

"Fresno," I told him.

"Well, it's a small world. My wife's sister lives there and we're moving to Fresno. It's my last week in this job." He polished a bar glass as though it were an art treasure which belonged in a museum.

My intuition immediately stood at attention, and I decided to tell him that I was looking for a couple to supervise meals and housekeeping for my new business. I looked him straight in the eye and told him the nature of that business. He set the glass down gently and laughed heartily. He and his wife, Sadee, both in their mid-sixties, had formerly managed the household affairs in the same kind of business in Las Vegas.

I hired him on the spot, and never regretted my intuition. Printus, tall and thin, was the perfect counterpart to his chubby wife, and as a couple they were dynamite—efficient, neat, warm and lovable characters with abounding good humor. Neither were shocked at the nature of the business. They had worked in a house of prostitution before in Vegas... but then, prostitution is legal in the state of Nevada. It was not in California.

I went to work immediately and placed advertisements for "models" in newspapers in San Francisco, Los Angeles, San Diego, and Portland. The ads read that they must apply in person only, on a specified date and time, to such-and-such a suite, in a major hotel. I planned a group interview, and once the girls had all arrived in the suite, I bluntly told them that this was for a prostitution service. Many walked out in a self-righteous huff, but I was to find that this was a smoke screen. They would usually call back later and agree to work.

I had three telephone lines installed in my apartment across town. I was the only one who answered the telephone. The girls were told they must make a reservation for times that they were available to work, and would be restricted to no more than two days per reservation.

Either Printus or I picked them up at the airport. Many were married with families, and I was quite certain I never knew their legal names.

The men were also always transported to the house, and never permitted to drive there. I advertised in men's magazines statewide, and paid the head housekeeper in many of the best hotels to put sticker ads in the telephone books placed in guest rooms.

I made $6,000 my first night! It was easy to become addicted to that kind of money, and I was to later find that a money addiction is far more habit-forming than any addiction to drugs or alcohol.

This sudden infusion of money into my life was the blessing I had always looked for, but it had its dreadful downside. I had begun to live a secretive life, adopting a new identity in order to conceal what it was I did for a living. The subconscious strife began to take it's toll over the years of living a life incognito.

But the money was incredible, and there were humorous highs at times. One morning, after the house had been opened for awhile, I answered the doorbell. No one ever just "dropped by" so this had to be a stranger.

I opened the door to find, a tall African American gentlemen, nicely dressed in suit and tie. "Good morning," he said pleasantly, like he was here to award me the Publishers Clearing House prize money.

"Yes?" I eyed him up and down, trying to figure out why he was there.

He pulled a rather grimy California Private Investigator's license from his wallet. "I'm sorry to bother you, but I'm going to just level with you, lady. I'm investigating a gentleman who comes here quite often." He showed me a picture of one of our customers.

My toes began to curl slightly in my high heels.

He shifted a slightly chewed cheap cigar to the other side of his mouth. "Now, there no sense dancing around this. Why is he coming here?"

I smiled broadly and lightly touched his sleeve. "Well, I'll be truthful with you," I told him. "You see, I don't know how to put this delicately, but he's a very good friend of mine and also a transvestite. He doesn't want his wife to know, of course."

The P.I. shook his head in understanding.

"We're friends, so I allow him to come here and dress up in my clothes. I paint his toenails and let him parade around a bit. Get's it out of his system…that's all."

"Oh, I see," he said, and smiled in a conspiratorial fashion. "I do hope you'll keep his little secret, and not betray this confidence."

His tone suggested the poor man had found himself diagnosed with a fast-growing cancer. "You can count on me," he pledged and accompanied his statement with a broad wink. I closed the door and leaned against it, while fanning my face. "Good grief, Printus, I think I just won the Academy Awards for this year!"

Sadee laughed until tears ran down her plump, apple-like cheeks.

In the fifth year of unbelievable prosperity, both the girls and customers began prodding me to allow them appointments in hotels. I finally gave in, against my better judgement. It was the beginning of the end...

CHAPTER THIRTY-EIGHT

After five years, I was arrested for pimping and pandering. Other than the arrests, I don't remember any of it.

I was more frightened than I'd ever been in my entire life. In court, I became hysterical. It was a flashback to that day when I had been in court with Mama, when I was eleven years old.

I never heard what the judge said. I had no idea that I was going to prison. Mr. Boree, my lawyer, had assured me I would never go to prison on a first offense. There were no record of my drunk driving arrests.

When I was being taken to the holding tank to be transported back to jail, my attorney handed me a copy of my evaluation that had been sent to the judge—the evaluation of the court psychologist, together with a report of a telephone interview with Jeri. She had told the psychologist that I'd always been unmanageable. She'd said, "Pegi will start out by crying. She'll cry uncontrollable. It'll be like someone turned on a water faucet." She told them all about her long battle with me as a foster child. How hard she'd tried to help me, and how ungrateful I had been.

The evaluation by Dr. Allan Hedburg was totally false. It almost seemed to me that the report was about somebody else. I kept going back to the first page to make sure my name was on it. I could hardly believe it all. Many of those things had taken place during my drinking phase, but most of it was completely wrong. I'd already been sentenced, though, so there wasn't anything that I could do.

The only thing Jeri said that was correct was that I'd cry non-stop. She said it was only an act, which it certainly wasn't!

Jeri also told the psychologist that I received almost $260,00 from the railroad after my first husband's death. It was $10,000. Thirty-three hundred for each child and myself. My childrens' money was put in trust, but she told Dr. Hedburg that I'd squandered all the money that was my childrens' estate. She wove a lie that I had lived my entire life on large settlements, by suing hundreds of people, and I'd embezzled thousands and thousands of dollars from my ex-husband. She also said that I'd received thousand of dollars after Jeff's death, which too was not correct.

Dr. Hedburg also asked her if I had seen my siblings while living with her. Jeri said, "Why, she never asked to." She also said that I'd had an ongoing sexual relationship with my brother Brian.

I loved Brian, but I didn't like him. We were both drunks, but he was worse. I was only around him for a few months in my adult life. He spent seventeen years in the Navy, then lived in Louisiana most of his adult years, and died there. Mickey was the one I was close to.

None of Jeri's garbage was true. But once she had been questioned, I didn't stand a chance. I'll never know how Dr.

Hedburg even found her, because I hadn't told him anything about her. She ended up being my judge and executioner with her way of convincing others. Of course, her credibility always surpassed mine, but this was the ultimate betrayal.

When I was drinking I knew I had done many bad things, but the majority of the report was fabricated and I didn't have a chance to say these reports weren't true. I'd already been sentenced and was on my way to prison before I had the opportunity to read them.

In the end I was processed like a slice of cheese. The judge stated that although this was the first time I had ever been in real trouble, it was evident I should have been imprisoned years before.

That's what it was all about. I should have been imprisoned years before, not for the crime that I'd committed. My sentencing was based on my past life, not my crime. When I was arrested, I didn't tell anyone about my past. I lived two separate lives. My life was carefully compartmentalized.

It wasn't that I didn't want anyone to know. I'd just never had one person stand by me. If I could have taken a chance and shared my past and my arrest with somebody, chances are I would have been abandoned one more time. The matter could have been turned around and used against me, as had been done with Dr. Hedburg. I couldn't chance that. Everyone in my past had always turned from me for things I'd never done to them.

At first, I was sentenced to a ninety-day observation. My attorney Mr. Boree told me that such a sentence was for first-time offenders of non-violent crimes. He also told me that I'd stay in receiving and wouldn't go into the yard with the main population. That was a major relief. He said I'd see counselors and a psychiatrist; I'd be watched daily, and a full report would be made of my actions. At the end of the ninety days, I'd be taken back to court along with the report, and my sentencing would be based on the observation, not on my crime. After I began to calm down that didn't seem so bad.

When we arrived at the gate of the California Institute for Women in Fontera, the deputies removed their gun belts and put them into a bucket, which was pulled up by the guard in the tower. I squinted, trying to get a look at the compound. I couldn't make out anything but blobs of lights that made the building look like a long motel. Far in the distance, I saw what looked like the runway of an airport.

The next thing I knew, I was in a small room where I was fingerprinted for the hundredth time since my arrest, and my photo was taken again. I always wished I'd kept it, it was so horrible. Next, I was escorted to a small room where Officer McNair came at me with plastic gloves and metal tongs, and gave me a plastic bucket. She paused to put on a medical gown.

"Never know what you'll catch around here," she said. "Strip," said another female guard. "Put all your belongings in the bucket."

After I had stripped the commanding officer, holding long tongs in each hand, went through my clothing. Then she stuffed them into a drawstring bag with my name tag on it.

"You never know what a prisoner might bring into the prison. I have to be careful. I don't want to catch anything." She repeated this like a mantra to herself.

Behind me were two stall showers without doors, which looked out toward the guard's station. The wall between the shower was lined with shelves that held supplies. I was instructed to shampoo all hair areas, using the green bottle. After I had finished the shower, the guard told me to turn around and face the wall. I did as I was told.

"Bend over and cough for me," she instructed. That was a weird command, but I tried to comply.

Officer McNair yelled, "Spread those cheeks." When I didn't move, she screamed at me again, "I told you to spread your cheeks!" A few seconds later, she hit the counter with the metal tongs and hollered again, "I told you to spread those fucking cheeks, goddamn it!"

I was shaking. My mouth was stretched so far I was afraid it wouldn't go back to it's original shape. Besides, my arms were growing weak from holding them up, pulling on my mouth for so long. I had my two fingers in each side of my mouth, stretching it as wide as I could.

Once she realized what I was doing in misunderstanding her crude laughter bounced off the mildewed tile walls. She threw me a towel the size of a wash cloth, yelling to other CO's, "This one just fell off a turnip truck." She told them what I'd done, and uproarious laughter echoed around the shower stall.

"Put on the clothes in the plastic bucket," she directed. I was issued a muumuu, three pairs of white socks, three pairs of cotton panties, a sweat shirt, and a pair of thirty- nine-cent rubber thongs. I was given a toothbrush, tooth powder, Ponds Cold Cream, stinking yellow soap, my bed linen, and one towel.

I'll never forget the iron "clank" of the cell block doors, followed by an electrical pop—steel-on-steel.

Finally in my cell, but not settled, I listened to the sounds of screams and cries, names called out, echoing around me all night long. Those two sounds, the clank of the locks, and the human cries will never leave me.

Many years before, I'd watched a television series called, "One Step Beyond." That was how I felt right then—as if I'd crossed over that invisible line. Sitting on the bed, I stared at the walls that seemed to be closing in on me. The judge's words echoed in my head. I could still see his mouth moving as he had said, "I want you to know that you are a danger to society. Women your age don't get into a business like this. Because of your age, I'm giving you the maximum sentence."

I'd lost my freedom.

I found out that those prisoners with long-term sentences didn't like those of us with short terms. They knew we'd be leaving soon. Some of them were never leaving. My own cellmate was a killer.

The only kindness shown inside the prison walls was for personal gain. Sexual favors were given to guards in exchange for drugs or an extra blanket. Lesbians manipulated others into submission. Violence, sex, sex crimes, and cruelty, both physical and mental, were routinely committed by inmates and guards alike.

I was shocked and terrified. I continually prayed, "Oh, dear God, please help me. Is this what I have to live with the next ninety days?" I wondered if others only prayed when things went bad. I knew I would have plenty of time to think about it. Perhaps the answers would come. "Please God, I beg of You, give me some relief! I know this isn't the worst place in the world, but to me it is the end of the world. Please God, give me the strength to see this through."

I felt like I had in the past when I'd run up the steps and pounded on the door begging Jesus to help me.

Dr. Cotta prescribed three Elavil at morning and bedtime. The medication was too strong, and I hallucinated. At four o'clock one morning, I was awakened by wild cats coming through the window at me, and my cries awakened my roommate. I begged her to tell me there really weren't any wild cats. I knew there weren't, but I could still see them. "Here, here...I'll catch one," she said. "See, it's not wild. Just your imagination. Just listen to me, and everything will be okay." My attorney had told me I would be under observation daily by counselors and psychiatrists. But the other inmates told me we were not under watch, nor monitored. Instead, I was to have only two appointments, one with a counselor and the other with a psychiatrist. How could they possible judge our sentence with only one appointment? For the prisoners' nighty-day observations, the appointments with counselors and psychiatrist were key to any hope. Our whole evaluation was based on just two interviews, however, most of them lasted several hours.

My first interview lasted forty-five minutes, but the one with the psychiatrist, Maria J. Jamakas, PH.D., was over in less than ten minutes. How in the world could they make any type of evaluation of an inmate based on ten minutes? The report she sent to the court was fifteen pages long.

I realized they had already made up their minds long before the interview, based on Jeri's report. Where else could the psychiatrist have gleaned fifteen pages of analysis from a ten minute evaluation?

Noise was my worst enemy. It was unbearable—crying, screaming, wailing, and cursing. Lovemaking noises continued for hours.

I stood in the long line weekly for tooth-powder, bath soap and toilet tissue. Most of the time my toilet tissue was stolen. Then I'd have to use a rag which I washed after each use.

The dorm inmates gathered together to decorate for the holidays. All of us together came up with many good ideas. It was the only time that we got along amiably.

Right after Christmas, I was sent back to Fresno for my hearing, and was sentenced back to the California Institution of Women for three years. I can't begin to tell you what the judge said in court that day. I was back into prison so fast, I hardly had time to discern what had actually happened. I felt like Dorothy being sucked into the vortex of a dizzying cyclone, but instead of landing in Oz, I found I had landed in a grim, dangerous environment, imprisoned with hard core criminals.

When I arrived in prison, the first thing I did was to figure out what I could learn from this experience. How could I take what had happened to me and use it as a tool to work for me? It may have been an unrealistic goal as most of the people in prison were so hateful, and they couldn't have cared less about another human being.

While I was there, I decided to write my story.

The task began as an exercise to fill the long, lonely days and nights. I found by escaping into the past I could hide from the gray, unfeeling drudgery of the present. I'd never been any place where I felt I could talk about my life and those babies. I started to write, moving words, replacing one with another. I kept moving all the words around, word by word, paragraph by paragraph, chapter by chapter. And what had begun as an exercise became a prescription for finding myself under all the layers of heartache, abuse and betrayal. As the words flowed they peeled back layers of scar tissue which had formed a thick keloid over my feelings, my self-esteem...my heart.

After a couple of years, as I re-read my story one day, I looked at all those words and realized I'd finally found myself and rebuilt me. I had really found Pegi and in doing so, I was able to meld the two Pegi's together into one healthy woman, but two surprises awaited me. They were both catalysts to work a miracle.

CHAPTER THIRTY-NINE

Finally the day came for my parole. I was being sent to Turning Point in Fresno to do my last ninety days. I was excited to leave. Several people tried to tell me how sorry I'd be, but I knew nothing could be worse than prison. I thought it was by far the worst place I'd ever been.

Within twenty-four hours, I sincerely wished I could be back at C.I.W.

I was called into the office to talk with my parole agent, Mr. Faulk who said, "I want you to know that after I read your record, I really didn't want you here with me. But this is your first time in prison, so it's totally out of my hands." Is he telling me that I'm the worst person to ever be here? That's impossible, I thought, my hands twisted restlessly in my lap.

"I'm here to tell you that if you make one little slip-up, you're gone, shipped back to prison."

His words made me so mad and confused. It was unbelievable! I was living with eighteen hardcore heroin users. There were syringes everywhere. They put them inside toilet paper spools, in the hems of drapes, in the freezer—you name it. I was the only one not on drugs, so what could be so bad about me? And the things that were going on there were far worse than I ever thought of doing. One was stealing credit cards out of the mail boxes in the area where we lived. Another was renting cars and selling them to be taken to Mexico and telling the rental agency that they'd been stolen. And here he thought I was bad.

While at Turning Point, one counselor betrayed me by using a letter I had written to a friend back in prison. I had described what was going on at this agency. I had written about one counselor who often let prisoners out at night to roam the streets. He always told them that if they weren't back by five o'clock the next morning, they'd be reported as escapees. The counselor, who discovered the letter I was writing, took it and showed it to the staff, asking if they had been allowing all those terrible things to happen. The guilty staff member told the inmates what I'd done. Every one of them was furious with me. I could have been killed by any one of them, and it's a wonder I wasn't.

It may have been neurotic but I still had my own soap that I carried in a soap container. I had my own car hidden blocks away and kept my cosmetics locked in the trunk. That way I didn't have the hassle of having to share with the addicts. I really was fearful of the heroin addicts and Aids. Later, I did bring soft gel into the ward, but I made sure that they were in containers with pumps. Then I didn't mind sharing.

From the days of living with Jeri trying to make me wash those Kotex, I couldn't bear to share anything that I put on my body or face. While in prison I learned that Hepatitis B could be spread from fingernail files, mascara, and many other cosmetics. Many inmates had Hepatitis B.

As part of my parole, I now had a job. I rode the bus to work at Valley Children's Hospital. On the bus, I would tell everybody who'd listen that I was just out of prison and in Turning Point. I rocked back and forth in the seat and talked. I'd tell about my Mama drowning her babies, about being abandoned, about not being able to see my siblings, not knowing where one of my sisters was. I'd never been able to even think about all this much less speak of it. I needed to hear my own voice tell of it. I talked and talked, never shutting up. I repeated the stories hundreds of times a day. Many of the passengers would say something about me to the driver.

The bus drivers always said, "Oh, her. She's nuts. She doesn't even know what day it is. Nobody's home upstairs." The day came to leave Turning Point. I had looked forward to this day, thinking it was never going to arrive. But when it did, I was frightened out of my wits. I didn't want to go. It would be like abruptly leaving the womb prematurely. I wasn't prepared and couldn't understand why I was feeling as if some cord was being cut away.

Had I become dependent on the system? That had to be it. I was institutionalized. The one thing I had maintained all along wouldn't happen to me, had happened. Now I knew why all those inmates had returned back to C.I.W. We all had become lost without the regimented helm of the system to guide us and therefore felt like orphans left on life's doorstep without our course being rigidly charted. I lost my job at Valley Children's Hospital and couldn't get another one. I was desperate. I started through the many services such as Older Americans, King of Kings, Alternative Sentences, and many others. There are hundreds of these services. They would grab me immediately when they heard I'd been in prison. They knew I qualified and would bring government funds into their offices. The amount I heard was thirty three hundred dollars.

None of these services intended to hire me, though. They had no jobs to send me to. In reality, all it did was pay the salaries for their office. At one of the services, the woman who interviewed me was so ignorant, that I had to show her how to fill out my application.

I finally figured out what these services were about, and how they played the system. I called the director at King of Kings in Fresno.

"Mr. Allen, there really is no job for me in your organization, is there? You get government grants off people like me, don't you?"

Mr. Allen couldn't answer me. The telephone line went dead. I called him back on several occasions, and he'd never talk with me.

Shoplifting stories from prison came to mind, and soon I began shoplifting. I became the retailer's nightmare, walking away with two or three thousand dollars worth of merchandise every day. I sold everything for half the ticketed price. If I had something I couldn't dump, I'd have a yard sale and sell it.

It's common knowledge that when a parolee finishes their first year clean, they are taken off parole. That wasn't what happened with me. But I didn't want to rock the boat, so I didn't ask any questions.

I rummaged through all my scraps of material to see what I could do that would bring me in some money. I came up with jockstraps. Fancy jockstraps. I made sequined jockstraps and leather ones, jockstraps decorated with lace, silk, fur, roses. You name it, I had it. I worked day and night, sewing jockstraps.

But how was I going to market them?

One night in a fit of desperation, I walked into a gay bar with hundreds of jockstraps over my arm. I came out with over fifteen hundred dollars.

Thank God, I was on my way. I began doing alterations, some for dry cleaners. I rented out a bedroom with a private bath to the manager of K-Mart. From then on, my life started on an upswing.

A friend in Fresno introduced me to Jim. His wife had died two years earlier. As we got to know each other I discovered that I'd known his first wife, Betty. She too was a sober member of AA.

Jim was soft-spoken and quiet.

During the next few hours, it became obvious to me that he was very lonely. He was kind, gentle and understanding. He accepted me precisely as I was. He was the first person who had ever done that.

Now that we'd met, we became even closer friends. He was the only person in my life who had given me equal status. I'd never before experienced that kind of understanding.

Jim and I were best friends for almost two years. He was somebody I trusted, the first safe person to ever enter my life. Our first goodnight kiss was a long time coming. The suspense made it even more special. It was worth waiting for. This genuine, sincere, loving man made my heart open like a rose to sunshine. And this was a heart I had thought had died in the snows of alcohol, abuse and betrayal.

When our relationship changed, from that of just friends, I was worried about his future because of my past. I told him, "I'm just a lemon."

"Oh, no you're not," he answered back.

"What will your church and the community think of you marrying a felony?" I asked.

"I don't believe there's anything you could do that would reflect on me," he said, grinning. "You see, only I can do that. I've been with the school district long enough, and I have a good reputation. Another human being couldn't reflect on me."

I was deeply impressed by his attitude. From the deep well of his religious conviction, he poured forth rivers of gentle qualities; that of being caring, loving, and quietly unshakable. I'd never experienced that kind of love before. He was my hero, possessing all the maturity and strength that I'd been reaching for all my life. Jim was willing to take on a cripple. To justify his incredible and revitalizing belief in me, I had to prove I could walk.

Jim and I were married two years later. We had a small wedding at home with Jim's son and my daughter Shaunda present.

When I first found this incredible guy I was sure it wouldn't last, because he was just too nice. Fortunately, I was so exhausted from years of trying to make the wrong people love me, I relaxed and gave Jim a chance to show me how remarkably loveable he was—and how nice it was to be happy for days, weeks, months on end. I actually caught myself thinking, *He's nice to me, but he's nice to everybody! How will I ever know if he really loves me?*

Jim became my eighth husband, although I'd had only one divorce; all the other marriages ended in annulments. Much later, Jim told me that the first time I knocked on his door and he looked at me, Betty whispered to him, "This is she. This is the one you'll marry." She knew she was dying. Jim has been the kindest person to enter my life.

He's loving and my most beloved friend. He's fabulously sensitive, encouraging, and worshiped by his kids in school.

By coincidence, my new husband lived in Porterville, one of the towns close to where I'd lived with Mama and Daddy.

In truth nothing was familiar to me. My eyes darted nervously about prodding scenes from my childhood. It wasn't at all like I'd remembered. After all, it had been forty five years. But the name, Porterville, haunted me—the fact that I was back, living in a town where I'd suffered so much abuse. As I walked in the alleys behind the bars, even though nothing was familiar, I was reminded of the women who had looked down on me as a little girl, begging quarters and rifling through the garbage dumps and trash cans for food. Would I be accepted now, I wondered?

CHAPTER FORTY

Months later Shaunda called to tell me Hunter had died. It was early morning. That night, she called again to tell me that Jeri passed on, just ten hours later. It had to be coincidence; she didn't love him that much but he loved her dearly.

I felt nothing. I had buried them years earlier. I'd dealt with it more than ten years before. I knew this day would eventually come. While I had loved them both very much, I hated them at the same time, but I felt that I owed them both so much. After all, they took me in when nobody else had wanted me. Crazy, huh? I believe they had just as hard a time with me as I did with them. I believe they didn't know better.

I helped Shaunda clean out their home. On the refrigerator were many pictures of Jeri and Hunter with Herman.

I hadn't seen Herman in years, and thought I'd totally gotten over him, but that little soft spot, that secret place that held the strange bond between us, had never quite died.

A thrill shot through me as I stood there, staring at his picture one more time. Oh my God! I thought I'd shaken him forever. It bothered me more than a little bit. He was my first love, and I'll always have a place in my heart for him. First loves remind us of who we were and how far we've come. So I made a mistake. And perhaps someone else can benefit from the lessons that came, in part, at my expense. That's what growing is all about. The relationship left its imprint. With his manipulations of my friends and family, he'd ripped my heart from me. For the first time, I really knew it. He was still lying to friends and family that I continued harassing him by sending him copies of all my published stories. I certainly wish I had those published stories, as I never knew that I had been published.

I made a startling discovery. Hidden in the bottom of a chest was an envelope with three tiny pictures of me. One picture was the one in the red raincoat; the other two were taken at the carnival when I had begged the stranger for money, years before.

I was fifty years old, and had never had a picture of myself under the age of eleven. I don't know where those pictures came from, or how Jeri had gotten them. For her own mysterious reasons, she had never shared them with me. Shaunda and I carried out three large, black plastic bags full of prescribed medication. Jeri had managed to hide her addiction for more than fifty years. Jeri and Hunter left my daughter their inheritance. I was grateful to them that they did. I certainly hadn't expected it for myself, although I was saddened that my son, Danny, couldn't have received any of it. Nobody knows why. That's just the way Jeri was. I felt sad for him, as he was young at the time, and was hurt at their obvious exclusion of him.

Shaunda said later that it was because of Danny's drug use, but her's was as great and she spent most of it on drugs and men.

Shaunda had a tough life. Beginning at the age of twelve, she raised her two brothers, one a newborn, and Jeff, who was three years younger than she. She married at seventeen to get away from home. Her husband was older, and he had a five-year-old son.

Then she had her own baby, Monyka. In the middle of my drinking, she took her brother Jeff for a while, and she cared for her in-laws, who lived next door, until they died. After my last divorce, she took in my son Danny, who was into drugs. Then she took me during my prison arrest. It was as if we reversed roles and she was the mother and I the child. Then she brought Hunter and Jeri back to Woodlake and took care of them until they both died.

As badly as I wanted to rise out of the quagmire of my past and be a better mother than my Mama, the quicksand of some mysterious generational demon pulled me right back into her mold. As a child I had taken on Mama's responsibilities with my siblings, and as history repeated itself with me, Shaunda had accepted these very same responsibilities. The Bible says the sins of the fathers are visited upon the children from generation to generation. It must pertain also to mothers.

I will always be grateful that I had the opportunity to live with the Crosbys, however, I blame Tulare County and Child Protective Services for what happened to us. Our lives were chipped away by the welfare system. The system is a rich, powerful organization. They could buy their way out of anything. For each child CPS takes away from his or her family, they receive $80,000 from Social Security.

With that abundance of money and resources I would think they could figure out a way to save the family, rebuild it, teach them how to become better parents. It could be done, and CPS would still be just as rich and powerful.

I should have seen all my brothers and sisters weekly or monthly. The welfare system could have implemented visitation rights. They should have gotten the best help possible for me and my siblings. I also feel that I should have been questioned about the things that went on in the Crosby household. They should have checked the school and looked at my grades. I truly feel that the system had everything to do with the problems all of us children have had throughout our lives—of being plagued with suicides, depression, alcoholism, and drug abuse. All of us had problems. I have to ask myself why.

My brothers and sisters and I will never get a refund on our childhood. The welfare system and CPS literally stripped us of our rights. Throughout the years, they collected millions of dollars in government funds for our care, but they used it to maintain their system, and to hell with the children. CPS took my life from me, and I can't get it back.

It's very important to keep siblings together. When I lost my brothers and sisters, a part of me died a big, important part. I always dreamed of suing. When I was of an age to sue, I had such low self-esteem and blamed myself for our abandonment, therefore, I wasn't able to sue anyone.

There will always be some birth parents who shouldn't be parents and won't want their children; therefore, there will be a need for foster parents, and there's a significant place for them. Parents and foster parents both have the power to do devastating damage to children.

In my opinion the dirty system really isn't for the children. It operates to perpetuate itself, feeding like a parasite on the lives of babies—small boys and girls. It feigns to be helping, but the main goal is to feed itself. When is it going to matter what a child thinks and what a child feels? Children are treated like pieces of junk, or furniture, for the courts to move here, there, and wherever they seem to fit the best, while using monies to fatten more jobs and a larger system.

If Child Protective Services were really concerned with the child, they would make sure the children had all the help available through counseling and maintaining the children's relationship with the family, whatever it takes.

Americans are at a fever pitch over child abuse these days, and haven't done very well at preventing or diminishing it. How can they, when a system is getting richer over it? This country desperately needs the family unit. At a time when many families are disappearing and juvenile problems are increasing, families need to be creating bonds and thinking about how to protect our children and the family unit.

The absence of such childhood experiences is just as dramatic and enduring.

The bond between biological parents and their children are severed too quickly, by public services in the name of assisting the child, but the children are left in the middle. The courts turn a blind eye to the rights of the children. I know there must be hundreds and thousands of stories like mine.

I'm the same, but I'm different. While I may be a product of my history, I can't change what has happened to me. I must accept the fact that it's not profitable to sit around and cry about my misfortunes.

All I can change is what I'm doing now, and if I become more responsible, most of my troubles will disappear. I'm not responsible for what happened in the past, but I can live responsibly now. I learned a better way to fulfill my needs within the confines of reality.

If nothing else, we all change with age, or by our own experiences. I changed because of what happened to me and the choices I made. Finally, I've victoriously freed myself from the dark shadows of my childhood. I never realized how much my future was rooted in my past. I was driven so hard by the terror of it that I would try to ensure a different future at any cost. Not all changes really free us from the pain of our personal history.

I wallowed in self-pity, thinking it was justified because of my childhood. I soon learned that as an alcoholic, I couldn't afford justified self-pity. Poor me, poor me, pour me...another drink.

Today I can tell you that my overwhelming power of self-pity has been removed. It has been replaced with overwhelming gratitude. I missed a special kind of teaching that should have been established during normal growing up. Responsibility is usually learned in a child in early years from parents or school, instead of as a mature adult, as in my case.

As the many examples of abandoned children show, man is not driven by instinct to care for and teach responsibility to his children. Children ordinarily learn through a loving relationship with responsible parents, or involvement that implies parental teaching and example. Responsibility is taught by relatives, teachers, ministers, and friends with whom children are involved.

I had to gain responsibility now, focusing on the present. I suffered from a type of personality disfunction which was a mental illness displaying thoughts and behavior which were unacceptable to society. I was "sick."

Most counselors believe that a person is born perfect, was all right at one time, and fell victim to a series of life experiences that caused deviant behaviors. That wasn't the case with me.

The consequences were so great, or the pain so bad that I had to admit my life was out of control because of my behavior. My behavior was unacceptable even to myself, but I didn't know where or whom to turn to for help. To look at what went wrong didn't help.

I came to understand that it made little difference what went wrong with the relationship I had with my mother or father. I had to know what was going on in all aspects of my life. The details of my life were the material I needed.

The little girl Peggy still emerges at times, though not often. Today, I can put her back when she appears. She still frightens me threatening that the day will come that I will no longer be able to put her in her place.

I still live with dreams of flying just out of reach of people who are trying to get me. I'm wearing a long, white gown. In the distance, the little girl Peggy is running away. She is looking back and up at me, wearing the same tattered dress. I have the dream two or three times a week. It must mean something.

My problem is now more than ten years old. Some try to understand, and I know that some can't. I did find out one thing about my life growing up. I was so focused on the things that I hated about my mother, (I didn't want to be like her) that I missed all her better qualities. Mama was a victim herself. I believe that Daddy would have killed her had she left him. Today, if I dwell on what Mama did to me more than ten years ago, then I haven't forgiven her. My mother did what she had to do to survive. It was clearly my redefined relationship with my mother which freed me from the past.

Probably in real truth, I should have given up my children, but I could never give them up because of what happened to me. Rational people were a threat to me, and therefore it was difficult for me to conceptualize a loving heavenly Father when my earthly one had been so frightening. But there was an experience to come which would be the culmination to all my healing.

Jim's faith was deep and abiding, but I couldn't seem to find the button to turn mine on when we started going to the Terra Bella Church of the Nazarene. I'd searched for God all my life. As a little girl, I had pounded on His door night-after-night, and He had never answered me.

Now, through Pastor Don, and the love of others in the church I finally learned the truth. Jesus was the one knocking on the door—the door of my heart. And I was the one who had to open the door! The answers of true forgiveness were inside this experience—forgiveness of Mama, forgiveness of Daddy, forgiveness of Jeri, forgiveness for myself.

I was told that when you're in Christ, you are a new creature, born again. If that's the case, though I never had a belly button birthday, I couldn't bring myself to celebrate an AA sobriety birthday, I guess I can now celebrate my "born again" birthday.

EPILOGUE

In 1955 when I went back to live with mama and Earl, and they thought they were having a baby. There never was a baby. Just a guess, mamma first symptom of menopause.

Mickey is sober, living in Louisiana. He's near his children. He's purchased five acres and built a small home. His wife of more than twenty-five years didn't know that we'd ever been abandoned. Mickey still can't talk about it.

Mickey had a massive heart attack in July 1997. He's just a six-foot-two toddler.

I haven't seen Scotty in almost forty years. I flew to Florida and spent a month with him. He died the following September. He's been a Christian for many years.

Daddy died at the age of forty-one. I never saw him again. I never knew what happened to Patches. I still think of him.

Mama served a year in jail for abandonment, and Daddy didn't do one day. The system hasn't changed much today.

Brian never married. He spent seventeen years in the Navy. He always had a weak stomach. If one of my children so much as sneezed or had the sniffles, he'd run off to puke.

Brian was a terrible drunk, and he wet the bed until the day he died. He'd get so drunk, no one could understand a word he said. He spent a year with me in California because he was running from someone. Someone had broken both of his arms, but he wouldn't tell me who. I never pushed; he wouldn't have told the truth anyway.

Mickey always said that Brian was a Mafia hit man. When Mickey lived in California, his house was staked out by men in big black limousines with dark windows who looked like criminals.

Brian's body washed ashore in 1980 in Louisiana. Mickey said that the Mafia drowned him while on a fishing trip, and that they had a huge insurance policy on him. Mickey also said that the funeral home in Minden, Louisiana, wanted to know who Brian was because his funeral was the largest service they'd ever had.

As children, my three brothers lived with Tom Jones in Elderwood. His wife Anne lay drunk in the back bedroom. She never cooked or cleaned for the boys—Tom did it all and he had several foster boys. Tom was a great old guy, and his main concern was for the boys and their mental health. He let our mother spend weekends with the boys without obtaining permission, feeling that if the boys could see their mother and have a relationship with her, it would be easier for them. Tom believed that the boys wouldn't have as many problems if they were allowed to bond with Mama. That could be why my brothers didn't have as many problems as I did.

I always knew where Kathy was. She stayed with the Marshalls in Farmersville. When she was sixteen, Mickey and I went to visit the Marshalls one morning while Kathy was at school. We told Mrs. Marshall that we wanted to get to know our sister. We told her that if she wouldn't allow it, we'd meet her at school or when she got off the bus. Either way, we were going to know her. We left that day telling her we would give her one week to talk to Kathy and explain everything about her family.

The very next day when I came home from work, Kathy was sitting on my doorstep. We've kept in touch over the years. We now live within twenty miles of each other.

Kathy was molested by Shelly's first husband when she was nine years old. When she told Mrs. Marshall, she said, "And what did you do to cause that?" She continued to allow Kathy to be alone with the husband. This man works for the Tulare County Schools today.

Rita lived with the family of the Chief of Police in Tulare. When she was seven, they gave her up. Then she was adopted by a family in Dinuba. They moved to Ventura, and I lost track of her. I spent more than thirty years looking for her before the Maury Povich show found her in 1992.

When I first started gathering information for my book, I went to the Tulare County Courthouse to look up old records. I found some that said I took the Welscher Bellevue Test in 1948, and it showed that I had an I.Q. of 130. The Rohrschack showed that my intelligence was average. It stated that I had difficulty identifying with people, had problems bonding with others, and was extra-sensitive.

I found a record from Juvenile Hall for Mickey and myself.

In the report about Jeri and me, the social service wrote, "the Crosbys live in a lovely home in Three Rivers, Calif. The home overlooks the river, with a majestic view of the mountains. The Crosbys don't want Pegi back. They feel that she will cause them to have a bad reputation in the community."

What does all that have to do with what went on inside that home? Social Services seemed to think that just because a home is lovely, overlooking the river with a beautiful, majestic view, with lovely foster parents, that everything is wonderful inside that home.

Wrong.

Only I can give myself a bad reputation, not anyone else. I don't believe the Crosbys were ever told that I was retarded or even borderline. That was Jeri's way of covering up for all the things she'd done to me. Had I been a scholastic achiever in school, I wouldn't have had the time to be a servant to Jeri. After all, that was the reason she got me in the first place.

If in a small way my story can relieve another person, other parents, or children who have carried the same burden, it's worth telling. Writing gave me the courage to see what was done to me by alcoholic parents, Child Protective Services, foster parents, and the prison system.

Only I can know what it was like to grow up in different homes without love and security. What the Crosbys offered me was not love, but control. Jeri only loved me when I did what she wanted. If I didn't do what she wanted, her love was used against me. They weren't there for me, I was there for them.

I showed all the characteristics early in my childhood of being an abused child, and what Jeri did was play on my weaknesses. Hunter was pleasant, never outwardly abusive, although he had no strength. In many ways, the fact that he never said anything to Jeri about what she did to me, was abuse. Despite everything, I adored them both to the day they died. Crazy, huh?

"Healing requires forgiveness" of the abuser. I can't wish for "rehabilitation" of my abusers, for that would become another dream that wouldn't come through; however, the key to freedom is forgiveness and truth—the real truth, not distorted.

I went through my entire life thinking I was not worthy of anything. Possessions and things were more important than me, therefore, the only real love I would know would be my own.

Nothing ever, ever wipes out child abuse, but I hope that no living soul will ever have to follow in my footsteps and carry all the secrets as long as I did. But I know that someplace out there, someone will. It happens every day.

Look at the children the system and judges have ripped away from loving homes today, whether it be natural parents or foster parents. Think about Baby Jessica and Baby Richard. It will be years before the damage to these children can be measured, and none of us will be around to see. Those who are will wonder, what happened to her? She's always been this way. We've done so much for her, given her everything, and look how she turned out.

I can pick up a newspaper on any given day and read a story like mine. According to California's Office of Criminal Justice Planning, a woman is abused every fifteen seconds. Experts say that domestic violence goes on behind closed doors and is often unreported. Husbands beat the love out of their women.

Just this morning, I read a story about a woman who killed eight tiny babies at birth. Why? She couldn't give them what they needed.

Most victims of abuse grow up to be juvenile delinquents, then marry abusive men. The cycle goes on, never ending.

An abused wife will divorce her husband because he is abusive, then turn right around and marry a man just like the one she divorced. Unless the victim gets treatment, this pattern is never broken.

The U.S. Advisory Board of Child Abuse and Neglect, established by Congress, found abuse and neglect at epidemic proportions. At least two thousand children, ninety percent of them under four years old, die each year from abuse and neglect in the home. That's five children every single day.

The answer is not to throw more money at a system which uproots the family, scattering and separating children like leaves in a windstorm. The answer is in nurturing the family unit, educating parents, and closely monitoring the habits in the home. Foster parents have their place, but the rights of the children should be carefully taken into consideration, and again, closely monitored. This is the only way the system will repair itself and offer hope and healing for abused children.

Through the years I'd hear from her...not much. One morning the telephone rang, "Hello."

"Pegi, this is your mother's sister, Aunt Anne. Your mother is dying, Pegi. She needs someone, one of you kids to be here with her. Will you come?"

"No, I can't Aunt Ann. Where was she when I needed her?"

"What do you mean?"

"When she left us! Why did she leave us? Six of us, and she never tried to get us back! Aunt Ann I've had a horrible life because of her, and you want me to come and care for her. And not only that Aunt Ann, I remember trying to ask you some questions one time and you told me to keep my mouth shut. That your husband didn't know that Daddy had almost killed you. So where were you Aunt Ann? When you went back to Texas, I don't suppose you knew that they later abandoned us. But why didn't you go back to California and bring Mama and us kids to Texas?"

"Well, Pegi I never knew they abandoned you."

"You didn't?...Well what do you think happened to six little kids?" I hung up the phone.

I didn't talk with Mickey all the time as I didn't always know where he was. He drug his family and moved from town to town. I could leave a message for him at his in-laws land they'd give him a message. I had to wait until he called me. It was a few years later when I did hear from him. "Did you go to Mama's funeral," I asked.

"No. No I didn't Pegi. But my kids went. They loved her. She was good to them."

"I'm glad she was good to somebody. She certainly wasn't good to us."

"Aunt Ann really got mad at me because I wouldn't go and care for her while she was dying," he said.

"Oh she did me too." I told him.

It's been almost 45 years now, since Mama died. I have grown up and matured some. I understand so much more today about life and the life of a battered mother, I have been there also. I wish it could have been different with Mama. She wouldn't talk to me. And that's all I wanted.

In the spring of 2014 I went with Connie, who lives in Springville to our old home. The gates were open for the first time. And the owners were there. They told me they had owned the property for 30 plus years...They came up on weekends and rebuilt the old cabin. Daddy had not burned it down as Scot had said. The old outhouse was still standing. The property looked good, although I wouldn't want to live there again. It brought back much memories. For the first time since that visit I no longer have flashbacks. That alone has been a blessing...A FINAL ENDING.

In 2000 I found the man who molested me was our landlord when we lived in the little house across the street from the hospital. One of his relatives told me. He had molested all his children and grandchildren and other around town. Of course the man is dead today.

I guess no one ever knew that we had been abandoned. As my siblings started raising their families, they never told their children. Why did we not talk about it? For me, the pain was far to great. And Jeri was threatened when I'd speak of my family.

I appeared on the Maury Povich Show in 1992. After thirty years of searching for my sister, Jeannie. We were finally reunited on the show.

Brian drowned in Louisiana in the early 1980's. He never married and was the worst of drunks. Mickey, Scott and Jeanie have passed on. I was able to find some of the Bearden's and went to Texas to meet my dad's oldest sister in 1998. Kate just passed away in 2013 at 96 years old. Many cousins came to meet me. They all said Grandmother Bearden spoke of six grand children that just disappeared. It still amazes me how 6 children can vanish. My sister kathi is still very bitter. I finally was able to put it to rest, all though I cry at the mention of any of it. There were eleven children in daddy's family and nine in moms, wouldn't you think with 20 aunts plus their spouses, that they could have found us and taken us in to keep us together?

In 1936 my grandfather Bearden was killed in Rochester Texas, by the Haskell County Sheriff. His three sons had gone into town the night before and got into a drunken brawl. The sheriff locked up the three boys. My grandfather being the wealthiest farmer in Rochester, went into town the next morning to get his sons out of jail. The sheriff wouldn't release them. My grandfather took out a knife and was going to stab the sheriff, when the sheriff shot and killed him.

With only grandmother Bearden to run the two farms my dad and his brothers had no jobs. Grandmother Bearden sold the farms. My dad and mother moved to California where there was work in the fields. Aunt Kate told me all the Bearden boys were awful drunks. Must be a strong gene in my bloodline as for me and all my brothers are drunks.

In 1936 one's wealth was measured by the size of their home and the amount of property ones owned. Therefor my grandfather was considered wealthy.

At my church a man told me his mother was a Bearden. With help from his daughter we found his grandfather and mine were brothers, and they grew up in Dallas, Texas. I also found another cousin in this area on the Burleson side but not sure just how close we are related. It's very emotional for me to know that I had cousins so close and never knew. He has Burleson children living in Three Rivers by the name of Burleson. From this Burleson I learned that I did hair for a client who had married a Burleson and I never knew.

Her first husband had been a Burleson. When he died she remarried and moved to Three Rivers. Now her name was no longer Burleson. It is truly a small world. Jeri would turn over in her grave had she known I had relatives living in Three Rivers. As she said, I came from junk. Sure wish I could share it all with her today.

In a way it's comforting for me to know that I did have a spot or place somewhere in life. I'd like so much to go back to my name "Bearden" which was so freely taken from me. That's truly whom I am.

I live not far from the place where I spent the first years of my life. I was well into my fifties before I was on the road to healing. Finding it easier to write about my past than to speak about it, this book was instrumental in that process. I have chosen not to close the door on my past, but have instead, have thrown it wide open to serve as an inspiration to others everywhere. I am able to turn the stumbling blocks in my path into stepping stones for the future and hope that readers of this book will be able to do the same. My story is one that is sure to inspire readers everywhere.

I live in Porterville California, with my husband Jim. I breed and raise yorkies and continues to write. I also have a African Grey, named Max who I just adore. Max is truly a Kick and he has quite the vocabulary.

CREDITS

First Edition: WHAT'S A BIRTHDAY MAMA?
BAREFOOT ANGELS.
THEM UGLY BEARDEN'S.
Television: THEEVIDENCE.ORG
Television: FAITH FOR TODAY.

BAREFOOT ANGELS.
BIOGRAPHY/AUTOBIOGRAPHY—
PERSONAL MEMOIRS.

Criminal Justice Planning, a woman is abused every fifteen minutes.

I can pick up a newspaper on any given day and read a story like mine. According to California's Office of seconds. Experts say that domestic violence goes on behind closed doors and is often unreported. Husbands beat the love out of their women.

Most victims of abuse grow up to be juvenile delinquents, then marry abusive men. The cycle goes on, never ending. An abused wife will divorce her husband because he is abusive, then turn right around and marry a man just like the one she divorced. Unless the victim gets treatment, this pattern is never broken.

The U.S Advisory Board of Child Abuse and Neglect, established by Congress, found abuse and neglect at epidemic proportions. at least two thousand children, ninety percent of them under four years old, die each year from abuse and neglect in the home. That's five children every single day.